# Friar Felix at Large

# Friar Felix at Large

## A Fifteenth-century Pilgrimage to the Holy Land

## H. F. M. PRESCOTT

GREENWOOD PRESS, PUBLISHERS
WESTPORT, CONNECTICUT

TO
D.M.M.

# Acknowledgments

I wish to express my thanks to all who have given me help in the making of this book, and especially to Miss Joan Evans, Miss E. A. Frances, Miss O. Bickley, Mr. Malcolm Letts, Dr. and Mrs. V. Erhenberg, and Mr. D. M. B. de Mesquita; to Mrs. Agnes Arber and Dr. D. H. Valentine for botanical information; to Professor A. J. Hutchings for transcribing from old into modern musical notation; and to Professors G. R. Driver and T. W. Thacker, Messrs. A. F. Beeston, C. Rabin, and R. Walzer for interpretation of Arabic words and names. Finally I wish to thank Miss E. Costello and Mr. I. G. Robertson for their unfailing kindness and help.

I am indebted to Messrs. Longmans, Green and Co. for permission to quote from Robert Bridges' translation from *The Confessions* of St. Augustine in *The Spirit of Man*.

# CONTENTS

# ILLUSTRATIONS

# FRIAR FELIX AND OTHERS

FRATER FELIX FABRI, he called himself, or F. F. F. for short. Haeberlin says that his name was Schmidt, his family noble, and their arms "a globe argent on a field sable." Not much is known of his life, except for those two periods when he went on pilgrimage, in 1480 to Jerusalem, and in 1483 to Jerusalem, Sinai, and Egypt.

He was born about 1441 at Zürich.[1] Brought up at the Dominican convent at Basel he learnt there, besides "religious and holy writ," at least something of gardening, so that in his wanderings he was curious of plants and flowers. He cannot have been much more than a boy when he left Basel for Ulm, for according to his own reckoning he must have come there about 1453–54.[2] Even before he left for his first pilgrimage he had seen a little of the world. In 1457 he was at Pforzheim, perhaps for study. In 1467 he was at Aix, and in 1476 in Rome. By that time, or soon after, he was preacher at Ulm. He was at Venice in 1486 and 1487 for the Comitia Generalia of the Dominican order.* He died at Ulm in 1502.[3]

Besides his Latin *Evagatorium* and a German account of the same pilgrimage, he wrote a *Treatise on the City of Ulm*,[4] which contains information about the noble and mercantile families of the city, and some local description; a *Historia Suevorum*, a work entitled *De Monasterio Offenhusano;* a lost work on the siege of Rhodes; and according to Haeberlin an account, separate from that of his first

---

* Davies, *Breydenbach*, Introd., p. v, states that Felix was provincial of his order for Germany from 1486–87. Haeberlin, pp. 17–18, examines a similar statement but disagrees with it.

pilgrimage, of his stay at Venice in 1480 and the journey as far as Corfu.[5]

But it is the book which he called his *Evagatorium* which is his great work, and, if we knew nothing else at all of him but what is to be found there, we should still feel that we knew Brother Felix very well.

The title itself was one of his pleasant but ponderous jokes. "I am resolved," he says in his dedication, "that this book shall not be called a Pilgrimage, nor a Journey nor a Voyage, nor anything else at all, but I have determined that it shall be truly entitled, named, and known as the Evagatorium Fratris Felicis Fabri," and we may translate that as we will by "The Wandering," or "Rambling," or "Straying of Brother Felix," or perhaps by "Friar Felix at Large."

This "little book" he offered to his fellow Dominicans of the priory at Ulm, "not," he hastened to warn them, "as containing nothing but the authentic scriptures." No. This was a book to be read "with pleasure and amusement in the intervals of more fruitful studies, or on holidays, thereby eschewing idleness and obtaining recreation. Therefore," said he, and we cannot know whether apologetically or with a chuckle, "therefore I have dared, among great things and true, grave things and holy, to mingle things silly, improbable, and comical." [6]

In all this, nicely balancing himself between depreciation and commendation of his own work, he spoke the truth, except when he called it a "little book," for the *Fratris Felicis Fabri Evagatorium* contains the most varied, profuse, and entertaining medley of piety and frivolity, shrewdness and simplicity, observation and credulity, all heavily garnished with classical and theological learning, and illuminated by the Friar's own good humor and inexhaustible gusto of living. But in the nineteenth-century edition it runs to three volumes and nearly fifteen hundred pages.

Before we follow him upon his two journeys however, it will be well to try to set him against the background of his time, and among some of the vast company of pilgrims who made that same journey during the fifteenth century and left a record of their experiences. That company was drawn from every Christian country, and the literature of their journeys combines devotional reflections with personal experiences; jumbles together pagan myths, Christian belief, and garbled history; records the measurements of the Holy Sepulcher and the chant of little Moslem boys at school; and in addition may offer to the reader such advice, information, and instruction as is now to be found in the volumes of Baedeker.

In the fifteenth century the stream of pilgrim travel to the Holy Places of Palestine still ran full. The flow had begun more than a thousand years before, and throughout the later Middle Ages the devout and adventurous had made that journey in ever-increasing numbers. In the next century the supply was to dwindle, as the northern nations left the Roman Church; but even before that time came events had taken place which shifted the whole balance of political and commercial power in the Mediterranean; and as these events affected the conditions of pilgrim travel, it is necessary that they should be briefly stated.

For our purpose the century may be divided into three unequal periods by two momentous happenings. The first of these, the fall of Constantinople to the Ottoman Turks, brought to an end the existence of that empire which, rather than anything in the west, was the true heir of Rome. Yet the Turkish victory of 1453 neither began nor ended the advance of the enemy, who already at the beginning of the century had been threatening the weakening defenses of the Eastern empire, who by the year 1500 was master of the greater part of the Balkan States, and who, less than twenty years after that, was to bring down the rival Moslem power, that of the Mameluke sultans, and so to add Egypt and Syria to the Ottoman Empire.

It was Venice who, for the sake of her own colonial

possessions and the trade upon which the whole fabric of her power was built, must succeed to the part played by the Eastern emperors. After the defeat of her great rival Genoa, Venice was unquestionably the first maritime and commercial power in the Mediterranean, and from 1456 the only Latin state still having a foothold on the Greek mainland. As such she must stand face to face with the growing power of the Ottoman Turks, sometimes at open war, sometimes in an uneasy, humiliating, and costly peace.

Yet for all the drain upon her riches which this meant, and for all the hazards which the continually perturbed state of the Levant set in the way of the steady flow of trade, she still prospered. If one trade route were blocked her merchants would be found at the westward gates of another. Timur's smash-and-grab raid in the first years of the century and the destruction of the kingdom of Armenia obliterated the old communications across Asia Minor; the fall of Constantinople barred the Black Sea to the West; but there were still two main outlets at which Venetian merchants might tap the rich Eastern trade; that is to say the ports of Beirut and Alexandria. To these, as well as to the Barbary coast, to Flanders, to rude and distant England, the Venetian State sent a regular and carefully regulated service of galleys and sailing ships.

Beirut was the port for Damascus, and to Damascus, jolting slowly upon the backs of slouching camels, came out of Asia, Persian gums, silks, precious stones. At Damascus gathered the merchants of many nations; de La Brocquière, who was there in 1432, speaks of Genoese, Venetians, Catalonians, Florentines, and French, as well, of course, as Jews and men of the various races of the Levant and of the Near East.[7] So important was this northern Syrian trade route to Venice, that the Republic kept consuls at Damascus and Aleppo, and on the coast, at Beirut and Tripoli.[8] And, besides the service of galleys to Beirut, every June another fleet sailed for the sake of the Syrian cotton crop.[9]

But of greater importance than any Syrian market in the commercial system of Venice was the port of Alexandria, since there was to be found the chief Mediterranean exchange for the spice trade. Ivory, silk, pearls, precious stones ranked high among the merchandise of Venice, but spices far higher, with pepper first among all spices. What, at the other end, the spice trade meant to the West can be read upon the pages of any medieval account book or cookery book, and the reflective student of such domestic records may observe how again, here, the cook's ladle has had its share in ruling the world.

At the markets of Alexandria Venice was the chief of all the European nations. In spite of all the perverse vagaries of the mameluke sultans, whose greed might send up prices to a crazy figure and whose gusts of fury might inflict upon patrician Venetians a slave's flogging, to the Republic the game was worth the candle, since customers in Germany, France, England must pay what price she chose to ask.

But in 1487 Bartholemew Diaz rounded the Cape of Good Hope, and eleven years later Vasco da Gama brought his ships into the port of Calicut. Here, abruptly, ends our second period. What the opening of the Cape route meant the Venetian merchants themselves at once recognized. When the news of Vasco da Gama's successful voyage became known "all the city of Venice was greatly impressed and alarmed, and the wisest men held that this was the worst news that could ever come to the city." [10] They did not need to be told that cargoes such as their own, so often transshipped and passing through so many hands, could not compete with those bought, as the Portuguese were buying, in bulk and on the spot.

What they foresaw took little time to become apparent. In 1498 there was so much pepper in the Alexandrian market that the Venetian merchant captains lacked money to buy all that was there. Four years later, at Beirut, the Venetians could find but four bales, and even in Alexandria there was little to be had. From this time onward that scarcity was to continue. Occasionally there were no spices at all to be bought; usually the galleys must return half empty, while the price of their merchandise, because of its rarity and because of "the exorbitant dues exacted in every one of the Sultan's dominions" had been increased a hundredfold.[11]

So the fifteenth century closed, in the Mediterranean, upon a changed political balance and upon a shift in trade which helped to tip that balance still further. For the Portuguese had not been the only seafarers to attempt a new way to the Indies, nor was it only the Cape route to the Spice Islands which had been opened to the nations of the Atlantic seaboard. Between the voyage of Diaz and the arrival of Vasco da Gama at Calicut, Columbus had reached his "island of Antilhe," and it was not long before Europe knew that a continent lay to the west and believed it to be a continent of unimaginable riches. A man did not, in 1500, need to be very wise to guess that in the future trade, and with it power, would begin to run into unaccustomed channels. Not even the wisest could have known, however, that before the new century's end what the Portuguese had won from the Venetians Englishmen would be tearing from the hands of the Portuguese.

But this is to look forward too far, and our pilgrims of the fifteenth century were not looking forward at all but back toward certain stupendous, all but incredible happenings, localized at a village, in a small city, and upon the shores of a little inland sea. It was to that point in time at which, they believed, time had been broken into by eternity, that they looked, and so, with a faith not, perhaps, always so simple as we in this age are inclined to think, but unshadowed by the perplexities, sorrows, and angers of sixteenth-century religious controversy, they set their faces toward Jerusalem. Upon that journey only a very few were greatly concerned either with commerce or with politics except as the vicissitudes of these threatened their safety or comfort. It is not therefore on such subjects that the accounts of pilgrims may most fruitfully be searched, but for petty arrangements of daily life, trivial difficulties and enjoyments, profound beliefs and emotions, manifestations of religion comical, pathetic, perfunctory, or sincere—in a word for the humanity common to these pilgrims and ourselves.

Of that baker's dozen of fifteenth-century pilgrims who went to Jerusalem either before or after or actually in the company of Felix Fabri, and to whose far less voluminous narratives we shall go from time to time for some anecdote or comment which adds to our picture of the pilgrims' world, the first made the "Jerusalem Voyage" in 1413. Margery Kempe was the wife of a burgess of Lynn, the mother of fourteen children, a woman who had bustled and blundered through life trying to make money by brewing, but the beer would not prove, or by running a horsemill, but the horses decided one day that they "would rather go backward than forward." [12] Margery, already troubled by religious hysteria, saw in these untoward speculations the directing hand of heaven. More and more she longed for some form of religious life; she took to roaming from shrine to shrine in England. Her husband—"he was ever a good and easy man"—went with her, suffering her vagaries with an exemplary patience. She tried for a long time to persuade him to take with her the vow to live chaste. Always he refused. At last "it befell upon a Friday on Midsummer Even in right hot weather, as this creature [Margery] was coming from York-ward, bearing a bottle with beer in her hand, and her husband a cake in his bosom," he told her that, upon conditions, he would agree. So the two of them, kneeling together beside a wayside cross, made their vow, and then "ate and drank together in great gladness of spirit." [13]

But whether it was to worldly vanity or to devotion that her abounding energy was turned, Margery Kempe must be egregious. Even after her first conversion she had worn "gold pipes upon her head, and her hoods with the tippets were dagged. Her cloaks also were dagged and laid with divers colors that it should be more staring to men's sight." [14] Years after, when she had forsaken such vanities, she attempted to bully the Bishop of London and the Archbishop of Canterbury into giving her permission to wear a white gown and a ring, but they disliked the idea of "so singular a clothing," and though she talked to the archbishop in the garden at Lambeth "till the stars appeared in the firmament," and though she roundly rebuked him for "the great oaths swearing" of his household, she had to start on her pilgrimage in a less striking garb.[15]

That autumn she sailed from Yarmouth, a pilgrim with all the uninhibited fervor of the earliest times. So voluble, so aggressive, so lachrymose was her devotion that those in whose company she sailed lost patience with her. Either, they said, she must eat meat and drink wine at meals as they did, must "leave her weeping. . . . and not speak so much of holiness," or they would no longer have her with them. Of course she refused their terms; of course she continued the pilgrimage, sometimes in touch with the unwilling, protesting company, sometimes alone; now despised and mocked by them, for her piety was of that sort which invites, which even delights in, contumely; now vindicated by the approval of more discerning and spiritually minded persons. She sailed from Venice with the fellowship, but on board ship a priest stole one of her sheets and her maid deserted her; at the end of the voyage she professed herself to be in charity with them—"and if any of you hath anything trespassed against me, God forgive it you, as I do." [16] But she was not any the less scrupulous to record their ill behavior.

It was at Jerusalem and in the Church of the Holy Sepulcher that she was for the first time visited by the faculty of "crying in contemplation." "Plenteous tears," she had had before, "and many boistous sobbings," but this went beyond measure, and was a "crying and roaring . . . so loud and so wonderful that it made the people astonished." The gift, or affliction, was to grow upon her until "once she had fourteen in one day," and it was to cause her considerable unpopularity, folk at home complaining that "she howled as it had been a dog . . ." ". . . Some said it was a wicked spirit vexed her; some said it was a sickness . . . some banned [cursed] her; some wished she had been in the haven; some would she had been at sea in a bottomless boat . . ." [17]

Her return journey, and indeed her whole life after, was passed in this atmosphere of hysterical and militant devotion. She provoked and clearly enjoyed opposition, having always the most religious conviction that it was her duty to exhort and if necessary to rebuke. "To them that doubted not nor mistrusted not in their asking, her crying greatly profited to increase of merit and of virtue. To them that little trusted and little believed peradventure was little increase of virtue and of merit." [18] One who could use such a summary and subjective method of dividing the sheep from the goats is unlikely to have placated opponents. Many must have found her intolerable, and it is not surprising that "there was none so much against her as her daughter [in-law] that ought most to have been with her."

Yet, at the comfortable distance of over five hundred years, it is possible to like Margery Kempe, if only for the sake of the pungent Chaucerian flavor, the mass and drive of her personality. And we may add to this, upon the credit side, her treatment of her husband in his old age. For he, good man, when over sixty, "as he would have come down from his chamber barefoot and barelegged, he slithered or else failed of his footing, and fell down to the ground from the gresses, [stairs] and his head under him . . ." Torn between the claims of affection and piety Margery chose the humble way, "and kept him years after as long as he lived, and had full much labor with him, for in his last days he turned childish again, and lacked reason . . ." [19]

On Monday, February 27, 1417, a Gascon noble, a cousin to the Count of Foix, left his home to make the "Jerusalem Voyage." This was Nompar, lord of Caumont, of Castelnau, of Castelculier, and of Berliguières, a young man of twenty-seven years. With the opening of the second part of the Hundred Years' War France had become once more a battleground; so disturbed was the country that de Caumont did not take the ordinary pilgrim route, by Venice, but made for Barcelona, there to find shipping. Before he left he drew up a series of "Ordonnances" for his people to observe while he was away; they are mostly of a moral nature—lay folk are to live in peace together, priests are to be constant in prayer. For de Caumont was a man of deep and gentle piety; he knew the waste and wickedness of war and lamented them in words that come home to this generation, since men still "do not cease to make war, to take towns, to kindle fire, to force women, and to destroy the folk that cost Our Lord so dear." [20]

It was in the true spirit of pilgrimage that he left the wife and children he so greatly loved—the wife to whom he always refers as "m'amye," "my darling," and the "young and innocent" children for whom, two years before, he had written a book of moral precepts, the opening words of which are like a window giving upon a medieval springtime: "I, lord of Caumont, being twenty-five years old, was walking in a fair flower garden where many birds sang sweetly and graciously." [21]

The young man made his pilgrimage, received knighthood at the Holy Sepulcher, and returned in safety. But he was not to live out his life at home, ruling the folk he knew and walking in the "fair flower garden" of his castle. He was one of those who stood by the English overlords who had held Guienne for so long. In 1443 Charles VII disinherited him in favor of his younger brother, and Nompar, Seigneur de Caumont, came to England, an exile, and died there three years later.

After de Caumont come two more Frenchmen, the first of Flanders, the second a man of Guienne; both noblemen and both servants of those dukes of Burgundy who, from their capital at Dijon among the vineyards, ruled also over Brabant and the wealthy stirring towns of the Low Countries. Much of the history of France in the first half of the fifteenth century was determined by the friendships and enmities of the Burgundian duke. A sixteenth-century Carthusian, pointing to the hole in the skull of Duke John made by his assassins at Montereau, could tell the king of France of that day, "Through this hole, Sire, came the English into France," and speak the essential truth, for it was to avenge his father's murder that Philip the Good threw all his power into the scale against the Orleanists, among whom he reckoned the king of France, and allied himself with Henry V of England, the victor of Agincourt.

We are not concerned with the political results of that alliance—and what they might have been but for the early death of Henry no one can now guess—but the connection between Burgundy and England is interesting when we consider these two pilgrims. For quite apart from self-interest and the hard realities of statecraft, Henry and Philip were drawn together by one common and hereditary aspiration. Henry's father had fought for the Cross in Prussia and made the Jerusalem pilgrimage. Philip's father had been taken prisoner at the fall of Nicopolis (Nikopol), fighting against the Turk; his grandfather had reached Venice on his way to Jerusalem only to be turned back by a temporary ban laid by the Republic upon the passage of pilgrims.[22] With such precedents, and given not only the political circumstances of their day but also the character of the two men themselves, it was not unnatural that the thoughts of both king and duke turned toward the old Western and Christian ideal of crusade.

At the beginning of the century the eyes of Christian princes had been drawn to the Levant by that catastrophic attack on the growing Ottoman power by Timur, "the Scourge of God," who swept like a whirlwind through Asia Minor and Syria, leaving, as traces of his passage, ruined and empty cities, and, outside the shattered walls, tall pyramids built up of the skulls of their defenders. For a few years after that colossal raid, of which, in fact, the force was spent almost as soon as Timur died on his way to conquer India, it seemed possible for Europe to hope that the tide of Ottoman conquest had been checked, since Mohammed I, son of Timur's captive Sultan Bayazid, had to rebuild the unity of the Ottoman power in Asia Minor; the Turks had lost nearly all their European possessions except Adrianople, and were soundly defeated at sea by the Venetians off Gallipoli.

It was upon this seemingly hopeful prospect that Henry V, a captain never defeated in the field and in 1419 the arbiter of western Europe, looked out. A superb soldier, with a nature at once cold and fanatical, he began to dream of a greater crusade than his father's venture in Prussia. Let but the schism of the Church be healed, and he might lead the English archers, as well as the combined chivalry of England and France, to recover the Holy Places. Nor was he a man to allow even such a grandiose ideal to remain without its foundation upon exact knowledge of those practical details which determine strategy.

It was therefore to make a preparatory military reconnaissance that some time probably in 1421 Gilbert de Lannoy, the Fleming, chamberlain to Philip of Burgundy, "undertook the Jerusalem voyage by land at the request of the king of England, and of the king of France, and of Monseigneur Duke Philip, chief mover." [23]

De Lannoy was a good choice. A man of war from his

youth—his first taste of fighting was gained in a raid upon
the Isle of Wight—he had already made the Jerusalem and
Sinai pilgrimage. This time he set off for the Holy Land
neither as an ordinary pilgrim nor by the ordinary pilgrim's
route. He went first as ambassador, accompanied by a herald,
through Prussia, Poland, and Russia, distributing gifts of
jewels from the king of England to those rulers through
whose territories he passed. From Constantipole he sailed to
Rhodes and there deposited the golden clock intended for
Sultan Mohammed but made superfluous now by his death.
At Rhodes also he left all his company but two; the rest
"were very displeased at that," but now de Lannoy must
travel without ostentation, "so as to accomplish my inspec-
tion more discreetly." [24]

He began his investigations in Egypt, covering them
under the convenient pretense of pilgrimage to Sinai, and
then moving northward into Palestine. The result he recorded, and had two copies made of it: one for the king of
England, one for his own master.

"This is the report Messire Gilbert de Lannoy, Knight,
made. Upon visits to divers ports and rivers by him paid, as
well in Egypt as in Syria . . . By the command of the most
high, most puissant, and most noble prince King Henry
of England . . . whom God assoil." [25]

"Whom God assoil." De Lannoy had not yet returned
from this journey of investigation when Henry died at
Vincennes with his last thoughts on the Holy City. "Lord,"
he had prayed when he caught in the chanting of the priests
the name "Jerusalem," "Thou knowest that mine intent hath
been, and yet is if I might live, to re-edify the walls of
Jerusalem."

De Lannoy's report was written to supply information
on the military strength and strategic layout of Egypt and
Syria. Not Calvary and the Holy Sepulcher but the walls,
towers, ditches, the water supply of Jerusalem; not the errors of heterodox Christian sects but the fighting qualities

of Syrian, Saracen, Turkoman, and Egyptian were his concern. It is idle to hope to find in such a document any disclosure of the writer's personality. All is as it should be, terse, concentrated upon the military object. The interest of the treatise, apart from the very precise information which it gives about the Holy Land, lies in the motive which had caused it to be compiled.

What Henry, with his genius for war, had purposed and might have achieved continued for Philip of Burgundy as an aspiration, not so much to reconquer as to defend what was left of Christian power in the East. For after the accession of Murad II in 1421 it soon became apparent that the Ottoman power had paused only to consolidate itself and now was on the move again; Venice lost Salonika, Serbia was defeated, Hungary devastated, and Greece suffered the first of the Turkish attacks.

Yet for years Philip of Burgundy kept the Holy Places in mind. He paid for a hospice for pilgrims to be built at Ramle; he presented to the Franciscans at Mount Sion, for the Chapel of the Last Supper, a magnificent set of tapestries, interwoven with gold.[26] How seriously he in his turn contemplated the possibility of a crusade it is not easy to say. He had de Lannoy's report to go on; he also caused to be translated, under the title *Advis directif pour faire le passage d'oultre-mer*, a Latin treatise then commonly ascribed to the fourteenth-century Burchard of Mount Sion.[27] He certainly considered one project of intervention after another, and even when Constantinople had fallen he held at Ghent the great Feast of the Pheasant. Edward III had sworn upon the White Swan to recover his kingdom of France; in the same tradition of chivalry the duke swore upon a living pheasant, collared with ruby and diamond, to rescue the lost imperial city.

But a little more than twenty years before that he had sent out upon "a distant and secret journey" his chief esquire

carver, Bertrandon de La Brocquière.* De La Brocquière
went to Jerusalem; he was balked of the Sinai journey by an
untimely fever, but what he next set out to do was something
far more hazardous, was in fact, so they told him, impossible.
For he had undertaken to cross Asia Minor to the Turkish
capital, Brusa, and so by way of Constantinople home.

He went north to Damascus to make inquiries and satisfied
himself that at least he knew how to begin. His companions,
Burgundian nobles like himself, tried to persuade him to take
ship with them to Venice and so home. He refused. They
sailed from Beirut and he remained. At Damascus once more
he bought "a little horse," which, he says, turned out to be
very good; the clothes of a Saracen slave; a sword which he
must keep secret; and some other necessaries. He knew no
word of Turkish, Arabic, Hebrew, or Syrian, but a Jew
wrote down for him a list of useful phrases in Turkish and
Italian.[28] So provided, he joined a caravan making a homeward journey from Mecca to Brusa, a man so fearless that he
could be friendly with all and could therefore find friends
among even the wild Bedouin, a man who believed anything
was possible to one who had health, a strong constitution,
and some money. He was a devout Christian, and would visit,
at some risk, such a holy place as Nazareth; but he had the
ordinary interests of a gentleman too. He noted down the
Turkish method of burnishing and tempering steel; of shoe-
ing, feeding, and training horses, and the horsemanship of
their riders.[29]

At last, after about a year spent in the journey, he reached
Burgundy, "and I appeared in his [the duke's] presence in
the same clothes in which I had left Damascus, and I had led

---

* In his account of his adventure, written many years afterward, de La
Brocquière speaks as though his journey had been undertaken on his own
initiative. But the entry quoted above, discovered by M. Ch. Schefer,
Le Voyage d'outremer, Introd., p. xvii, shows clearly that the "secret journey" for the expenses of which the esquire carver received an allowance
of £200 was a mission entrusted to him by the duke.

in the horse that I had bought in the same town, which had carried me into France." The horse, the clothes, a Latin translation of the Koran, and a life of Mohammed written at his request by the Venetian consul's priest at Damascus, he presented to the duke.

Our next pilgrim is yet another Frenchman, Louis de Rochechouart, Bishop of Saintes, who made his pilgrimage in 1461.[30] A very positive, even a domineering, young man we may guess him, who, coming into his bishopric only the year before and upon a disputed election, was bold enough to go off at once to the Holy Land and pugnacious enough to start proceedings against his Chapter even while in Jerusalem.[31] This character we might even guess from his writing. "I think" and "in my opinion" are phrases which often recur, and he obviously was one who thought for himself and as he says preferred to write down what he himself saw rather than what he had read. If he quotes an authority— and he frequently quotes Bede—he will add perhaps "with whom I agree," but he will notice when things which he saw differed from Bede's account.[32] He listened and learned much while at Jerusalem from "Friar Laurence the Sicilian," but he will record a fact which from his own observation "is quite obvious" before remarking that "Friar Laurence, on the other hand, says to the contrary." A man, we must suspect, of a sharp tongue, he will interject, on occasion, a tartly humorous remark: Pilate's house, he says, "is in these days fairly well built, and pretty good; I do not know if it were so in the ancient time, but anyway it is good enough for a judge." [33] In the same spirit he pithily describes the assistant Saracen interpreters as "two little thieves." [34]

Yet he was a man who had friends—for one of whom he kept his journal and for whose benefit he notes the use of pitch from the Dead Sea upon palm trees and vines "to prevent ants and slugs getting up to the bunches of fruit. But you, Master Peter de Mamoris, following the advice of

Palladius do this in a different way with axle grease and ashes." [35] He had too, I think, a kindness for animals; why, otherwise, should he take the trouble to notice that, though there was plenty of rain water in the cisterns of Jerusalem for man and beast, yet "the sparrows find it very difficult to drink. For they must go down into the depths of the cistern, or they may not drink. But Master Stephen Talivelli provides them with water at his window, and pretty near all the sparrows of the city gather there." [36]

From his pilgrimage he returned to long years of strife with his Chapter. More than once imprisoned and constantly at odds with them and with their supporters, by 1486 his reason, though he was now only fifty-three, became impaired. It is a sad ending to the story of a man whom in his writings the reader has come to like.

Three years before Bishop Louis, and again a year after, William Wey, an English priest of the royal foundation at Eton, made the Jerusalem journey, having already accomplished the popular English pilgrimage to St. James of Compostella.[37] Closely connected with his account, so closely indeed that we can almost treat the two as one, is that of another English pilgrim, occasionally, but I think erroneously, called "John Moreson." * These two, either of whom copied from the other, or one or both from a common source, be-

* *Informacõn for Pylgrymes unto the Holy Londe*, ed. G. H. Freeling, Roxburghe Club, 1824. The supposition that "John Moreson" was the name of a pilgrim seems to have been founded upon the following sentence: "There passed from Venice . . . certain pilgrims toward Jerusalem in a ship of a merchants [*sic*] of Venice called John Moreson." But it is clear that the name is either that of the ship or of the owner of the ship, and it is not difficult to recognize under the English disguise the name Giovanni Morosini. As Venetian surnames used for ships were generally put into the feminine, it seems that the name of the merchant owner was intended. The date of the voyage is given in *Information for Pilgrims unto the Holy Land*, ed. E. Gordon Duff, Introd., p. ix, as 1481, 1487, or 1492, and he holds that the writer copied from Wey. The editor of *Expeditions to Prussia and the Holy Land by Henry Earl of Derby 1392*, p. lxiii, gives the date as about 1430, without stating a reason.

long to a type of pilgrim literature differing from any of those that we have yet considered. In both the account of the voyage is brief; the real purpose of the record is correctly stated in the title of the second, *Informacōn for Pylgrymes unto the Holy Londe*. Instead of the self-revelation of Margery Kempe, the gentle but chivalric piety of de Caumont, the concise military notes of de Lannoy, de La Brocquière's lively narrative of adventure, Bishop Louis' sharp personal observations, we have, in spite of a seasoning of copybook religion, the true guidebook, full of plain, homespun, useful fact: the mileage between towns, rates of exchange, a long and very informative shopping list, a tariff of fees and tips to be paid in the Holy Land, word lists of Greek, of "the language of Moresque" and "of Turkey," and, in as mercantile a spirit, an exact record of the indulgences to be gained at the Holy Places.

There is nothing in either that is personal, and yet perhaps their flat utilitarianism reveals a trait in the national character. And there is besides something in each which, like straws on a wind, tells us that already in England a wind was blowing, and that it blew from off the sea.

In William Wey's account of his journey to Compostella he drops a remark which in the arid narrative gives us a sudden glimpse of the tumbling waves of the Channel. "The first part of England," says he, "seen and perceived by our sailors is called Browsam Rocks; the second is called Long Ships, and these are three rocks; the third is called Popylhopyl; the fourth, Mount's Bay, the fifth Lizard, of which people say—

'Be the chorel [churl] never so hard
He shall quake by the beard ere he pass Lyzarde.' "

He gives us, as well as that rhyme, another, not this time either English or of the sea. For he writes down a stave of music and the words to it, under the heading "Cantus parvulorum Hyspanie saltantium ante peregrinationes pro blankys et splintris."

And the song of the little Spanish boys turning cartwheels for coppers in front of the pilgrims was as follows:

"Sancte Jaco a Compostel da vose leve a votir tere,
 Sancte Jaco bone baron de vose da de bon pardon,
 Bona tempe, bona vye, bona vente, bon perpassi,
 Da istys kee sunt assen una branck a vowse curtese." [38]

And even in the wooden prose of the *Informacōn for Pylgrymes* there is a single phrase which, it seems to me, is a presage of what is to be found, so richly strewn, throughout the pages of Richard Hakluyt.

"In the seven and twenty day"—so runs the opening sentence of the curt narrative of the voyage—"there passed from Venice under sail out of the haven at the sun going down, certain pilgrims . . ."

So we come, not quite twenty years after William Wey, to Friar Felix himself, and at once in his narrative find ourselves in the midst of a profusion of trivial, precious, and very human detail. Nor is Felix's own account of those two pilgrimages of 1480 and 1483 the only one which we have to draw on. Curiously enough, each time he went to Jerusalem the Friar traveled in the company of two other men who were to leave accounts of their journeys. On the "autumn voyage" of 1480 went Santo Brasca, a Milanese, and an anonymous person, probably a clerk and almost certainly from Paris. Again, for the journey of 1483 we have as well as Felix's own, the records of Bernhard von Breydenbach and Brother Paul Walther.

It was a dangerous voyage indeed upon which pilgrims must embark in the summer of 1480. Venice had just made peace with the Turk after a war that had lasted seventeen years, but that war had been disastrous to her; not only had the long and costly effort drained her strength and wealth, but she had lost Negropont, though her tightening hold over Cyprus gave her some compensation. Yet, if Venice was at peace, and splendidly entertaining the Turkish ambassador, that did not mean that there was peace in the Levant. Already, before the pilgrims left Venice, a Turkish fleet had raided and sacked Otranto, and the Knights of St. John were fighting in Rhodes for the Cross, and for life, against a great and sustained Turkish attack.

With the Paris pilgrim we come nearer to the diarist, that product of Renaissance individualism. He assures the reader that during the journey he wrote down "in the evening what during the day I had seen that was worthy of notice, keeping faithful record of those things which follow, not adding to them nor leaving out anything that was true, so far as we could know it by our eyes." But we are not yet very near, for what he thought worthy of record is hardly at all personal to himself, and not often concerned with those trivialities which, in the diary of the ordinary man, are, for posterity, above rubies. His eye, however, was quick and keen, the eye of a man who knew when he had left behind his familiar things and embarked upon the great experience of foreign travel. "Susa," he says, after a long list of French towns and cities, distinguished occasionally by some such brief remark as "bonne ville," "ville," "chasteau," "Susa is the beginning of Piedmont, where they begin to reckon the distance by miles; the clocks begin to strike differently from those in France" for they strike at noon twenty-four hours; also after this place the women do not wear hoods any more but only coifs and kerchiefs.[39]

Venice he describes with enthusiasm and particularity, often referring it for comparison to distant Paris. "They say that there are more boats in Venice than there are horses or mules in Paris, and that more ships come there in a year than horses pass through Paris." Sometimes too he will surprise the reader by a tiny detail, picked out from a crowded scene. The Turkish ambassador, who arrives in Venice while the pilgrims wait for their galley to sail, goes glorious in red velvet, flowered with cloth of gold; at Modon (Methone), on the voyage out, the Frenchman notices another Turkish envoy in black velvet with a pattern of leaves of cloth of gold.[40]

Santo Brasca, the Milanese, made the pilgrimage in far greater comfort than did Felix, the clerk of Paris, or even the German nobles of the party. A wealthy young man, and of a noble house, when he concluded the account of his pilgrimage with a set of instructions for any who might come after, he prescribed, as part of the luggage of every pilgrim, two sacks. The first was for patience, but the second must be full of money: 200 Venetian ducats was the sum he advised, though 150 would do, 100 being necessary for any man "who values his life and is used to living delicately in his home," and 50 for sickness or any other emergency.[41] Money and his Italian nationality together insured that the "patrono" of the galley, a notorious skinflint, if no worse, should treat him "as a son"; that treatment included the advantage of living and eating with the captain, an advantage which Brasca candidly admits.

So, with a quick, amused, interested glance, the young man went his way among the other pilgrims, paying more attention, or at least describing with more particularity the

dress and customs of the "Moors" and the curiosities of the
bazaars of Jerusalem than the Holy Places themselves,
though it is true that he records, as no other, the prayers
and chants used by pilgrims. He was sympathetic enough
toward the discomforts and sufferings of his companions, but
while German knights were dying of fever in the galley at
Larnaca, Santo Brasca spent an agreeable few days in Nicosia
with a Lombard merchant, returning to the ship in leisurely
fashion just in time to sail, and in such ample comfort that
even when he and his host spent a night under canvas they
were served from silver.[42]

Those two fellow pilgrims who were at Jerusalem with
Felix in his second pilgrimage, Bernhard von Breydenbach
and Brother Paul Walther, present, curiously enough, a striking contrast not only each with the other but each also with
Felix himself. Of all men few could be so impersonal as, in
his book, is the noble chamberlain of Mainz, von Breydenbach; few more full of personality than Brother Paul of
Guglingen, friar of the Fransciscan convent at Heidelberg,
and Brother Felix himself. But again, no two men could be
further apart in spirit than the cantankerous, self-tormenting
Paul, and Felix, in whose record pleasant meetings, kind-
nesses received, laughter, friendships, good food and good
wine take up so much space.

Bernhard von Breydenbach, a layman, for all that he was
canon of Mainz, was already, when he made his pilgrimage,
a man of importance, being a member of that opulent Chapter which, when rebuked by the pope for self-indulgence,
excused themselves by saying that they had more wine than
was needed for Mass but not enough to turn their mills
with. Red-haired, with his full red beard,[43] he moves im-
portantly though indistinctly in the background of both
Paul's and Felix's narratives. His own book is a curious pro-
duction. Determined to produce a work worthy of himself
and his subject, he went to the length of taking with him, as

far as Jerusalem at least, an artist, "the learned and ingenious Erhard Rewich," * so that he should cunningly draw and reproduce upon paper things fair and lovely to the eye. Nor was this all. Distrusting his own powers as an author, von Breydenbach also procured Friar Martin Roth, "an eminent and venerable Doctor of Divinity," as Felix calls him, to write the book for him.[44] Friar Martin Roth may have been all that Felix proclaims, but the author of a book of travel is sadly handicapped when he has not himself made the journey. The result of Breydenbach's expenditure is a beautifully printed and illustrated volume, containing colored woodcuts representing various ports of call on the way to the Holy Land, and also some of the many races and sects of Palestine. But as an account of a pilgrimage it is a dry thing. Much of its space is taken up by exposition and refutation of the beliefs of Moslems and of heretic Christians. To give weight to charges against the Jewish race there is a laborious calculation of the amount of compound interest which the usurer would receive at the end of twenty-two years upon the loan of a Frankfurt florin; the total reaches 5,691 florins, 16 shillings, and a few odd coppers. Apart from this, and a couple of receipts against fleas, worse, and seasickness, there is nothing in the account of the Jerusalem journey but what is to be found in the common stock of pilgrim records.

The book of Brother Paul Walther the Fransciscan bears the same title as that of the prosperous cathedral dignitary from Mainz, but there is nothing else in them that is alike. With Friar Paul we are once more in the world of Margery

---

* Davies, *Breydenbach*, pp. xxix–xxx, considers that Rewich certainly printed as well as illustrated von Breydenbach's book, possibly borrowing for this purpose Peter Schoeffer's type, but cf. E. Gordon Duff, *Early Printed Books*, London, 1903, p. 33.

Von Breydenbach, *Peregrinatio* [f. 104b], states expressly that Rewich accompanied him to Sinai; he must therefore, it seems, be identified with that Erhard who in Felix's list, *Evagatorium*, II, 107, is described as "companion, esquire and servant" of the count of Solms.

Kempe, a world where the heavenly powers contend with Satan for the human soul, and through which that soul moves, supremely self-aware. Like Margery the friar must reveal and justify and betray himself, in something of the spirit of the great diarists but without the zest and dash of the Englishwoman's egotism. His book, as well as being an account of his pilgrimage, is something of a *Pilgrim's Progress*, something of a tragicomedy, told in a Latin of grotesque barbarity and by a method all his own, largely in a series of dramatic dialogues. Goaded always by his own nature, jealous, introspective, emulous, he went through life, finding his present company and profession always unendurable, hoping always by change to attain peace.

The first words of his book put the unhappy man at once before us:

"When I considered how many years, eighteen or twenty, of my youth I had passed in poverty and toil as a wretched poor scholar, I betook me, not for my soul's salvation but for bread, to a certain order of Religious, the order, that is to say, of the Holy Sepulcher, and put on the black habit with the red cross. After a year's probation I professed the Rule of St. Augustine. But alas, in that order neither did I progress in things of the spirit; rather I squandered in worldly vanity and profitlessly wasted eighteen years." [45]

Even when, "not by my merits but only by the grace of God," he experienced conversion and later joined the Franciscan order, peace was no nearer. "Though I was able, in confession and by preaching, to hold out a helping hand to many, to myself I profited nothing, inadequate and inept as I was." Once more he sought about for some refuge, and seemed to find hope of it in a plan to go to Jerusalem, and there, remote and in quiet, to reside among the Franciscans of Mount Sion.

He received license to do this and set off upon his journey. But always his puritanical conscience tormented him. At a friendly Italian convent, "in bodily comfort and peace," with good food well cooked after the fashion of the Italian brothers, and most delicious white wine, he found to his horror that he ". . . began to grow amazingly fat . . . 'O wretched Brother Paul' I said within myself." [46]

Not that all his self-depreciation prevented him from holding the conviction that the Heavenly Powers were keenly interested in his case. If he had a stomach-ache, it was sent to him "de alto." If, in a midnight expedition in the Holy Land, the untimely braying of his donkey might betray the presence of the pilgrims to lurking robbers, he had but to utter an argumentative prayer, the donkey was silent "at last," and the whole party proceeded in safety, with the exception of some of the Saracen escort, who, being pagans, and therefore upon the periphery of Brother Paul's pious influence, were allowed to fall from their horses during the journey.[47]

Brother Paul's technique of prayer resembled that of some modern revivalists. In perplexity he would address one of his reasoned and explanatory petitions above, and wait until "there came clearly into my mind the words . . ." which gave the solution of the difficulty. Sometimes the answer was as homely as it was detailed. While crossing the desert he suffered from what was probably a "desert sore": in great distress he prayed to God and St. Catherine, and received in answer exact directions as to treatment: "Take salt and put it in water . . . ," and so on.[48]

In his relations with his fellow men he was carping, suspicious, difficult. As regularly as Margery Kempe, he was in the right, but he lacked her superb overriding confidence. Sometimes he will dress his failings in the most decent of disguises; sometimes he will reveal them with that nakedness of statement which is the true diarist's gift, showing himself not as he wished but as he knew himself to be. At Hebron it was from the highest motives and with a flood of the most rational arguments that he resisted the rash desire of the other pilgrims to steal by night into the mosque in order to see the tomb of Abraham.⁴⁹ But at Alexandria he tells an anecdote which betrays the coward without attempt at concealment. His companion, disregarding Paul's prudent counsels, got into trouble with "a black Ethiopian" who began to throw stones. Twice hit, "my friend began to throw stones himself, but the Moor shouted to other Moors. One of these ran up, and I fled, crying loudly to my friend 'Run, run quick. You'll do no good, but only make him more angry with us.' "⁵⁰ That such a man as this should have dared the Sinai journey and even offered himself as one of the missionary friars required to teach Christianity to the people of the semimythical Prester John in Abyssinia gives the measure of his desire to escape from the irritations of human contact.

At the risk of delaying too long over Friar Paul I shall let him tell the story of his quarrel with that other friar, by name John Wild, whom he had chosen at Heidelberg to accompany him on his pilgrimage. They were in Italy, on the road to Venice, where Brother Paul hoped to arrive in time to catch a galley going to the Holy Land.

"But as we went it happened that my companion caught a catarrh or cold in the head, and he began to be downhearted and to trail along far behind me, and the more I hurried the slower he came on, so that it looked as if he was doing it to spite me. Before that I had been able to tell from what he said that he would have liked to stay several days in every convent and place. And it seemed quite clear to me that what he wanted was to have an easy time, but I would not let him . . . so we were on bad terms with each other though neither of us had said anything. Yet at Verona I said to him, 'If you are ill, say so, and stay here . . . !' He answered 'No.' However we stayed that Sunday in Verona."

On Monday, after Mass and a meal, they set off again, "and again, just as before, he followed a long way behind, but I dragged him along as best I could, through Vincenza and Padua to Venice."

At Venice, to Brother Paul's chagrin, they found that the

galley had already left. It was Brother John's opportunity
and he took it, abusing the other for a hard man who would
listen to no one. " 'What's the good of all your running
now?' " said he. Paul gave no answer, but prayed for patience.

Since it was impossible either to sail, or, without the Provincial Vicar's permission, to remain in the Franciscan convent at Venice, the only thing to be done was to seek the
Vicar at Mantua. So back they must go, hardly speaking to
one another for twenty German miles, "but we marched as
if alone, one in front, the other far behind, divided both in
body and mind but always within sight of each other," and
as he went Paul turned over in his mind all the wrongs he
suffered—how he had trusted Brother John, had chosen him
from the other fathers and brothers, had received his promise of loyalty and service, "and now he refused these, and
was loyal only to himself, providing himself secretly with
this and that which he needed, and forgetting all about me."

With such inflammable material it was only a matter of
time before there was an explosion. And that evening, when,
as Brother Paul put it, "the borders of the Mantua duchy
were approaching to us," [51] the moment came. Brother Paul,
far ahead as usual, found that they had lost their way. It was
too much. It was also a chance of getting his own back after
the fiasco at Venice. "I became possessed by a terrible spirit,
stood still, and waited for my companion.[52] When he came
up I shouted furiously, 'I'm surprised at you: you were in
this country before I was and you have no idea of the
way . . .'

"And I threw in his teeth certain times when he had failed
me; and what yet he would do, I knew not. At that he
promptly demanded permission to leave me, saying, 'If I
don't please you, dismiss me and let me go.' 'I shall be delighted,' said I at once, 'to do what you ask.' And I added,
'When we come to the Convent I will tell you so before the
fathers so that they also shall know why we separate.' "

But first they must reach the convent, and as they went on "in silent rage . . ." accompanied, no less, by God and the devil, they were met by some men of the country who warned them that, late as it was, they would be unable to cross the water which separated them from the convent where they hoped to spend the night.

Their only alternative, since it was too late to turn back, was to go on to another within the city. But there, in the gate, they saw customs' officials who, for fear of plague, were examining those who would enter as to where they had come from and what was their business. It was an awkward corner, but Paul, though almost despairing, was, after prayer, able to resign himself to God's will.

"And just listen what happened. Who, hearing this will doubt that God did not do a miracle . . . For at once the divine mercy touched me, and I came cheerfully up to the men sitting in the gateway, greeted them pleasantly and went on. And they greeted me again, and said nothing else at all, nor did anyone stop us going in, but when we were within the gate a man came to us, as if he were a porter, and said, 'How did you get in? What's all this now? Where have you come from?'

"My heart sank, but I answered with the truth; I would not lie; and I said, 'We have come from Vicenza.'

"He was silent at once, said no more, but bade us go in peace."

That was a great moment for Brother Paul, but a greater was to come. For not only did a man encountered by chance "in a piazza" confirm, by his astonishment, the friar's triumph, but at the convent the brethren showed the most gratifying amazement.

" 'How,' " they asked, " 'did you get into the city? Who spoke for you? Did you tell a mighty lie? Did you give surety?' . . .

"I answered, 'Our Lord helped us by his special grace.' "

"Ipsi dixerunt, 'Credatis firmiter,' " and what they said

I am tempted to translate by a modern locution: "They said, 'You're telling us.' " [53]

So much, for the moment, of Brother Paul. He and Brother John Wild reached Jerusalem and there Paul remained until in the summer of 1483 there came, among the pilgrims of that season, a number of German knights and churchmen, among whom were the chamberlain of the cathedral chapter of Mainz and Brother Felix Fabri of the Dominican house at Ulm.

The last of our pilgrims came to Jerusalem in the final decade of the century when there was peace between Venice and the Ottoman Turks, and before the recent discoveries of the Portuguese had visibly affected the wealth and splendor of the Republic. Not yet was it apparent to Italians that power was passing to the ruder nations beyond the Alps, and even if power were lost all the graces of life still remained. Men born in the rich and profuse Renaissance civilization would, for yet another half century at least, believe, as Venetian ambassadors to the court of our Tudor kings believed, that nowhere so well as in Venice would the unruly young barbarians be tamed by the experience of living in a truly civilized state.

So Canon Pietro Casola, of a noble Milanese family, made his journey, in 1494, looking down, from the height of his urbanity, upon the jostling crowd of all those pilgrims whose homes were north of the Alps.

"I always let the Ultramontanes—who trod on each other's heels in their haste to leave—rush in front." [54] That was his practice, whether he were disembarking at Jaffa or visiting the Church of the Holy Sepulcher. "As soon as I saw that the crowd of Ultramontanes had diminished, I went again with my lighted candle . . . and I touched the places and relics . . . without any impediment." [55]

With men of his own race and class he kept none of this disdainful distance. The little supper, to celebrate the pilgrims' departure from Venice, which Casola himself cooked, "Milanese fashion, especially a pasty," [56] must have been a cheerful affair, for the old man close on seventy, cultured, witty, sophisticated, was ready to laugh, even at himself, as he laughed when in a night alarm at Ramle, "half asleep as I was, I fell from the plank [on which he slept] to the ground in such a way, that there was not a single pilgrim who came to grief . . . except Casola who fell off from his perch." [57]

This dignitary of the church, deeply learned in matters of liturgy but disillusioned and seasoned by sixteen years as secretary at the Milanese Embassy in Rome, looked at the world with a gaze at once critical and amused. The simple fervor of the true pilgrim was not to be found in one who could poke demure fun at apostle and evangelist, suggesting that the then Cathedral of St. Peter in Venice was bare of ornaments because "St. Mark, who was his disciple, must have stolen them." [58]

At Venice it was "to while away the tedious time . . ." that he went visiting the neighboring monasteries, and in these it was not the sanctity of the relics which he comments upon but the beauty of architecture, the gold and carving of choirs and stalls, a façade of marble and gold, a Pietà, "sculptured with such art and genius that, setting aside the figure of Christ, all the others seem . . . alive . . ." [59] His interest in relics, when he does specially mention them, is more that of an archaeologist than of a worshiper. The complete body of St. Simeon at Zara moved him to astonishment. It is, he says, "perfectly preserved, there is nothing in the world lacking. . . . The mouth is open and in the upper jaw there are no teeth; I was not surprised at that, because he was very old when he died . . . I went several times to see the relic . . . And the more I looked the more it seemed to me a stupendous thing, most of all when I remembered the time of his death, which could not be less than fourteen hundred and ninety-three years ago." [60]

Not even the sanctity of Jerusalem itself could disturb the equilibrium of his aesthetic judgment. Coolly and deliberately he set down his opinion of that goal of pilgrim desires, and it is a poor one. There is "one beautiful building, that is its Mosque. . . . I saw nothing else beautiful in the said city." [61] Led about the usual tour of the Holy Places, he preserved his detachment. He had, he said, borrowing and elaborating Brasca's fancy, brought with him on pilgrimage three sacks, the first containing patience, the second money, the third faith (by which, I think, we should understand "belief"). So, describing a sight-seeing expedition in Jerusalem, he says, "When we had seen what the friars had wanted us to see—opening the first and third sacks where it was necessary . . . we arrived at the Hospital all hot and covered with dust . . ." [62] And it is quite clear that he enjoyed, far more than this trip with the friars, another day's outing when he was shown round Jerusalem by "a very agreeable Moor."

It might seem fitting that we should end our list of pilgrims with this Italian, since the close of the century, and more, the close of the whole Middle Ages, may be said to be theirs. Yet it was, indeed, far more an opening than a close, and through the door which Italy had set wide came stalking the young crude nations, staring, fumbling, quarreling, but with the future in their greedy hands.

So the last of all our pilgrims is one of Casola's despised "Ultramontanes," a German noble, by name Arnold von Harff. In spite of all the traditional record of indulgences, in spite of the number of pages upon which von Harff, with rosary, script, and pilgrim staff, is depicted kneeling before the Three Kings, or St. Peter, or the crucified Christ, his book is far less a record of pilgrimage than of travel. His journey was made in company not with any band of pilgrims but with merchants going about their business. And if he did not go as far as he said, yet he claimed to have gone to places which were the bourn of no pilgrim travel—to India, Madagascar, and the Mountains of the Moon.

It matters little, for our purpose, whether he went to these places or not, whether or not he saw the white lions and white elephants at the court of the king of Phasagar [63] or the children playing in the streets of Lack with pearls and precious stones. What matters is that the claim was made, and that von Harff stood with one foot already in a world in which the pilgrim was to become a rare bird, a survival, a freak; in which pilgrim galleys no longer sailed regularly from Venice; in which an adventurous mind sent a man gadding either into strange ways of thought and belief or out upon strange seas and round about the globe, but not along the ancient routes of pilgrim travel.

## CHAPTER II

# LEARNING TO BE A PILGRIM

OF all our pilgrims only three—Margery Kempe, Friar Paul, and Felix—tell anything of the events and emotions which led them to take the pilgrim vow. Those which concerned Margery and Paul we know already; what Felix reveals is not only more copious but in a completely different vein. Not for him were the struggles by which a willful and unbalanced enthusiast won her way to go on pilgrimage; still less did he share those goading doubts and resentments which drove Paul Walther out from the convent.

What set Felix longing to make the journey was first his earnest desire to understand, in order to preach, the Scriptures; and second that temperament of the born traveler which, unconsciously but most vividly, he betrays in his narrative. The first he can well justify by reference to St. Jerome; had not that saint said that "as they who have seen Athens will the better understand Greek history, and they who have sailed from the Troad . . . to Ostia on Tibur the third book of the Aeneid, even so he will more clearly understand the Holy Scriptures who has beheld Judea with his own eyes"? And Felix drives the point home by recalling how mere laymen "return [from pilgrimage] arguing about the evangelists and prophets, talking of theological matters, and sometimes refute and inform learned and erudite persons when there is question of some difficulty in Holy Scripture." [1] As for his temperament Felix was too far from an introvert to be aware that he had such a thing.

It is true that he had his own perplexities, but they were strictly practical, and in retrospect, when his two pilgrimages had turned him into a seasoned traveler, trifling. At the time, however, they seemed to be formidable, and "I ran about hither and thither more than I need have done, to obtain advice." For what about leave of absence? What about money? What about the perils of the journey? "I was frightened. I feared for my life. I dreaded the sea too, which I had never yet seen, but of which I had heard much." [2]

The first person whose advice Felix sought was Count Eberhart of Württemberg, but he refused to commit himself further than to say that, like matrimony and war, a journey to Jerusalem, though good in itself, might turn out badly. "A noble old knight," whom Felix next consulted, and who himself had made the pilgrimage, declared that only his age prevented him from repeating it. A nun, "famed for her devotion, and remarkable, some thought, for holiness," was even more encouraging. " 'Go! Quick! Quick!' she answered with extraordinary joyfulness, 'make your journey. Stay no longer, and God be with you in the way.' " [3] These words, spoken perhaps by Elizabeth Krelin, whom Felix mentions elsewhere as "most dear to me in God as spiritual mother, and in Christ as daughter," were enough for Felix. From that moment he began to make his preparations.

Difficulties were soon overcome; a friend in Rome got the pope's license for the pilgrimage. As for money, when Felix showed the license and confessed his intention to his dear friend and Prior, Ludwig Fuchs, that was at once provided, for the Prior himself and the provincial general of the order furnished what was necessary. Moreover, when word of the Friar's intention got about, he found himself invited to act in the capacity which later would have been described as that of "bear leader" to a young gentleman of Bavaria, whom his father wished to dispatch, not upon an educational "Grand Tour," but upon the pilgrimage to Jerusalem, there to receive knighthood at the Holy Sepulcher.

"Give me my scallop shell . . ."

wrote Sir Walter Raleigh when the pilgrim had ceased to be a familiar sight upon English roads for about as long as, today, the stagecoach:

> "Give me my scallop shell of quiet,
> My staff of hope to lean upon,
> My scrip of faith, immortal diet,
> My bottle of salvation,
> My gown of glory, hope's true gage,
> And thus I'll take my pilgrimage."

That retrospective description of the pilgrim's outfit may stand for Felix and for his "young Lord George von Stein" in all but two particulars. Felix would wear, instead of the gray gown of the pilgrim, the black and white habit of his order, and both he and young George, instead of the scallop shell of St. James of Compostella, would fasten the red cross of Jerusalem upon the black or gray hat. Otherwise the staff, iron-pointed like an alpenstock, the scrip and bottle were necessary for all pilgrims.

The scrip and bottle, "not for indulgence, but only just enough to keep body and soul together," were for use upon such expeditions as those which, in the Holy Land, took the pilgrims beyond reach of the bazaars of Jerusalem. Our English pilgrims exhort their readers, with earnest particularity, "when ye shall ride to flume Jordan, take with you out of Jerusalem bread, wine, water, hard cheese and hard eggs," [4] the very same meal upon which Felix was to fall and roll when thrown from his ass, so that when he opened the scrip he found all his food ground into the smallest crumbs. Being very hungry Felix sat down to the crumbs "and ate those mixed up bits with delight . . . regretting only that they were so few," for on his pilgrimage, he explains, he took and ate without turning a hair food which, in the comfort of home, would have disgusted him. [5]

How Felix carried his money, and where he put all those brooches, rosaries, and rings which he carried in order to lay them on the Holy Places, he does not say. Men worth plundering, like Bernhard von Breydenbach, carried their gold stitched into a belt. Felix will have found some safe place for such a ring as that which the mayor of Ulm entrusted to him, passed down as it had been from father to son; certainly the ring came safe back to its owner, and Felix calculated that its value, in the mayor's eyes, had been exactly doubled.

In the year 1480, just at that season in which, as Chaucer knew, men long to go on pilgrimage, namely on April 14, Felix, having preached his farewell sermon, mounted his horse, and with Prior Ludwich Fuchs set out for Memmingen, where he should meet "Master George." Of the start from the convent at Ulm he says nothing; the parting from Fuchs was what mattered; at Memmingen next morning the two friends kissed, not without tears, the Prior insisting that Felix should promise to remember him at the Holy Places, to write (if he might find a messenger), to come back soon. "Then sadly he left me, returning with the servant to Ulm, to his sons, my brothers there." That parting took away at a stroke all Felix's courage and all his delight in pilgrimage. "And I raged at myself for having entered upon it. All who would have dissuaded me I thought of now as my best counselors and true friends; those who had led me into it I reckoned my deadly enemies. At that moment I had rather look on Swabia than on the land of Canaan, Ulm was sweeter to me than Jerusalem; I was more frightened than ever about the sea, and . . ." (this is a most honest traveler) "if I had not been ashamed I should have hurried after Master Ludwig and gone back to Ulm with him, for that was what then I most longed for." [6]

Shame, however, did prevent that flight from the unknown; Felix, with the young man and his servant, set out for Innsbruck, and by the time they reached the Alps the

Friar is able to use one of his favorite words, for already they were traveling "merrily," having discovered, as they came to make each other's acquaintance, "that we and our tastes agreed well together." So that though they had lost their way, and though, having no common language with the people of the inn, they could use only signs, their night at Bassano, with as much of the local red wine as they liked to drink, must have been cheerful.

So much, without any information about mileages, or rates of exchange ("let those who want such, read other books of pilgrimages"),[7] without even a mention of relics seen and revered upon the way, is all that Felix says of this first stage in their pilgrimage, which landed them at that great port of pilgrim travel—the city of Venice.

Even before the fifteenth century Venice had monopolized the pilgrim traffic to Jerusalem, and, as with her other concerns, had organized it with a thoroughness and precision which belong rather to the modern than to the medieval world, the state itself often fulfilling the functions both of the shipping company and the travel agency, and when allowing individual enterprise, minutely and jealously controlling it.

Directly he reached Venice the pilgrim found himself the object of almost fatherly care on the part of the state. There were inns for him to put up at, and license to keep such an inn must be sought from the Senate.[8] But it was not enough that his lodging should be respectable; the crowds of pilgrims which poured into Venice each pilgrimage season must be shepherded about the strange city and protected from those who would exploit them. For this purpose, since a time long before that of Felix's pilgrimage, the Venetian State had regularly appointed officials called *Cattaveri*, and, under them, a number of "Piazza Guides." At the beginning of the century two of the twelve Piazza guides must be on duty during every week, keeping, from dawn to dusk, their station either on the Rialto or in the Piazza of St. Mark, and these two must have command of more than one foreign language between them. Human nature being what it is, these guides at one time began to make a practice of taking the dinner hour off. This would not do; it was enacted that while one dined the other must remain on duty; later the Senate softened, and the dinner hour was allowed.[9]

The business of these officers was to interpret for the pilgrims, to help them to obtain the correct exchange for their money, to see that they were not fleeced in the shopping so necessary for the next stage of their journey, to bring them into contact with the captains of the pilgrim galleys, and to a certain extent advise them in the agreements which were then made. Over all these activities the Cattaveri kept a sort of watching brief; appeal could be made at any time to them, the contract between captain and pilgrims must be handed in at their office three days before it was signed.[10]

The records of the Venetian Senate show what vigilance and ingenuity were needed in order that the profiteering tendencies of innkeepers and guides might be thwarted. But the battle against their peccadilloes was as nothing to that against the greed and insubordination to statute of the captains; all of them of the great noble houses of Venice, and by the circumstances of the case removed for the greater part of the voyage from supervision by the state.

From as far back as the early years of the thirteenth century the Senate had laid down regulations which, if observed, should insure the safety and comparative comfort of their pilgrim clients. Every pilgrim galley sailing from Venice must have a cross painted at a certain level on the hull; this served the same purpose as our Plimsoll mark, lading with relation to this cross being graded according to the age, and hence the seaworthiness, of the vessel. So many sailors, so many rowers, must be shipped; sailors in the earlier century, and again during the dangerous times of the Ottoman advance, must be provided with arms, must be over eighteen, must take an oath to look after ship and tackle, and

not to steal more than five small soldis' worth. Captains must
be at least thirty years old.[11] In order to prevent these noble
captains from merely painting up ancient and unseaworthy
craft, the magistrates were instructed to send experts to inspect these before sailing, and the Venetian governors at
various ports were made responsible for seeing that the
captains of the pilgrim galleys did not load them up with
any more merchandise than was agreed upon between captain and pilgrims.[12] But this list of provisions, regulations,
prohibitions could be prolonged almost indefinitely. Let us
sum it up by saying that no possible opportunity seems to
have been lost by the Venetian captains for making something "on the side" out of the pilgrim traffic, and that such
sharp practice was nosed out and forbidden (as we shall see,
vainly forbidden) by the state, through a period of more
than three hundred years.

The great flow of Jerusalem pilgrims to Venice was ac-
commodated for the journey in three different classes of
vessels. For the rich, the "V.I.P.'s" of the period, there was
the galley, hired out by the Venetian State to the noble pilgrim. For the poor there was the sailing ship. For the vast mass
of pilgrims there was the regular service of galleys, timed
to leave Venice at two seasons of the year, that is to say soon
after Easter and soon after Ascension Day.

The practice of hiring a galley to persons of wealth and
importance was considered by the Venetian State as part of
their foreign policy. With the enlightened self-interest fitting in a nation of splendid shopkeepers, the Senate in 1392
declared that it was "wise and prudent to oblige the princes
of the world . . . having in view the facilities and favors
which our merchants trading in those ports may receive and
obtain." [13]

Though so candid about their motive, the Fathers of the
State seem to have been less truthful about the terms of their
bargain in this case. The minutes of their meeting state that
the galley in which Henry of Lancaster, later Henry IV,

passed oversea to the Holy Land was lent, furnished, and
stocked free. The earl's account books tell another tale;
a payment of 2,785 ducats goes down under the heading of
"Skippagium" [14] for the hire of the galley. However the
Signory voted 300 ducats to be spent on a farewell entertainment before Henry sailed and another 100 for a similar
function on his return. And, one way or another, the sprat
caught its mackerel, for when Henry of Lancaster became
Henry King of England in 1399 he promised to treat all
Venetians as his own subjects.

Lancaster was by no means the only great noble to whom
the Senate hired out their galleys for the Jerusalem journey.
His enemy, Mowbray of Norfolk, in 1399; a Portuguese
prince in 1406; and others throughout the fifteenth century
made the pilgrimage in this way. [15]

While the great went overseas, each with his own household, in a galley, lent or hired by the Venetian State, the
poor would travel most cheaply in a sailing ship. When the
writer of the *Informacōn for Pylgrymes* sailed with "Luke
Mantell" each of forty-six pilgrims on board paid as he could
afford 32, 26, or 24 ducats for his return fare to Jaffa, with
food included. Devout captains sometimes carried friars "for
the love of God." The less devout took them at a reduced
rate, charging 15 to 20 ducats for the voyage out and back. [16]

But the ordinary run of pilgrims traveled in the regular
service of pilgrim galleys, though even among these ordinary
pilgrims there were often to be found great men who,
whether from motives of humility or parsimony, arrived
in Venice and took their passage without advertising their
wealth and rank. This practice caused the Signory considerable anxiety, ". . . on account of the abominable way in
which princes, counts and other foreign noblemen who
went disguised as pilgrims, to the Holy Sepulchre, on board
our galleys, had been and were actually treated" by avari-
cious galley captains. What such treatment could be we
shall see later, for Felix and his companions sailed with a

captain notorious for his avarice and bad faith. The Venetian State, acutely sensitive to the opinion of such great persons, ". . . considering how much they can injure or aid those of our merchants and citizens who pass through their countries," [17] could only continue its unending battle against the erring captains.

Apart from keeping constant watch over the condition of the pilgrim galleys, and this might mean, as in 1473, the condemning of a vessel which had seen twenty years' service, the state did what it could to protect the pilgrims in the formal contract, made between them and whatever captain was to carry them overseas. Enactment and re-enactment follow each other in the minutes of the Senate; but in spite of all, at the end of the century it was necessary to decree that captains must find four sureties to be bound to the amount of 250 ducats each for the observation of the contract; the injured pilgrims should be compensated by the sureties, and the defaulting captain punished by the state.[18]

The pilgrims themselves, profiting by the long experience that lay behind them, did what they could, in these contracts, to safeguard themselves, and there is a common form which the contract usually follows. The fare was more or less fixed by custom. Surian, in 1500, says that pilgrims were charged according to their quality, and that the sums ranged from 30 to 60 ducats, with 13½ ducats for sight-seeing expenses in the Holy Land.[19] In 1483 Bernhard von Breydenbach's party, which sailed with Agostino Contarini, paid 42 ducats each; Felix and his company, in the ship of Pietro Lando, paid 40. The *Informacōn for Pylgrymes* on the other hand says that you must pay 50 ducats for "freight and for meat and drink . . . for to be in a good honest place, and to have your ease in the galley and to be cherished." Casola, fourteen years later than Felix, but traveling with the captain of Felix's first pilgrimage, paid 60 gold ducats. But this was to cover his keep "by sea and land" and a place at the captain's table.[20]

This fare covered more than the transport to and from Jaffa. On board ship the captain was to provide a hot meal twice a day with good wine (but, said the pilgrims, there was always plenty of water in it), and "to each of us a bicker or small glass of Malvoisie" every morning before breakfast.[21] In port, on the voyage, pilgrims provided their own food, unless it were an "uninhabited harbour," where the captain must feed them. Once arrived at Jaffa it was the duty of the captain to arrange and pay for the transit of the pilgrims to Jerusalem; that is to say "all dues, all money for safe-conducts, and for asses and other expenses, in whatever names they may be charged . . . or in whatever place they have to be paid, shall be paid in full by the captain alone on behalf of all the pilgrims without their being charged anything . . ." [22] The anxious precision of the clause indicates what pitfalls were known to lie in the path of over-confiding pilgrims.

This "lump sum" payment, satisfactory in one way to the pilgrim, had its drawbacks. It was necessary to stipulate that "the captain shall let the pilgrims remain in the Holy Land for the due length of time, and shall not hurry them through it too fast . . ." The "due time" was a fortnight from landing to departure, and as we shall see, Felix in his first pilgrimage was denied even this short period.

Other clauses, among the twenty or so which may appear, seek to insure the pilgrims against the captain keeping them waiting, and wasting their money in Venice; against his calling at unnecessary, unusual, and strange ports on his way; against his trying to prevent them going out of Jerusalem to the Jordan. It is stipulated that he shall protect the pilgrims from the galley slaves; shall, if a pilgrim die on the journey return half the fare to his executors; shall not interfere with the goods of the dead man; and shall, if possible, put into port for the burial. A sick pilgrim shall be given a place to lie out of the "stench of the cabin"—but that might mean no better refuge than one of the rowers' benches.[23] Not only the pilgrims but the Venetian State itself tried to prevent the captains of the pilgrim galleys from adding to their legitimate profits by private trading on the homeward run. In 1417 two captains were prosecuted for crowding the pilgrims with their merchandise; next year, though it was admitted that the officers and oarsmen had the right to trade, their merchandise must not overflow into the ship but must be contained in boxes; in 1440, and again twelve years later, trading was forbidden to the captains. But prohibitions and prosecutions were in vain.[24]

On his first pilgrimage Felix sailed in the galley of one of the most notorious of these patrician profiteers. Agostino Contarini, Agostino dal Zaffo ("of Jaffa") as he came to be known, had already begun his long career as a pilgrim captain, and had begun it badly, since in his voyage of 1479 he had found himself succeeding to the inheritance of a nasty quarrel between the captain of the previous year and the Saracens. That had meant loss instead of profit; even in 1480 he thought it wiser to bring as a present to the Saracen governor of Syria one of the famous glass vessels of Murano. He was therefore determined to recoup himself. The state allowed him to raise his charges to 55 golden ducats for each pilgrim [25] and throughout the voyage he saw to it that wherever he might he would spend a little less on, or wring a little more out of, the pilgrims; or would cheat the Saracens; or would do a little private trading on his own account.

At Ramle, when he must pay dues to the Saracens for every man who went up to Jerusalem, he tried to pass off fifteen of the pilgrims (without their knowledge of the deal) as sailors of the galley's crew, ". . . so that he should pay for them only half the tribute, although he had had from each 55 ducats. And certain of the pilgrims passed as crew, and the others were refused . . . and thus the said captain's trick failed, although he made a lot on those who passed." [26]

At Jerusalem the pilgrims fell foul of him again, for he would not provide them with an escort to make the Jordan expedition, though this, they insisted, had been included in the contract. At Ramle on the way home he demanded a ducat and 8 *marcelins* from each of them for the hire of donkeys; those stouter spirits who refused, and who continued to refuse, were brought to order at Jaffa by the threat that they would be left behind.[27]

When all were on board he kept the ship waiting at Jaffa from "Thursday to Friday evening" in order to trade; and his merchandise must have added to the discomfort of the pilgrims, for already "our whole galley was cluttered with the 600 or 800 ducats' worth of good Jaffa cotton which was the result of the trading ventures of the officers and crew. Nor was the captain yet satisfied, for at Cyprus he loaded up with ". . . lovely salt, white as crystal . . . in fine pieces like tiles, four or six fingers thick . . ." from the salt lake at Larnaca.[28]

Fourteen years later Agostino dal Zaffo, still in the pilgrim trade, had not changed his ways. Casola, a friendly critic, thought that the amount of Cyprus carob beans brought to the galley at Limasol was "stupendous. . . . sufficient to supply all the world . . ." At Crete, on the homeward run, the pilgrims, "satiated with so much malmsey and muscatel . . . began to say to the captain that he must take them away from there, and that if he wanted to trade in malmsey or anything else he could do it at his good pleasure, provided he sent the company to Venice." [29]

Apart from the momentous affair of their agreement with the galley captain the pilgrims' most serious business in Venice was shopping for the voyage. It is remarkable and I think curious, that Felix himself, even in the full flood of his reminiscences of his second pilgrimage, says little of this, though quite a lot when he comes to describe the setting out from Jerusalem of the pilgrims for Sinai that same year. At Venice he briefly remarks that "we went to the market and bought all that we should need on our galley for the voyage—cushions, mattresses, pillows, sheets, coverlets, mats, jars, and so forth . . . I bade them buy a mattress for me stuffed with cows' hair, and I had brought woollen blankets with me from Ulm . . ." [30]

Other pilgrims are far more particular in their lists and earnest in the advice that they give. You must have a feather bed and bedding, pillow slips and two pairs of sheets. You should buy the bed mattress and pillows from a man near St. Mark's. They will cost you 3 ducats, and when you come back you can sell them again, even if "broken and worn," for half that. You should also buy a chest and see that it has a lock and key. Buy barrels, two for wine and one for water. The best water for keeping is to be drawn at St. Nicholas, and when that is used up fill the barrel again at any port of call. As for wine, there is none so good for the voyage as that of Padua, "which is a little wine, bright red, and not strong." The wines that you will find on the voyage are so strong that they cannot be drunk (fearful things are said of the effect upon the inner man of Cyprian wine: drunk neat it will burn up the entrails, therefore dilute it with anything up to four quarts of water).[31] A wise man will keep his Paduan wine to drink on the return voyage.[32] It is well to have "a little caldron, a frying pan, dishes . . . saucers of tree [wood], cups of glass [an unexpected refinement] a grater for bread . . ." [33]

Although the pilgrims while on board ship were provided with two meals a day by the captain, they did not build much upon these, "for some time ye shall have feeble bread and feeble wine and stinking water so that many times ye will be right fain to eat of your own." [34] So, besides flour and firewood they would buy hams or salt ox-tongues; [35] Englishmen took bacon; Italians would take "good Lombard cheese" and sausage; all would take cheese of some sort, eggs, bread, and biscuit, ". . . that is bread twice baked which keeps without going bad, and it is so well baked that it is as hard three days after as it is at the end of a year." [36] Fruit was important, dried apples and dates, figs and raisins, spices too, unless you were prepared to eat tasteless food, so take "pepper saffron cloves and maces a few as ye think need, and loaf sugar also." [37]

An Italian adds such refinements as sugar "of the best quality" and above all fruit syrup, ". . . for it is that which keeps a man going in that great heat . . ."; [38] some syrup of ginger to be used, but with discretion, after seasickness; quinces, unspiced; "aromatics flavoured with rose and carnation," the necessity for which is made sufficiently clear by an Englishman's vivid description of the lower deck on a galley as a place "right evil and smoldering hot and stinking." [39] The Italian adds also, with startling modernity, "some good milk products." [40]

Besides all these it was well to "hire you a cage for half a dozen of hens or chickens to have with you . . . And buy you half a bushel of millet seed at Venice for them." [41] Nor would even this bulk of provision be sufficient: wherever the ship touches on the voyage the pilgrim "should furnish himself with eggs and fowls, bread, sweetmeats and fruit, and not count what he has paid to the captain, because" (it is a wealthy Italian speaking) "this is a journey on which the purse cannot be kept shut." [42] In addition to all that he brought the rich and influential pilgrim might, while at Venice arrange, as von Harff did, for letters of credit. [43]

Having provided as far as possible for all needs, the pilgrims almost always found themselves forced to wait upon, as they were convinced, the pleasure of the captain, or, as he regularly maintained, a favorable wind. This delay, during which the pilgrims fretted, and which the anxious state tried by successive legislation to restrict to reasonable dimensions, the pilgrims would fill in by sight-seeing, sacred or secular. But in 1480 Felix, still numbed by the "temptation" of homesickness, which "caused me to be dull and stupid both in viewing places of note . . . and also in writing accounts of them," says nothing at all about the beauties of that city, which his fellow pilgrim, the clerk from Paris, describes with such enthusiasm. Neither the curiosity and fascination of water instead of roadway, "the little barks and boats [which] go through the streets," nor the "twelve to fifteen hundred bridges, big and little, of stone or wood," nor "the fair houses which they call palaces," drew from Felix a word of notice. It is the Paris pilgrim who so carefully explains and so palpably admires the splendors of mosaic work: "the little pieces and bits of glass the size of a small silver penny . . . in gold and azure and other right rich colors . . . of these little bits are made the vaults and walls of the churches, all showing characters of the Old and New Testaments, and to each of these characters a writing, which describes the character, and the writing is made of the little bits, and the pavement is made up of small pieces of stone of all colors, in the shape of beasts, birds, and other most beautiful designs." It is the Paris pilgrim who describes the massed splendors of the treasure of St. Mark's, displayed at Ascensiontide, the "images, angels, chalices, patens, vessels, and chandeliers, all of gold, huge, thick, massive, and garnished with precious stones of price inestimable and of every color." While the Paris pilgrim climbed the campanile and looked down upon "the sea and the town," and "round about the town, towers, castles, churches, abbeys, houses of Religious, monasteries, hospitals, and villages . . . all in the midst of the sea"; while he visited the Arsenal, and stared at the reception of the Turkish ambassador and admired the nightly illuminations on the towers of Venice,[44] Felix, for all we know to the contrary, moped in the inn of St. George, yet making friends, in spite of his melancholy, with Master John, the innkeeper, and Mistress Margaret, and with the big black dog, all of whom were to welcome him so warmly on his arrival at Venice three years later.

With this heavy mood upon him Felix passes by his first visit to Venice without a word. He and Master George came there, made their agreement with Agostino Contarini, and waited for the day on which they might sail, as all the rest of the pilgrims then gathered in Venice must wait. This company, scattered as yet among the many inns, included noblemen of various countries, "priests, monks, laymen, gentle and simple, from Germany . . . and France, and especially two Bishops, that is of Orleans and of Le Mans," besides English, Scots, Spanish, and Flemings. To the disgust of some of the noblemen there were as well no less than six wealthy matrons, who, though "through old age scarcely able to support their own weight . . ." intended the pilgrimage.[45]

When at last the ship was ready to sail, news came which, to the expectant pilgrims, was a heavy, almost a disabling blow. A ship arriving in Venice reported that the Grand Turk was besieging the Knights in Rhodes and that the seas of the Levant swarmed with his ships. Whether to go or stay became the question which sowed "troubles, discord and quarrels" among the pilgrims, especially as the Venetian Senate refused to guarantee in any way the safety of the pilgrims themselves, though it did not prohibit the voyage, the galley being covered by the Turkish safe-conduct.

It was therefore after a period of painful indecision that on Thursday, June 7, "just before dinner time, all the pilgrims aboard, and the wind fair, the three sails were spread to the sound of trumpets and horns and we sailed out to the open sea . . ."[46]

When he came to write his book for the stay-at-home brethren at Ulm, Felix dealt thoroughly with the subject of ships, and from his account and that of Casola we learn much of the disposition of the pilgrim galleys and the routine of life aboard.[47]

Felix, according to his custom, goes right back to the elements, and enumerates three kinds of ships "which are great, middle-sized and small ones," refers to the reputed

invention of the first ship, and so, working his way gradually
onward to the present and the particular, declares that he
will deal only with the galley, "an oblong vessel which is
propelled by sails and oars."

But here it is necessary to explain what is only implicit in
the descriptions of the Friar and of Canon Casola. The pilgrim galleys formed part of the merchant fleet of Venice,
and by this time were vessels of much greater draft than
the fast war galleys. A large merchant galley could load
two hundred and fifty tons of cargo below deck, so that
she rode low in the water, and must depend for the greater
part of her voyage upon her sails, being, in fact, practically
a sailing ship, with the added convenience of oars for use in
entering and leaving port. So Casola will state, though without explanation, that during his voyage the oars were little
used, and Felix will remark that "when the sun rose, the
galley slaves began to work the galley along with their
oars," or that "before it was fully light the slaves rowed the
galley out of the harbour as far as the corner of the mountain, where we committed her to the wind."

Again, though both Casola and Felix mention biremes and
triremes, and Felix explains that one is "rowed by pairs and
pairs of oars" and the other "by threes and threes of oars,
because on each bench it has three oars and as many rowers,"
neither he nor Casola makes it clear that these benches were
set at such an angle with the ship's side that the oar of the
rower at the inboard end entered the water aft of that of his
neighbor, and this man's oar aft of that of the rower nearest
the gunwale.[48]

Apart from this the two landsmen give a fairly exhaustive
description of the galley. They speak of its narrow build, of
the three masts, of the iron prow "made something like a
dragon's head, with open mouth . . . wherewith to strike
any ship which it may meet." Both were especially impressed by the ropes, "many, long, thick, and of manifold
kinds. It is wonderful to see the multitude of ropes and their

joinings and twinings about the vessel." Casola learnt with
respect the price of the great anchor cable, and doubted
whether "two Milanese waggons with two pairs of oxen to
each could have carried all the ropes" in the galley.

Starting from the prow, with its small forecastle and sail,
the two mention the rowers' benches, with the wide gang-
way between, laid upon chests of merchandise and running
from prow to poop. Felix alone concerns himself with the
rowers, most of them, he says, slaves of the captain, though
there were others, wretched enough but free, from Albania,
Macedonia, Illyria. They lived, ate, slept on the benches, if
necessary chained there in port lest they should escape.
"They are all big men; but their labours are only fit for
asses . . . They are frequently forced to let their tunics
and shirts hang down by their girdles, and work with bare
backs . . . that they may be reached with whips and
scourges. . . . They are so accustomed to their misery that
they work feebly . . . unless someone stands over them and
beats them like asses and curses them." When not at work
they would gamble with cards or dice, shocking the good
Friar with the incessant foulness of their language. Some
were craftsmen, plying such trades as that of the tailor or
shoemaker; all were traders, keeping their merchandise under their benches to sell when the ship made harbor, or to
the pilgrims; they sold, says Felix, excellent wine.

At the galley's stern rose the tall, three-storied poop, upon
which "the flag is always hoisted to show which way the
wind blows." When Casola made his pilgrimage the "castle"
was hung with canvas and with curtains of red cloth embroidered with devices of the Holy Sepulcher and the Contarini arms. In a latticed chamber in the topmost story was
the steersman "and he who tells the steersman how the compass points, and those who watch the stars and winds, and
point out the way across the sea." Below, on the deck level,
was the captain's cabin, and the place where "the tables are
spread for meals." Below again, when Felix made his first pil-

grimage, "the noble ladies were housed at night," and the captain kept his treasure. Casola describes this lowest compartment as without windows, and says that it was used for sleeping and for storing arms and tackle.

A little forward of the poop, toward the starboard side, was the captain's food store. Between this and the ship's side stood the kitchen, open to the air, with its "large and small cauldrons, frying-pans and soup-pots—not only of copper, but also of earthenware—spits for roasting and other kitchen utensils." There were three or four cooks, very hot-tempered men, said Felix, but excusably so, considering the restricted space, the number of pots and things to be cooked, the smallness of the fire, and the shouting that went on outside as men clamored to have things made ready; "besides that the labor of cooks is always such as moves one to pity." [49] Close and handy to the kitchen were the pens for the wretched animals, carried for food, but so ill nourished that by the end of the voyage they were little but skin and bone.

The pilgrims' cabin, "a kind of hall . . . supported by strong columns," was reached by four hatchways, and with ladders of seven steps, from the rowers' deck. It was spacious but unlighted, and here the berth space of each pilgrim was chalked out on the deck; one and a half feet was looked on as a fair allowance. In two long lines, at the feet of the pilgrims, stood each man's chest, but in the daytime mattress, pillows, and all must be rolled up, roped, and hung from a nail above the berth.

Below the pilgrims' cabin was the sand ballast, and this the pilgrims found a convenience, for they could lift the planks and bury in the sand wine, eggs, or anything that needed to be kept cool. Quite a different matter was the bilge water below, the stench of which was a sore trial to the pilgrims. But it was only one trial in many, for besides this they must suffer such inconveniences as smoke from the kitchen, rats, mice, fleas, and other vermin, but not (Providence being merciful in this to sailors) scorpions, vipers, toads, poisonous snakes, or spiders.

Comfort, and even peace, were rare on shipboard. Meals were a scramble for all except those noblemen who had their own servants and ate either on deck near the mainmast or by lantern light in the cabin. The ordinary pilgrim, when the four trumpets sounded for meals, must "run with the utmost haste to the poop," if he wanted to get a place at the three tables laid there; if he came late he must be content with a place on the rowers' benches "in the sun, the rain, or the wind." Even those at table were served in a hurry; they had malvoisie as an apéritif, and with the meal "as much wine . . . as one can drink, sometimes good, sometimes thin, but always well mixed and baptized with water." The food was, of course, cooked Italian fashion; at dinner a salad of lettuce in oil if there was any greenstuff to be had, then mutton, and some sort of pudding of meal, bruised wheat or barley; or else panada and cheese. On fast days salt fish with oil and vinegar took the place of meat, and there was a spongecake and a pudding. There was fresh bread only in harbor, or for the few days after; otherwise that biscuit of which the Paris pilgrim spoke, and which Felix describes as "hard as stones."

No sooner had the pilgrims finished eating than the trumpets sounded again, and they must get up from table so that this could be cleared and laid again for the captain and the other Venetian noblemen on board; who, though their fare was more frugal than that of the pilgrims, ate from silver, "and his [the captain's] drink is tasted . . . as is done to princes in our own country." [50]

In between mealtimes pilgrims often found time hang heavy on their hands. "Some . . . go about the galley inquiring where the best wine is sold, and there sit down and spend the whole day over their wine. This is usually done by Saxons, Flemings, and other men of a low class. Some play for money [it was the Frenchmen who, according to Felix,

were "gambling morning, noon, and night"] . . . Some
sing songs, or pass their time with lutes, flutes, bagpipes,
clavichords, zithers and other musical instruments. Some
discuss worldly matters, some read books, some pray with
beads; some sit still and meditate . . . some work with their
hands, some pass almost the whole time asleep in their berths.
Others run up the rigging, others jump, others show their
strength by lifting heavy weights or doing other feats.
Others accompany all these, looking on first at one, and then
at another. Some sit and look at the sea and the land which
they are passing, and write about them . . ." a feat of'concentration upon which one at least of our authors, Santo
Brasca, was rightly congratulated. *Mutatis mutandis*, the
description would not be unapt for the passengers of many
a liner today. One occupation, however, these later travelers
are spared, which in Felix's day "albeit loathsome, is yet very
common, daily, and necessary—I mean the hunting and
catching of lice and vermin." [51]

On deck, even in daytime, and whatever his occupation,
the pilgrim must be on his guard. He must not meddle with
ropes; he must not sit where a block will fall upon him;
during this very voyage the chief officer himself was killed
by a falling spar. Above all the landsman must not get in the
way of the sailors, or, be he lord, bishop, or even officiating
priest, they will throw him down and trample on him, so
urgent is work at sea, to be done, as it were, "with lightning
speed." If he sits down on the rowers' benches he is liable
to be assaulted by these rough and desperate fellows.

His property, as well as his person, is always in danger.
The rowers steal whatever they can lay hands on, but this
is not so surprising as the strange habit of thieving which
attacks even honest men at sea, "especially in the matter of
trifles, such as kerchiefs, belts, shirts . . . For example,
while you are writing, if you lay down your pen and turn
your face away, your pen will be lost, even though you
be among men whom you know . . ." And there are

other lesser perils. The pilgrim must be careful "where he sits down . . . for every place is covered with pitch, which becomes soft in the heat of the sun." He must beware if he leans on the edge of the galley not to let anything of value slip from his hand into the sea, or he will lose it, as a nobleman talking to Felix lost a rosary of precious stones and Felix himself his Office Book.[52]

If the day is full of discomforts and anxieties the night is worse. There is a "tremendous disturbance" while all are making their beds, with dust flying and tempers rising, till in disputes about the boundary for each man's berth "whole companies of pilgrims" take part, sometimes with swords and daggers. Even when most have settled down to sleep there will be latecomers who keep the rest awake by their talk and the lights they bring, which lights Felix had seen hot-tempered pilgrims extinguish, impolitely but effectively, with the contents of their chamber pots. And when all lights were out there were some incorrigible talkers who would "begin to settle the affairs of the world with their neighbours," continuing till midnight, and perhaps causing a fresh outbreak of noise and quarreling if some outraged companion called for silence.

For a man used to the quiet of his own cell rest was almost impossible. When all others slept Felix would be kept awake by the snoring of his fellows, the stamping of the penned beasts, and the trampling of the sailors on the deck above. The narrow bed, the hard pillow, the close proximity of his neighbors, the foul and hot air, the vermin, would drive him at last on deck, braving even the danger of being taken for a thief, to sit, "upon the woodwork at the sides of the galley, letting his feet hang down towards the sea, and holding on by the shrouds . . ."[53]

There, though waking, the pilgrim found some good moments, at least in fair weather, for "the ship runs along quietly, without faltering . . . and all is still, save only he who watches the compass and he who holds the handle of the rudder, for these by way of returning thanks . . . continually greet the breeze, praise God, the Blessed Virgin and the saints, one answering the other, and are never silent as long as the wind is fair." Their chant reminded the Friar of the cry of the night watchmen at home, "which cry hinders no one from sleeping, but sends many restless folk to sleep." [54]

But the freedom from anxiety necessary for the enjoyment of such rare moments cannot have been possible for the pilgrims who sailed from Venice at Ascensiontide in 1480, bound for Corfu, where they should find the Venetian Captain of the Sea and ask his permission to proceed on their pilgrimage. At Parenzo, their first port of call, they heard "horrible tales about the Turks." At Zara they dared not touch, for they heard there was plague there. Lesina (Hvar) they passed by in order to take advantage of a good wind, which changed presently and brought them to an uninhabited harbor on the Croatian coast; going ashore for diversion they found upon the beach "a corpse cast up by the sea, putrid and rotten"; a sign, so the sailors at once declared, of approaching disaster. Yet when, three days later, and after many unsuccessful attempts, a fair wind took them from that inhospitable coast they learnt from a passing Venetian war galley which they spoke that the contrary winds that had beaten them back into port had saved them from falling in with the Turkish fleet, even then on its way to sack Otranto. [55]

The fear of the Turk was everywhere. At Curzola (Korčula) and Ragusa (Dubrovnik) they found that folk had either fled from, or hastily fortified, their towns. On the hills at night they saw the alarm beacons lit, and as they sailed along the wooded Albanian coast they might remember the strong places which Venice had held there, now in Turkish hands, and regret the days when timber from those forests was used to build Venetian galleys, but now served for the ships of the infidel. [56] When they came to Corfu the

Captain of the Sea called them fools for their pains, advised them to turn back, and threatened that if they persisted they must make shift for themselves, for he would not allow a galley of St. Mark's to go into such dangers as those which lay ahead.

Small shame to the pilgrims had they yielded to such pressure. Many did yield, among whom were two of the greatest of the German nobles and the two French bishops. The rest, foolhardy or courageous but certainly obstinate, after a week of wrangling ignored both advice and prohibition. They had come, they told the captain, ". . . from France, Spain, England, Scotland, Flanders, Germany, and other regions and countries at great cost and outlay, determined to accomplish their pilgrimage or die, according as it was the will of God . . ." [57] They then made ready to leave and defiantly carried into the galley all that they had bought,[58] but once on board, being solemnized by their peril, they took an oath not to gamble, swear, or quarrel any more, but to have litanies sung by the clerks on board. Next morning the trumpets were blown, the moorings cast off, and "with joy and singing" they left the harbor, where the other pilgrims laughed at them from the quay, those turning back being, doubtless, embittered by the fact that of each man's 55 ducats Contarini had repaid only 10.

Upon the remainder of the voyage out we need not linger. At Crete even the Turkish merchants trading there charitably advised them not to put to sea. They persisted, passed the dangerous proximity of Rhodes on a favorable gale, touched at Cyprus, and so on the third day out of Larnaca got their first sight of the Holy Land and came safe to Jaffa.

They had dared and suffered much but, as it proved, to little purpose. At Ramle Agostino Contarini was seized and kept in prison for four days,[59] which time he, on his enlargement, took care to subtract from the pilgrims' time in Jerusalem, so that "we did not spend," says Felix, "more than nine days in the Holy Land, and in that time we rushed round the usual Holy Places in the utmost haste, making our pilgrimages both by day and night, and hardly given any time to rest . . . When we had hurriedly visited the Holy Places . . . we were led out of the Holy City, by the same road by which we had come, down to the sea where our galley waited." [60]

That was all, after six weeks at sea and many perils. Felix's first pilgrimage would have been a miserable failure but for one thing. When at Jerusalem the Friar "firmly determined that I would return again." It was this resolve which prevented him at once undertaking the journey to Mount Sinai in company with two English pilgrims who were setting out thither—that and not the fact that he and the Englishmen had no common language. It was also, I think, this resolve which restored Felix to himself, so that on the journey home he was able to observe, to savor experience, and to laugh.

He had in any case sufficiently recovered himself to be equal to snubbing an ecclesiastical superior, though certainly the occasion was just and the provocation extreme. The pilgrims, sick and weary for home, were held up for three days in the open roadstead of Lanarca; they were told that the galley must wait for two bishops of Cyprus who were to be passengers. When these arrived, with a great cavalcade and much gear, the pilgrims, crowded enough already, found themselves worse off than ever, and what made their discomforts harder to bear, they could not like their new companions. One of the two dignitaries Felix passes over in silence, but upon the other his eye was fixed with disapproval and growing indignation. For the bishop of Paphos, though a friar of Felix's own order, was "a young man, beardless and lady-faced, and behaving like any woman too." He wore a friar's gown, but it was of costly cloth, and colored "with a tail at the back like a woman"; his fingers were covered with jeweled rings; round his neck was a golden chain. Besides all this his manners were bad; he squabbled constantly with his servants and looked down on everyone, especially the pilgrims, whom he would not allow to sit down with him.

One day "a certain priest, chaplain to one of the pilgrim knights,"—the anonymity is not so consistently kept but that we may not recognize Felix himself—"a certain priest" asked the young man "to move up a little from where he sat." The bishop's only answer was a disdainful look. The priest, calling to mind how dearly he had paid for his berth and passage, determined to resist enroachment, and for a minute priest and bishop leaned heavily and angrily against each other in silence.

Then said the bishop, " 'How, you ass, can you dare to contend with me? Don't you know who I am?' "

" 'I,' " replied Felix, " 'am not an ass but a priest. It would be wrong for me to scorn a priest or despise a bishop, but I know a proud monk and an irregular friar when I see one, and I will contend against such with all my might.' "

At this point the bishop, forgetful of episcopal dignity, made that gesture with his thumb, "which the Italians use when they want to be rude to anyone." This brought in "the priest's knight" and other young knights with him, all shouting and swearing, so that the bishop, choosing the wisest course, fled to the captain's cabin, and came no more among the pilgrims.[61]

Felix certainly needed all his courage for the voyage that was before him. Worn out by their labors, by the heat, by having to sleep out-of-doors, by lack of wine and of good bread, by the hurry of their tour, the pilgrims returned to the galley in such a state that it "became like a hospital full of wretched invalids," [62] and it was the old women who, of tougher fiber than any man, nursed those who had scorned their company.

Worse suffering was to come. Contrary winds kept them at sea even when, knowing that the Turk had given up the siege of Rhodes, they tried to make that port. Water ran short; the sailors now could sell any that was not foul, "albeit it was lukewarm, whitish, and discoloured," at a higher price than wine. Soon "even putrid stinking water was precious and the captain and all the pilots were scared that we should run out even of . . . that." No water at all could be spared for the beasts; and Felix watched them with pity as they licked the dew from the ship's timbers.

"During those days of suffering," says he, "I often wondered how any man living on earth can be so pampered as to worry almost the whole year about the Lent fast, and the bread and water of Good Friday." (Was it Felix himself who so worried?) Now he found himself longing for that "white bread, fresh and good, and for the water, clear, cold, sweet and clean . . . Often I suffered so from thirst, and so greatly desired cold water, that I thought, when I get back to Ulm I will climb up at once to Blaubüren and there sit down beside the lake which wells out from the depths until I have slaked my thirst." [63] At last, however, they made the coast of the island, the sailors rowed ashore for water, the pilgrims drank, and at once, "like parched plants," revived.

They were held up in Crete by damage to the rudder. But Felix did not object to the delay. For one thing there was plenty for the pilgrims to watch. They might hang over the side and see the man who was to mend the rudder strip to his breeches and sink down into the water with hammer, nails, and pincers, to come up again, long after, with the work marvelously completed below the surface. Besides everything was cheap here, and especially that famous Cretan wine, malvoisie, "so we did not mind staying there, but enjoyed it." [64]

That same Cretan wine was responsible for a number of laughable accidents which Felix recorded, because "as I promised . . . I often mix fun and amusement with serious matters." So, when the evening trumpet blew to recall the pilgrims to the ship, those already on board might be diverted by the sight of their fellows lined up on the quay, too drunk to risk the steps down to the boats. Once Felix enjoyed the spectacle of a drunken servingman who pitched headlong from the steps into the harbor; he had been carrying on his back his master's gear, and though he himself was soon fished out by the boatmen, "the loaves of bread and all that he was carrying floated over him, and were all utterly ruined."

Even ecclesiastics, losing their dignity, provided entertainment for the rest of the company. A Dalmatian priest with whom Felix had become friendly, returning late and "lit up" to the galley, lingered on deck till it was almost dark; then, deciding to go below, he made for the nearest hatchway, and, forgetting that the ladder was always removed at sunset, stepped down. At the crash of his fall "the whole galley shook, for he was a big man and fat," and for a moment the rest of the pilgrims, lying in their beds below, talking, were silent in horror, till they heard his voice, angry and stammering, but not that of one seriously injured.

" 'There!' " said he, " 'I had the ladder under my feet and I went down three steps, and some one dragged it from under my feet and I fell down.' " He was told, " 'The ladder was taken away an hour ago,' " but he persisted. " 'That's not true, for I had gone down three steps already, and when I stood on the third it was dragged from under me.' "

At that the others began to laugh, and Felix loudest of all, for joy, he explains, that his friend had taken no harm in so great a fall.

" 'There!' " cried the Dalmatian, " 'now I am sure that it was you, Brother Felix, who dragged the ladder from my feet. Be sure that I shall pay you out before you leave the galley,' " and the more Felix tried to clear himself the angrier grew the other, swearing to have his revenge the very next day. But, says Felix, by next morning all was forgotten, so potent is the wine of Crete.[65]

After the pleasant days in Crete the pilgrims had yet another trial to face. Beyond Corfu they ran into a terrible storm, with wind and rain, lightning and thunder. Yet even here it is possible to discern in Felix that priceless gift, the enjoyment of mere experience.

"The rain . . . fell in such torrents as though entire rain-clouds had burst and fallen upon us. Violent squalls kept striking the galley, covering it with water, and beating upon the sides of it as hard as though great stones from some high mountains were sent flying along the planks. I have often wondered when at sea in storms how it can be that water, being as it is a thin, soft and weak body, can strike such hard blows . . . for it makes a noise when it runs against the ship as though millstones were being flung against her . . . Waves of sea-water are more vehement, more noisy, and more wonderful than those of other water. I have had great pleasure in sitting or standing on the upper deck during a storm, and watching the marvellous succession of gusts of wind and the frightful rush of the waters." [66] But, as well as the interest of the thing, this storm drove them fast upon their course, so, though "our beds and all our things were sopping," bread and biscuit spoiled with salt water, no fire in the galley, the kitchen awash, and all the pilgrims seasick, they bore it with patience.

And, except for one bad time when the anchor dragged and they nearly fell upon the rocky Dalmatian coast, the storm was the last of their ill fortune. After five days at Parenzo, on Friday, October 21,[67] "we reached the city of Venice and broke up our company, every man going to his own home," though Felix, ill and exhausted, spent a fort-night in bed at Venice and did not reach Ulm till November 16.[68]

## CHAPTER III

# SECOND PILGRIMAGE—ULM TO VENICE

FELIX had come home, having achieved the pilgrimage to which he had so ardently looked forward, and yet totally dissatisfied with his achievement. When, in the familiar cloister at Ulm, he tried to recall "the most holy sepulchre of our Lord, and the manger wherein He lay, and the holy city of Jerusalem and the mountains which are round about it, the appearance, shape, and arrangements of these . . . escaped from my mind, and the Holy Land and Jerusalem . . . appeared to me shrouded in a dark mist, as though I had beheld them in a dream . . ." Instead of being able to illuminate the Scriptures for others by reference to his own knowledge of the Holy Places, he felt that he knew less about these than before he had seen them, and when questioned could answer but lamely. Sometimes he was driven to reply "that I did not know whether I had really seen Jerusalem or no. And when they asked me whether I had any wish to go back again, I simply answered that I had," [1] an answer so laconic and spiritless that it must have caused the good Friar's friends surprise, if not anxiety.

Another man might have contented himself, though regretfully, with having at least acquired the *cachet* of a pilgrim. Not so Felix. The audacious resolve to go once more to Jerusalem remained fixed in his mind. He could neither renounce nor confess it, fearing equally to grieve Prior Fuchs by a second request for leave of absence or to receive from him a refusal of that request. But the hidden resolve worked in him, driving him to undertake the one kind of travel possible in the cloister. While inactive, "I read with care everything on this subject [Jerusalem] which came into my hands; moreover I collected [and he remarks elsewhere [2] that the collection amounted to the size of a large volume] all the stories of the pilgrimages of the Crusaders, the tracts written by pilgrims, and descriptions of the Holy Land . . ." [3] and "laboriously roved through pretty nearly all the Canonical and Catholic Scriptures, reading books, texts, glosses . . . I give you my word I worked harder in running round from book to book, in copying, correcting, collating what I had written, than I did in journeying from place to place upon my pilgrimage." [4]

The pilgrim narratives which he read and to which he refers by name, as well as those which he mentions only vaguely, range in time from that of Arculf in the seventh century to that of Master Hans Tucher, who had made his pilgrimage a year before Felix. The topographical accounts he used vary from such informed and judicious works as those of Bede and of the fourteenth-century Burchard of Mount Sion to the entertaining book of the parish priest of Sudheim in the diocese of Paderborn, usually known as Ludolph von Suchem—an author whose powers of beguilement can still, for all his lapses into fantastic incredibility, wring a word of pained appreciation from his modern editor.

It was presumably from Ludolph that Felix drew some of his most engagingly naïve classifications, some of his most astonishing and bizarre statements upon matters of geography and biology. At the entrance to the Mediterranean, so Ludolph declares and Felix echoes, where the African and European coasts are closest together, stand a Moslem and a Christian washerwoman, each abusing the other from her native shore.[5] Ludolph also supplies the information about that peril of the sea called "Troyp" after the fish "Troys," a terrible creature of the deep which can pierce the timbers of a ship with its beak, and which "cannot be forced away . . . save by a fearless look, so that one should lean out of the ship over the water, and unflinching look into the eyes of the fish, while the fish meanwhile looks at him with a terrible gaze." [6]

Observed fact and uncontrolled fancy jostle each other in Ludolph's pages. A "very truthful sailor" once told him of a fish which, having apparently snapped at a ship, left in the timbers a tooth "as thick as a beam, and three cubits long . . ." This surprised Ludolph, but it was nothing to what the sailor could do. For he next assured the passenger that there was one variety of fish which measured a mile in length. He himself had seen, off Sardinia, three of these. "They puffed out water with their breath . . . in vast quantity, further than a crossbow could shoot, and made a noise like thunder." [7] Ludolph was observant of the habits of birds, and when in Egypt took the opportunity of inquiring into the winter migration of swallows. He says that if he had time he could tell hundreds of stories about birds, and he does tell one which shows that the hobby of bird watching is not of such modern growth as one might have supposed. Two swallows, he reports, which were quarreling when in flight, fell upon the face of a man who was taking an after-dinner nap. This man wakened, caught the birds, "bound a girdle," says Ludolph, round each of them, and let them fly away; "and they came back every year with those same girdles to their nests." [8]

With Felix's knowledge of the Bible we need not concern ourselves, except to say that the book was as familiar to him as to any of Cromwell's Latter-day Saints, and that he quotes also, in comment and gloss, Josephus, Eusebius, and Jerome. But the supreme events which had taken place in Palestine brought, for the medieval Christian, anything connected with that country into the realm of theology. And since medieval theologians were encyclopedic in their habits of thought and study, Felix also absorbed a vast mass of statement and counterstatement upon questions of cosmography, referring in this to Aristotle, Dionysius, Diodorus Siculus, Ptolemy, as well as to such medieval authorities as Vincent of Beauvais, Albertus Magnus, Nicholas de Lyra, Peter of Abano; uncertain, when they differed, which to believe, but feeling strongly the tug of the contemporary craving to approximate opinion as closely as possible to the authorities of the Roman world.

In some respects the fifteenth century, for this very reason, held less enlightened views upon geography than had been current during the previous three hundred years. Writing about the year 1100, William of Conches could boldly claim that "the earth is an element placed at the middle of the world; it is at its middle as the yolk is in the egg; about it there is water, as about the yolk there is the white of the egg." Throughout the twelfth and thirteenth centuries concepts of the sphericity of the earth and the existence of inhabitants in the Southern Hemisphere were commonly held by scholars. Lambert of St. Omer and Albertus Magnus affirm both. Lambert thought that the dwellers in the antipodes were not of the race of Adam. "They have a different night and day which are contrary to ours, and so for the setting of the stars." Albertus held the view that a similar climate and also another branch of the Ethiopian race were to be found beyond the tropical belt. In the fourteenth century Sir John Mandeville, writing not for scholars but for the ordinary polite reader, takes for granted that the earth is a globe, and that "if a man found passages by ships that would go to search the world, men might go by ship all round the world, above and beneath . . . And always he should find men, lands and isles as well as in this country." [9] It has, in fact, been shown that Columbus himself borrowed, without acknowledgment, and acted upon in his great voyage, a passage from Cardinal d'Ailly, written in 1410, but itself a verbal quotation from the work of Roger Bacon.[10]

In turning thus to one of the authorities of the earlier Middle Ages, Columbus flew in the face of the scholarship

of his age, whose glance looked beyond the medieval to the
golden world of pagan culture, and whose geographical
opinions had been given a still more pronounced classical
form by the discovery and translation, in the early years of
the century, of Ptolemy's lost work on geography, so that
for a time any Ptolemaic statement became the dogma of the
orthodox.

In spite of this the tradition of medieval thought persisted, though what had at first been the conclusions of the
scholar, then the common belief of ordinary educated men,
was now despised as notions only held by the ignorant.
Yet Caxton was not ashamed to publish, as new, a treatise on
geography of a hundred years earlier, and Europe, it has
been said, was, in this matter of geographical knowledge "a
whispering-gallery, echoing every voice that revived to
speak in it." [11]

Felix, no great scholar or thinker, though a man with a
hearty appetite for knowledge, shows the uncertainty with
which the opinions of ordinary educated men swung between the classical and the traditional in geography. In the
library, as it were, he will refer with scorn to the beliefs
of the vulgar that "any place is the middle of the
world . . ." or that "mankind are spread all round about
the world, and stand with their feet the opposite way to ours,
so that each man has his own zenith, and each man treads
with his feet upon what to him is the middle of this . . .
world." [12] Such notions the Friar spurns, demolishing them
under the weight of the combined authorities of St. Augustine, the *Speculum Naturae*, and the Bible. Yet, when on
board ship, he will talk of the "sea's curvature," and of the
"height of the sea," as hiding from view the distant land.[13]

But it was not only the work of medieval writers which
was suspect for Renaissance scholars. The immense prestige
of Ptolemy's book was sufficient to make them turn a deaf
ear to the voices of recent and contemporary travelers and
sailors; so that only with unwillingness did the fifteenth

century assimilate into its cosmography the knowledge brought home by travelers such as the Polos and the missionary friars who followed them, and by the Portuguese seamen who discovered the Azores and the Canaries and painfully traced the true outline of the African coast.

Felix, with his bias toward orthodoxy in thought, is obedient to this unspoken prohibition, yet with a wavering glance toward less orthodox but fascinating speculations. It was not, he says, his aim to inform his readers of "the extreme edges of the world." If any wishes to know of these, let him go to the fourteenth-century Friar Oderic and to "the ancient histories of Diodorus." Or "let him study and consider the new maps of the world, and he shall find the regions of the East so far distant from us that according to modern geometers and mathematicians they who live there are to us antipodes, which however the ancients, such as Aristotle, Ptolemy, and Augustine could not admit. Yet today there are men worthy to be believed in secular matters who say that they themselves have been in the island of Cipango, a part of that region, who declare that they have seen another pole and other stars, woods of pepper and of cloves, gardens of spikenard, plains covered with ginger, fields of cinnamon, groves of Sethim wood, orchards of various spices; these and many other matters they claim to have seen with their eyes, and with their hands touched. Let these be read and pondered, and they will satisfy the curious." [14]

It would be interesting indeed to know what were those "new maps" of the world which Felix had studied as well as those of Ptolemy, and to which he recommends "the curious." Was he recalling the mappemonde which he saw upon the wall of the new Carmelite convent on the island between the city of Venice and Murano? [15] Had he studied maps in the houses of the nobles or burgesses at home, and was it already the fashion in Germany as in England in the next century, to hang these upon the walls?

Wherever Felix had met them it is likely that they displayed that same fissure which we have seen to exist in written treatises between the learning of the scholar and the experience of the sailor. In the planispheres and mappemondes devised by the learned, the as yet unexplored spaces were filled to taste, even by the more scrupulous, with legendary and mythological items.[16] Regardless of Portuguese discoveries, the cartographer might abruptly terminate the continent of Africa at about the latitude of Sierra Leone, or, when it was realized that this left too little space for the known extent of the Sahara, it might be more accommodatingly slanted off in a vaguely southeasterly direction. Even fifty years after Felix wrote, a man of the new school of precise geographical science would complain that maps were "worthless, although they have much gold and many flags, elephants and camels on them." [17]

That geographers thus lagged behind in assimilating recently discovered fact was not entirely their own fault. With regard to the knowledge gained by their sailors of the African coasts, the Portuguese were jealous monopolists, and saw to it that as little as possible of their discoveries should leak out. Their Academy of Sagres, their chair of astronomy at Lisbon were not maintained for pure love of knowledge but for the selfish, the almost cutthroat business of trade. Even when they employed such a cartographer as the Venetian Fra Mauro to produce a planisphere, he, it has been suggested, may have had to work without a sight of those preciously guarded sailing charts of the African coast which were served out to the sea captains at the beginning of each voyage and at the end must be returned to the Portuguese India Office.[18]

Apart from maps of the world Felix must certainly have studied maps of the Holy Land itself, but not all of these even attempted to give accurate geographical information.

John Poloner's map, drawn up in the early years of the fifteenth century, is lost, but he describes it with honest pride. Twenty-six colors, he says, he had used in painting it. "I have painted this kingdom [of Basan] yellow . . . All the land near this, which I have made white, is called Bethany . . ." He devised a code of signs, some of which sound surprisingly modern: the six Cities of Refuge were marked with three stars; battlefields were indicated by a sword.[19] About a hundred years earlier Mario Sanuto, writing with the aim of persuading the princes of Europe to recover the Holy Places, had added to his book a set of maps and plans, one of which shows the coast of Palestine and another the land itself, with an attempt to give the disposition of mountains and rivers. But Sanuto was an Italian and in his maps we can see the influence of the practical Italian seafarer and traveler, who expected to use a map in finding his way by sea or land. William Wey's *Itineraries* was also illustrated by a map of the Holy Land, but this is oblivious to utility.* Here we are in a world of tradition and fable; as is usual in medieval maps the east lies at the top, but little attention is paid to proportion or direction; there is nothing precise or succinct in this cartography, but an abundance of decoration—towers, domes, turreted cities, out of whose windows look disproportionately large faces, some comely, some villainous. An elaborate and fanciful representation of a walled town stands for Jerusalem. The vivid blue with which the Dead Sea is colored does not conceal the outlines of Sodom, Gomorrah, and the other Cities of the Plain, prone but otherwise undamaged beneath the water.[20]

Another type of map Felix was to see in actual use on board the galley. This, the Portolan chart, was no fruit of the scholar's brain, deduced from the statements of ancient or medieval geographers, but, even more than that of Sanuto, was the work of seamen, founded upon their own dearly bought experience and closely shackled by practical neces-

* I follow the editor in supposing that the map published as Vol. II of Wey's *Itineraries* is in fact the map originally designed to illustrate it.

sity to the most precise and pedestrian exactitude. These
charts, the first product of a true science of geography, had
been in use in the Mediterranean at least since the early
years of the fourteenth century, and probably much longer
than that.[21]

They confined themselves strictly to the business in
hand—to the coasts of the sea and the ports, among which
those providing good anchorage were marked in red; shal-
lows were indicated by a sign still used in modern sea charts;
hundreds of names of bays, headlands, rivers, were noted
down, and in them the measurements of distance, calculated
by the help of a network of loxodromes, surpassed in exactitude Ptolemy's own.[22]

Felix, when he came upon one of these, was impressed, not
only by the curiosity of the thing itself but by the marvel
and mystery of its use. On board the galley he saw "a chart,
which is an ell long, and an ell broad, whereon the whole
sea is drawn with thousands and thousands of lines, and
countries are marked with dots and miles by figures. In
this chart they observe and see where they are . . . when
the stars themselves are hid by clouds. This they find out on
the chart by drawing a curve from one line to another, and
from one point to another with wondrous pains." [23]

While Felix nursed his resolve at Ulm and pored over his
books of travel, he was secretly exploring every means of
realizing his intention of setting out for Jerusalem a second
time. And, as with his first pilgrimage, difficulties which
had seemed insurmountable melted away. A friend in Rome
got him the pope's license to go to the Holy Land; soon he
had timely news of a party of German nobles intending
the pilgrimage and only too glad to take with them as their
chaplain one who had already acquired the precious experience of pilgrim travel. It only remained to get the consent
of Prior Fuchs, but Felix, a coward where affection was
concerned, left this matter to the noblemen he was to ac-

company, who, raising it almost to the level of a question of local politics, enlisted the offices of the mayor of Ulm, and putting all the pressure they might upon the Prior, at last obtained his unwilling consent.

Now Felix could make his final preparations, though with as little parade as possible in order to spare the Prior's feelings. He let his beard grow, got his friends among women Religious to stitch the red cross on tunic and scapular, and perhaps procured those knee-high boots, "of costly leather, yellow and soft . . ." of which he was so proud, but which were to be the cause of disconcerting and unpleasant, though harmless, experience.[24] When all this was done he waited for the summons to join the rest of the party.

The messenger bearing that summons came to Ulm one Sunday evening—the evening of April 13, 1483—"as it was growing dark." Next day, after Mass and breakfast, Felix announced to the convent that he must leave at once. There were tears, farewells, and blessings in the church. Outside he mounted his horse, but the brethren would not yet let him go. They crowded round giving him their last injunctions— he must notice carefully all he saw, write it down, and bring it back for them to read. He promised, and is proud to record how exactly he kept his promise: "For I never passed one single day . . . without writing some notes, not even when I was at sea, in storms, or in the Holy Land; and in the desert I have frequently written as I sat upon an ass or camel; or at night, while the others were asleep . . ."[25]

This time Felix would not have his heart wrung by any second parting, and refused to let the Prior come any part of the way with him. He and the servant who had come to fetch him rode away, "stealthily, as though we were hiding ourselves, out of the city, crossing the river Danube by the gate which leads to the sheep-bridge," and thus, upon the anniversary of his first departure, set out upon that "most desirable and delightful" second pilgrimage of his.

He had hoped to meet "his lords" at Innsbruck, but find-

ing them gone he hurried on, alone now, for he had sent the
servant back, up to the Brenner in mud, rain, and snow, and
over the pass in intense cold catching up at Sterzing with
all the rest of the party, except one of the nobles who had
gone ahead. Beyond Brixen they had to pay toll at "a very
lofty and costly building" erected by Duke Sigismund of
Austria, but Felix did not apparently grudge that toll, for
where previously he had had to claw his way dangerously
between a rock and the precipice, leading his horse, now,
as a result of much blasting with gunpowder, there was a
road wide enough for carriages to pass. As far as Trent they
followed the valley of the Adige, not omitting to notice the
village of Traminer, from which "a noble wine . . . is im-
ported into Suabia . . . known as Tramminger . . ."

At Trent they stayed the night, and here Felix was called
upon, in his capacity as chaplain, to act as arbiter in a dispute
upon the ethics of tipping. They were sitting at supper when
in came a craftsman of the town with his wife, to entertain
the company with fluting, singing, and fooling, "which fool-
ery made us laugh heartily, in addition to the pleasure in
hearing the music." Innocent pleasure it seemed at the time,
but did it hide a device of the Adversary? For at the end,
when it came to a question of paying the performers, one
of the nobles refused to contribute. He was, he said, on a
pilgrimage, and would not give away money sinfully but
would give it to the poor. This put the cat among the
chickens. The lords, after arguing "long and angrily," left
it to Felix to decide, who, "though not without fear," pronounced himself against the overscrupulous nobleman. He
spoke boldly, and his ruling was accepted, yet the question
continued to trouble him, and it was with relief that he discovered, after his return home, that Gerson's "On Avarice"
confirmed his opinion. Flute players, jongleurs, and such
were not, provided their entertainment contained nothing
improper, in mortal sin; and besides, the fellow at Trent had

not been a professional but only performed before pilgrims "for their diversion and his own profit . . ." [26]

Their way now took them out of the river valley along the upper road to Feltre, where incessant rain held them up in a small inn full of Italian country people. It was a poor place and unaccustomed to noble visitors. Felix found the host and hostess "good simple people" who did their best, "but their lordships' servants were discontented with them." The rain, having fallen that night and most of the next day, stopped at dinnertime, so instead of staying in unsatisfactory quarters for a second night they started off and rode through an evening full of the sound of rushing waters, for the rain had swollen every torrent of the hills.

It was nearly suppertime when they reached a village which Felix calls Ower (probably Quero) and the first of those many hills which Felix, the born sight-seer, with as great an appetite for a view as any Victorian tourist, must insist on climbing, if possible in company, if necessary, alone.

The inn stood at the foot of this "delightful grassy hill." So, as they loitered in the courtyard, waiting for supper to be got ready, " 'See,' " said Felix to the rest, " 'if a man were on the brow of that hill, he would be able to see the Mediterranean.' " His companions were quick to take up the suggestion, though in no very cheerful spirit. " 'Let us,' they said, 'climb up thither, and see the sea, which perchance will be our tomb.' And straightway my three lords, and two serving men, and I climbed up the hill, which [how true to universal experience!] was much higher than we had thought." But the climb was worth while, for the view through the rain-washed air was equal to all Felix's expectations.

"Casting our eyes southwards, we beheld beyond the mountains the plains of Italy, and beyond . . . the Mediterranean Sea . . ." Even Felix was "something cast down at the sight of it . . . for as seen from these hills it had a terrible appearance. It seemed to be very close, and the setting sun shone upon the part which was nearest to us; the rest, the end of which no one could see, seemed to be a lofty, thick black cloud, of the colour of darkling air." [27]

During the next day's journey they left the mountains behind, and passing through "a flat country, very fertile, full of crops, fruit-trees, and vines," they reached Treviso where it was customary for pilgrims either to sell their horses or to leave them in charge of one of the innkeepers for the return journey. Felix and his company chose the first alternative and thus experienced the commercial methods of the excitable Italians, who "squabbled among themselves in a wondrous fashion, for they ran up to us, each trying to outstrip the other, and each interfering with the other's bargaining, and they poured abuse one on another, all alike, even old, rich, and respectable men fighting with one another like children . . . While this squabble was going on we stood still and held our peace, and we sold our horses well . . ." [28]

At Mestre, which they reached on hired horses, they had news of that member of the party who had gone on before them, for when they arrived they found not only supper ordered for them at one of the inns but also a boat lying ready on the Marzenego, which ran at the foot of the garden. Thus, like so many merchants and pilgrims approaching Venice, they were to begin the last stage of their journey by river, [29] and in a cheerful spirit, after enjoying the meal, they loaded the boat and set off, reaching before long that place "where the river glides out into the jaws of the Mediterranean, and so sailed into the bitter and salt water," chanting loudly and cheerfully the German pilgrim song, "In Gottes Namen fahren wir."

Yet this mode of travel, though agreeable, was not without its dangers. To begin with, the three lords and their servants did not travel light, so that, loaded with their baggage, the boat sank low in the water, and when they had a collision, off the Torre de Malghera, with a boat, "which some strong young men were rowing furiously . . ." there was nearly a nasty accident; nothing worse, however, came of it than a bad fright, as the two boats sheered off to the accompaniment of mutual abuse from their occupants. Nearer to Venice they were met by another boat from which they were addressed by the tout of one of the Venetian inns; as he was abusing the inn to which they were going, and expatiating upon the merits of the other, he lost his balance and fell into the sea. Our pilgrims greatly enjoyed his discomfiture; it added to the piquancy of the sight that he was wearing "new silk clothes." [30]

So, at last they reached "the famous, great, wealthy and noble city of Venice, the mistress of the Mediterranean, standing in wondrous fashion in the midst of the waters, with lofty towers, great churches, splendid houses and palaces," and passing along the Grand Canal as far as the Rialto, turned into another canal which brought them past the great Fondaco dei Tedeschi, where every German merchant had his counting house, and from which went out, to all the great towns of Germany, silk, spices, and other merchandise.[31] Leaving that on the right they reached at last the "sixty stone steps" which led up from the water to the inn of St. George—that at least was its correct name but among Germans it was "commonly known as 'Zu der Fleuten.' "

And here, "at the sign of the Flute," the pilgrims might feel themselves for a while at home, for besides Master John and Mistress Margaret, who welcomed them all, but Felix with especial joy as an old friend, "the entire household . . . and all the man-servants and maid-servants were of the German nation and speech, and no word of Italian was to be heard in the house . . ." This came as a great relief to the travelers, "for it is very distressing to live with people without being able to converse with them."

Not only were the guests welcomed by the management and staff, but even the "big black dog . . . showed how pleased he was by wagging his tail, and jumped upon us as dogs are wont to do upon those whom they know," a welcome which he was far from offering indiscriminately, for he was a dog, according to Felix, of highly developed national feeling. Men of every nation but the German were enemies, nor had he "grown accustomed even to the Italians . . . in the neighbouring houses, but rages against them as if they were strangers . . ." This racial discrimination he extended even to beggars and dogs, showing no animus against individuals of either of these categories, so long as they were German. Upon the animal's prejudice against Italians, German visitors had, so Felix reports, founded a theory of national antipathies. For as the dog is "the implacable foe of the Italians, so German men can never agree with Italians . . . nor Italians with us, because each nation has hatred of the other rooted in its very nature." [32]

The first business of the pilgrims on arrival in Venice was to book their passage for the Jerusalem voyage. This year they found that they had the choice between two galleys, for when on the morning after their arrival, having heard Mass at St. Mark's, they walked out upon the Piazza, they saw set up there before the west doors of the church, "two costly banners . . . on tall spears, white . . . with a red cross," as a sign that the galley captains were ready to accept bookings. Beside these banners the servants of the two rival galley captains, one our old friend Agostino Contarini, and the other Messer Pietro Lando, were waiting to tout for custom, and at once "each invited the pilgrims to sail with their master, and they endeavoured to lead the pilgrims, the one party to the galley of Augustine, the other to that of Peter; the one party praised Augustine and abused Peter, the other did the reverse." Their vehemence resulted in a draw; for the German nobles were unable to choose between them. Felix, it is interesting to learn, would have preferred to sail once more with Contarini, but "for peace's sake" did not interfere, saying only, when his opinion was

Venice in 1483

asked, that if he knew which captain would sail first, that captain he would choose. "Both, however, promised that they would begin the voyage directly, which I knew to be a lie." [33]

It was therefore decided that the pilgrims should inspect the two galleys which lay conveniently close in the Grand Canal. They went on board Messer Pietro's; it was a trireme, and besides that new and clean. Messer Agostino's, which they visited next, was the same bireme, "old and stinking," in which Felix had sailed two years before. Each galley captain regaled the pilgrims with "Cretan wine and comfits from Alexandria," doubtless with the same motives which, in a later day, moved one of the captains to serve his prospective passengers with "diverse subtleties as comfits and march-panes, and sweet wines," and the other with "a marvelous good dinner . . ." [34] Between their entertainment on the two galleys, and between the humble protestations and large promises of Lando and Contarini there was nothing to choose; it was the greater beam and therefore the greater stability of the trireme which made the pilgrims decide to call Messer Pietro to the inn to conclude with him the usual sort of contract which, on the last day of April, was signed and ratified before the prothonotaries, and the names of the pilgrims registered "in a great book"; it pleased Felix to know that his name was already written on one of its pages. "When this was done, we went in a boat with the captain to the galley, and chose a space for twelve persons"—the number of the party, including the servants—"on the left-hand side, which space the captain divided into twelve berths . . . and wrote each man's name upon his berth with chalk . . ." [35]

Even before the contract had been signed, Lando, abandoning pretense, had utterly refused to consent to that article in it which had stipulated that he should sail from Venice in a fortnight. Twenty-six days, and after that the first fair wind, was the best which he would promise; in the event, the pilgrims did not leave Venice until June 2.

It was Felix who, as both an ecclesiastic and an experienced traveler, suggested to the rest how this period of waiting should be spent. Owing to the peculiarity of the site upon which Venice stood, "flowery gardens or smiling plains . . . shady woods, green meadows, or delightful plantations of trees and flowers, roses and lilies . . ." were not available for recreation. Hunting was, for the same reason, out of the question; tournaments and dancing would have been improper occupations for pilgrims. As an alternative to all these the Friar suggested a daily pilgrimage to one or other of the many shrines of distinguished holiness in and around Venice wherein might be plucked "the roses and lilies of virtues, of graces and indulgences." Felix's companions accepted his suggestion, with one modification; let this pious program be, on occasion, carried out by shifts; those who did not go might hear from those who did, what they had seen.[36] The result, in the Friar's narrative, is an impressive account of hands, bones, complete bodies, fingers, arms, and teeth of great sanctity, and even so, by Felix's own confession, the catalogue is far from complete, for, says he, it would have wearied him to write down the names of all the churches they visited.

Venice offered, however, as well as such sights, others of a more secular nature which only the most puritanical pilgrim would ignore. Of the two great summer festivals our pilgrims of 1483 missed by a few days that of St. Mark, but they were there for the Ascension Day spectacle of the Espousal of the Sea, and for the Corpus Christi procession. On the first occasion, having first gone to Mass at St. Mark's, "both to attend service . . . and to see the grand sight," the German visitors followed the stages of the secular ceremony—the procession to the sea and the embarkation of the Doge in the Bucentaur, "a great ship fashioned like a tabernacle, painted, covered with gilding, and shrouded with silken hangings . . ." with all the bells of the city ringing, trumpets blowing, and priests chanting. In their hired boat they followed the Bucentaur as it moved from the quay with the flashing of three hundred oars, accompanied by a swarm of other vessels, which, during the actual ceremony of espousal, crowded round "with great press and jostling, and . . . such a noise with the cannons . . . trumpets, drums, shouting and singing, that they seem to shake the very sea." [37] They saw, or at least heard tell of, the diving after the golden ring * and the solemn service—for men only—at St. Nicholas' on the Lido; but they did not apparently attend even as spectators that great dinner, which early in the next century concluded the festival, and at which dishes, platters, and saucers were of silver gilt, and the tumblers who entertained the guests seemed to an Englishman "the most marvelous fellows that ever I saw, so much that I cannot write it." [38]

The Corpus Christi procession was no less splendid as it wound its way under the awning of white woolen stuff, around the Doge's palace and about the Piazza of St. Mark. The Doge himself, in his tiara and mantle, the ambassadors of foreign nations, the Patriarch, the vested priests, the Venetian gentlemen dressed "in cloth of gold—each more beautiful than the other—in crimson velvet, damask and scarlet . . ." the processions of the guilds, the children, both boys and girls, dressed as angels, carrying bowls of gold and silver from which they scattered rose leaves and flowers, the great processional candlesticks with candles of green or red, white or black wax, the bells, the singers, the sudden utter silence when the Doge entered the church for Mass, the "droll and beauteous pageants" of the Friars Preachers, the "gold and silver . . . precious stones and

---

* It appears to have been the custom, according to Fabri, VII, 99, when the Doge had wedded the sea by throwing the ring into the water from the Bucentaur, for many to dive in and try to recover it.

costly dresses," the "vanities . . . the extravagant dress of women and dissolute behavior of laymen"—all combined to provide a show, stupendous and unique, which filled pilgrims, whether as simple as Parson Torkington or as discriminating as Canon Casola, with amazement.[39] Nor, in this year, were the scrupulous distressed, as Brother Paul Walther had been, by the spectacle of the members of a Saracen military mission—"dogs, and right enemies of the sacrament"—given their own place in the procession.[40]

A side show, very popular in 1482 and 1483, drew both Felix and his party and Brother Paul. This was a young elephant, included by Felix in one day's sight-seeing with the relics of St. Barbara. Yet it is not the cheerful Felix but the uncheerful Paul who experienced most keenly and described most lovingly the astonishing design of this incredible creature. For he says, "surely this beast appears to me to be more amazing than any other beast on earth; for a man may hardly depict the form and habit of body of that same beast. Six years old was he at the time, and he was of the largeness of a large horse, but not such a long body like a horse [the friar's Latin, never elegant, is capable of the most atrocious grammatical blunders], but shorter and taller, altogether very ungainly. His color is neither white nor black, but gray, like a hairless black pig. He has nor hair nor mane nor bristles, but looks bald. He keeps his head bowed like a pig, little eyes like a pig. His nose is full six palms—spannen—long. He appears not to have a lower lip, so he uses his nose and upper lip. His nose he bends and raises, stretches and turns hither and thither; with his nose he does everything. He lifts his nose and opens his mouth, and allows his teeth to be seen. He eats fruit, and with his nose picks up corn, and bending his nose puts it into his mouth; and the same when he drinks water. . . . He has as well as other teeth two long ones, sticking out and up on either side of his nose, each more than half an ell in length. He has very wide ears, or ear-flaps, hanging down on the sides of his head, covering his gray, leathery neck. He has as well four large, round feet; he does not grow hooves . . . In his front legs are no joints except near the feet and near the body . . . His cry is terrific. And what shall I say of his strength?" So Brother Paul runs on, singing the prowess, the intelligence, the docility of the animal with a wholehearted appreciation which his fellow men signally failed to win from him. He must, one feels, have grieved if he heard of the end of the gifted animal, who, after a profitable tour with its owner in Germany, was crossing the Channel to repeat its triumphs in England when, a storm blowing up and the ship being in danger, the sailors threw it into the sea.[41]

Every man might, in fact, find sights to interest and entertain in Venice. The Arsenal was visited by all good tourists, who admired its dry and wet docks, the ships in building, and those being fitted out for the sea in the New Arsenal; they saw the workshops for the manufacture of tackle, and the swarms of artificers—women as well as men—who were employed; they saw the twelve powder mills, the "fine garden" where the powder was dried in summer, the stove which was used for that purpose in winter.[42]

Most people visited the glass works at Murano, which produced glass "of every colour." Casola stood to watch the work at the various furnaces; "and I saw, above everything else a glass chalice . . . but I would not touch it, fearing it might fall out of my hand." [43] Felix and his companions "shuddered" at the enormous fires and furnaces of the bakers, and observed with respect the competition models for the horse of the Colleone statue: one, in the church of the Minorites, was of wood, covered with black leather, one was of baked clay, and the third, presumably Verrocchio's own, of wax.[44] They could, as Casola did, enjoy the cheerful bustle of the early mornings, when the fruit and vegetable boats arrived from Chioggia.[45] And wherever they went there was displayed, for their admiration, the mercantile wealth of Venice, which, even to the critical Milanese, seemed inestimable, so that "it seems as if all the world flocks there . . . I see that the special products for which other cities are famous are all to be found there, and what is sold elsewhere by the pound and the ounce is sold there by *canthari* and sacks of a *moggio* each," as one might say "by the hundredweight and the quarter." The shops themselves seemed warehouses, so full were they of "tapestry, brocades and hangings of every design, carpets of every sort, camlets of every colour and texture, silks of every kind . . ." [46] Especially was this wealth concentrated about the Rialto, where "above the shops is a place like a monastery dormitory, so that each merchant in Venice has his own store full of merchandise . . ." [47]

The deportment of the Venetians themselves was a matter of interest to visitors, so great a contrast was there between men and women in both dress and behavior. The proud merchant princes of Venice, who, at the news of the birth of a son would say, "A lord is born into the world," and who, when on embassy or at a festival would go most magnificent, disdained show when at home and about their business. Like doctors of law in the universal long gown, so much de rigueur that a man going out without it would be thought mad, the black-robed men of Venice "go about the Piazze richly and decorously dressed, but the women richly indeed, yet not decorously. For they go about shamelessly, their shoulders naked as low as to their breasts—and as for other sins . . ." Brother Paul here leaves them to God.[48] Less puritanical observers than this Franciscan could not approve of the fashion, in dress and deportment, of Venetian ladies. Casola, old, experienced, temperate, pokes sour fun at the high heels, the curled false hair, which might be bought hanging from poles on the Piazza of St. Mark, the diamond and ruby rings, the painted faces, the bare shoulders—"they are not afraid of the flies biting them"—which might, he thought, please others, but did not please him.[49]

Felix, also shocked, or conscious that he ought to be shocked, comments unfavorably on the fashionable Venetian lady, making her the occasion for a classical flourish—"not Christian but Trojan women, and companions of Helen herself and of Venus." [50] All these critics were clerical; a layman, von Harff, remarked on the number and splendor of the jewels worn by even very young women, and considered the Venetian ladies the richest whom he saw in his travels, as those at Cologne were the proudest, those of Milan the loveliest, and those of Moabar the blackest. He did not think well of the Venetian fashion of making up the face, for when at night the heat made the paint run, it was unsightly.[51]

All this might be observed by any pilgrim as he went about the city. It was only an Italian, like Casola, who had the opportunity of seeing the Venetian interior. He was taken by the Milanese ambassador to visit a noble Venetian lady during her confinement. Upon the profuse and costly ornament of the small room in which she entertained a mixed company of friends, more than 2,000 ducats had, he learnt, been spent. "The fireplace was all of Carrara marble, shining like gold, and carved so subtly with figures and foliage that Praxiteles and Phidias could do no better." Gold and "ultramarine" adorned the ceiling; "there were so many and beautiful and natural figures and so much gold everywhere" that Casola could only doubt whether Solomon in all his glory had been more magnificent; as for the ornaments of the bed, "fixed in the room in the Venetian fashion" and valued at 500 ducats, and of the lady in it—but he will say no more, for "I fear I should not be believed."

The company in the room was no less opulently adorned: "twenty-five Venetian damsels, one more beautiful than the other," and showing "not . . . less than four or six fingers' width of bare skin below their shoulders before and behind," displayed so much wealth in "gold, precious stones and pearls," on heads, necks, and hands, that the visitors, impelled to turn upon them the same appraising, mercantile eye with which they had viewed the room and its furnishings, estimated the value of their jewels at 100,000 ducats.[52]

Yet, with all these spectacles, sacred or secular, to divert and occupy them, the pilgrims found their stay in Venice tediously long, and doubtless unpleasantly expensive. It was with relief that they heard, on May 25, that the Venetian State had intervened on their behalf and had ordered the galley captains to be off within the week.

They had certainly had long enough for their preparations, but when they knew that they would leave so soon the days seemed hardly long enough to do all that must be done. There was the doctor to be consulted and purges to be taken; there were churches to be visited whose patron saints were, by reputation, most likely to be of service to pilgrims. The archangel Raphael had been the conductor of Tobias upon his successful journey; the archangel Michael might be expected to protect against enemies; St. Christopher should bear them safely overseas; St. Martha, it was hoped, might, with her domestic bias, provide good inns or the patience to endure bad ones. There was also the bill to pay "at the sign of the Flute." Farewells must be said, last shopping done, the pilgrims' chests and other baggage taken on board.[53]

On Sunday, June 1, "very early before sunrise," Felix and his company carried down the remains of the stuff into the boat which they had hired to take them to the galley, now lying outside the harbor. They had a rough passage out and a rough night, and when at last they had ". . . arranged berths and beds to sleep in, with much disorder and labour and disputing, because we were not yet used to it . . ." and lay listening apprehensively to the rising wind, they were startled almost out of their skins by sudden shrieks from one of their companions. In the dark men hunted for their swords or tried to escape, believing that murder had been committed or a massacre begun. It transpired, however, that the screams were due to nothing more serious than a nightmare.[54]

Early next morning the captain came on board, so that as soon as it grew light the sailors began preparing for departure, hanging out the silken banners—the red pilgrim cross, the red lion of St. Mark, the della Rovere green oak tree on its blue field in honor of the pope, the armorial bearings of Messer Pietro Lando. Then, with "a fair wind, which was blowing the banners up on high," with trumpets sounding, galley slaves shouting, and the pilgrims chanting, the ship left her moorings.

"Within the space of three hours, [says Felix] . . . we had only the sky and the waters before our eyes . . . we had risen above and higher than the highest Alps, and could not see them, they being now, as it were, low down with the sea's curvature interposed between them and us. Being now out of sight of the world, the crew took down all the ornamental dressing of our ship, and gave it an everyday look as they made it ready for work." [55]

## CHAPTER IV

# LEVANTINE VOYAGE

THE party to which Felix was attached as chaplain consisted of four nobles and seven servants. Felix after his custom gives a list, adding to each name a brief description of its owner.

So he begins: "Lord John Werner von Zimmern, Count, a comely man and wise, remarkable for his grace of manner, and knowing Latin." He does not add that the count was a man of violent temper, who by pilgrimage was making atonement for having drawn his sword against his own father. Nor does he mention the tradition that Lord John came back from the East with a mermaid wife; but whether that story tells for or against the count's character the reader must decide for himself.[1]

Next comes "Lord Henry von Stöffel, Count of the Holy Roman Empire, an active, hardy, manly man . . . Lord John Truchsess von Waldburg, a very tall gentleman, conscientious, of a high and serious mind, and concerned with the salvation of his soul." (We at once conclude that it was this Lord John who grudged the fee to the flute-playing couple at Trent). Last of the nobles there was "Lord Bär of Rechberg, one of the great Hohenrechbergs, youngest of them all, but bolder, stronger, taller than any other, and more gay, more gentle, more generous."

From these we pass to the servants, who displayed an interesting variety of aptitude. There was Balthasar Büchler, so wise and experienced that the lords would listen to his advice almost as to that of a father. In Conrad Artus, the barber, they had a musician so skilled that his equal would be hard to find. Then there was an esquire, the old fighter

John "Schmidhans," as they called him, and another, very
different John, a country schoolmaster from Bebenhausen,
"a man of peace." The cook Peter was "a straight fellow and
a good chap" to travel with, because he bore hardship cheerfully. Their manciple and steward was the honest, careful
Conrad Beck, their interpreter Ulrich of Ravensburg, a
huckster by trade, who had learnt tongues and the ways of
Mediterranean ships on the galley slaves' bench. Finally
there was our friend Brother Felix.[2]

Outside the party of which he was a member we do not
yet hear many names of fellow travelers, though during the
long delay at Venice those who stayed "at the sign of the
Flute" must have made the acquaintance of many other
Germans, who had put up at one or other of the rival hos-
telries, at "the Mirror," or "the White Lion," or "the Black
Eagle," and we know in fact that it was at Venice that
Fabri struck up that close friendship with the Rumanian
Archdeacon John, which was to last throughout the pilgrimage.[3] Most of those in whose company Felix was to
make the pilgrimage to Sinai traveled, along with von Breydenbach, in the other galley, but even in Lando's galley we
hear only the name of a jongleur, "Bogadellus," and of a
knight, Jerotheus von Ratzenhausen, who was landed, sick,
at Rhodes, until at Cyprus Felix mentions by name Archdeacon John and several other pilgrims.

But we know that, with one exception, the company was
friendly, being unperturbed by the hotheaded and quarrel-
some Frenchmen of Felix's first voyage, while in some
Knights Hospitalers, on their way out to Rhodes, the pilgrims found "pleasant and loyal comrades . . . For on
board ship, as in places of study and at spas, very pleasant
and jolly friendships are made . . ."[4]

The exception to all this good fellowship was the one
woman who traveled in Lando's galley, Contarini having, as
it happened, gathered together in his ship all the other
women pilgrims. This woman had only arrived on board at

the last minute before sailing, in company with her husband, a Fleming, and Messer Lando himself. From the first the exclusively male company deplored this addition to their number, and the more bitterly because they suspected from her appearance that she was "restless and inquisitive." They were right. Even Felix, who, with some of the pilgrims, did his best for the sake of her husband, a decent man, to endure her "silly chatter and prying curiosity into things unprofitable," could not but be severe. "Those seven old women," says he, "in whose company I made the voyage before . . . made less noise and were seen less than this one old beldame, as she ran hither and thither incessantly about the ship . . . wanting to hear and see everything . . ." [5]

Felix himself was possessed of an equally insatiable curiosity, though directed toward matters which he would not have considered "unprofitable," and now, away from the study, he was in his element, looking, listening, trying, learning. He heard from the sailors of the mariners' marks on the Adriatic coast, of the qualities of a good harbor, of the rules which governed the salute of guns given by ship to ship. He learnt something of the pilot's craft in reading weather signs "in the colour of the sea, in the flocking together and movement of the dolphins and flying fish, in the smoke of the fire, the smell of bilge water, the glittering of ropes and cables at night, and the flashing of the oars as they dip into the sea." As we have seen, he also had explained to him the method of navigation by the pilot's chart. Mixed up with all the facts which he absorbed was information of that sort which Ludolph von Suchem's "very truthful sailor" purveyed, and Felix reports some highly improbable statements about the speed of ships. [6]

But as well as acquiring information, true or false, the Friar was getting his sea legs, and learning by practice some of the sailor's featness. He learnt to walk by night, in order to avoid the curses of an awakened galley slave, along the galley's bulwark, laying hold of rope after rope, a transit which he admits to be "risky and dangerous" but possible for one "not timid, and having a good head." [7] He learnt also to jump from the galley into a boat, and from a boat ashore, even in rough weather, although the boat alongside "was raised aloft by the waves higher than the galley, and then again sank so deep, that we on board . . . could not see it because of the waves between us. In such weather . . . whosoever wishes to get out of a galley into a boat, must stand on the steps of the galley, and watch carefully until the boat comes so near the galley that he can reach it by a leap . . . and he must leap the instant it comes so close, for . . . the next moment it is carried further away . . . and when he does leap . . . he cannot save himself from falling, either backwards or forwards . . . and those on board of it lift him up." After such an account Felix may well have felt that his readers at home would hardly believe that any would be capable of such feats of daring and address. But, he assures them, "after a man has been for many days battered with storms and hardships, and starved for want of food on board ship, when he arrives at a good port he will dare five dangerous leaps, rather than stay on board." Felix had seen even women "who at first . . . scarcely dared to look at the sea, who . . . became so bold by practice" that they could jump as well as the men.[8]

Their first port of call was Rovigno, a small harbor two miles beyond Parenzo. Here the pilgrims landed and Felix was able to give his companions the slip in order to climb up a hill for the sake of the view. The pilgrims had expected that the captain would wait here till the wind shifted, but instead they were recalled by the sound of the ship's trumpets; Agostino Contarini's galley had been sighted passing the harbor, and Lando was determined not to let him get ahead, for between the two Venetian noblemen there existed a deep-seated grudge, which they expected, though vainly, that their passengers should share, and which gave to the voyage something of the competitive character of a nineteenth-century Australian grain race.

Having sailed, they found themselves, after five days of contrary winds, forced to lie to off a deserted island for three days. Whatever were Lando's feelings at the delay, the pilgrims enjoyed the opportunity of making expeditions ashore. Felix, poking about among the rocks near the sea, was shown by one of the sailors a very tasty salad herb, which the sailor called *porcella;* he discovered also bushes of "the finest agnus castus." * This shrub reminded Felix of his boyhood, "for I learned about it at Basle, where it grew in our convent garden, and had been planted there by someone who came from the sea at the time of the Council of Basle. . . . So at sunset I returned on board the galley, taking with me my *porcella* . . . and my agnus castus for scent and for an ornament to my berth." [9]

That night, remaining below while the rest went on deck for supper, he enjoyed a very pleasant meal of the salad, and a restful solitude—for the Friar, in spite of his gregarious nature, frequently longed to be alone. "It was," he says, "unpleasant for me, and very distracting to my thoughts, to live entirely among secular persons." [10] At Venice he had made an attempt to detach himself from the party at "the Flute" and to stay at the Dominican convent, but was foiled by the kindness of the lords; and at Jerusalem we shall find him slipping away from the rest, in the select ecclesiastical company of his hosts, the Franciscans, or better still alone, for expeditions which were clearly to him the most enjoyable of all.

Yet after such refreshment the Friar was always ready to share in social pleasures. Next morning he and almost all the

---

* *Porcella:* probably one of the purslanes, which were much used in salads. *Agnus Castus:* a Verbenaceae, supposed to have antiaphrodisiac qualities. The crushed seeds were used by the ancients instead of pepper. Cf. *Evag.,* III, 364.

others went on shore again; though the weather was gloomy
it proved "a merry day . . . some ran about over the path-
less hills, while some sat and talked."

On the third day the wind changed and blew fair, continuing mainly so for a week. Now the pilgrims experienced the bright side of life on board ship, as they sailed
"along a very pleasant course wherein we had on either side
villages, castles, and cultivated ground." Night, with such
a wind, was as peaceful as the day. Even if Felix was unable
to sleep below he could watch, from the deck, the glow of
the lamp which hung above the compass in the sterncastle,
and listen to the chanted orders of the officer of the watch
to the steersman.[11] Only the captain and officers had to
endure the exasperation of knowing that Contarini's galley
had passed them once more.

On June 15, a Sunday, they reached Modon (Methone),
the great halfway house of Venetian trade with the East.
Here they found "Master Augustine's galley" in the harbor,
"and all his pilgrims . . . in the city." It was a merry meeting for the passengers. Both parties ate and drank together,
and disregarding the feud between the two captains, "we
brought them on board and showed them our galley, and
they took us to see theirs, and so we spent the day together
until vespers," separating only when the horns blew, and
all must return on board.[12]

Once more it was Contarini who got away first, and
Lando still further prejudiced his chance of reaching the
Holy Land in good time by deciding to touch at Crete.
This, though an act of filial piety on the captain's part, since
his father was Patriarch of Crete, would, he knew, be none
the less unacceptable to the pilgrims. In order to stifle criticism he therefore offered a roll of silk, to be played for at
cards. His device succeeded with the nobles, and particularly
with young Hohenrechberg who won the prize, but Felix
makes one of his few acid comments on this transaction.

"There was," he says, "much rejoicing, as fools rejoice, in our company, at our having won that piece of silk." [13]

Their call at Crete, though it caused delay, brought its own compensation. Failing to find an inn, they had to put up, "nobles, priests, or monks," at a brothel, "cleared" for the occasion. Felix has no word of condemnation for the proprietress, "a well-mannered . . . discreet woman," and a German, but then, she gave them "a glorious supper, with Cretan wine . . . and . . . ripe grapes, both black and white." Next day while the galley slaves, after their custom, traded their wares in the market place, the pilgrims improved the hours by visiting churches and monasteries. [14]

Rhodes, their next port of call, they entered by moonlight, and found Contarini's galley lying in harbor. This was satisfactory, but now they must part from their pleasant companions, the Knights of St. John. And now they left behind them also, though by accident, another fellow passenger. The Flemish merchant's wife, having "strayed away to some church outside the town," failed to rejoin when Lando, seeing the other galley weigh anchor, had the horns blown to recall the pilgrims, and in haste made off after Contarini. "Except her husband, no one was sorry," and "there was but little joy" when the determined woman arrived by boat at Larnaca five days later and rejoined the pilgrims. [15]

The second night after their departure from Rhodes was St. John's Eve, which the sailors kept as a high festival. At nightfall they lit twoscore lanterns and hung them from the maintop, then the trumpets blew, while the galley slaves and sailors "sang, rejoiced, chanted, danced, and clapped their hands. . . . I never had beheld," Felix remarks in an interesting aside, "the practice of clapping the hands for joy, to which allusion is made in the 46th psalm . . . Nor could I have believed that the general clapping of many men's hands at the same time . . . would have such great power to move the human mind to joy." [16]

The excitement of the festivity must have been too much
for the steersman, for when, next morning, Cyprus was
sighted, it was discovered that they were far off their course,
with the result that a complicated wrangle developed among
the captain, steersman, pilot, and sailors. It was not till the
evening of June 25 that they anchored at Larnaca, where
again Messer Pietro deserted his ship, having this time a wife
in the island, who was lady in waiting to the Venetian queen,
Caterina Cornaro. The pilgrims therefore were left in the
shadeless, shelterless roadstead to endure the delay as best
they could.

A little way to the east of Larnaca along the coast stood
up the imposing solitary hill of Stavro Vouni, the Mont St.
Croix of the Franks, a place of great sanctity on account of
the relic there displayed—the cross of "Dysmas, the penitent
thief." On the homeward voyage of Felix's first pilgrimage
Agostino Contarini had lain in harbor at Larnaca for a week,
waiting to take his brother off. A number of the pilgrims, and
the clerk from Paris among them, had taken the opportunity
to climb Mont St. Croix as well as to visit Nicosia. But Felix,
though he went to Nicosia, had not, strangely enough, shared
in the other expedition.

This time, however, the Friar was missing no opportu-
nities. Those who stood on deck listening, as he told "about
the barrenness of this port and the nature of the country"
and pointed out this or that place of interest on shore, soon
found that he was suggesting an expedition to climb the holy
mountain. At first, he says, they thought he was joking,
though those of his own party, who knew him better, may
have already been backing away unostentatiously from
among the crowd; certainly not one of them volunteered
to join in the expedition. Three German knights, however,
and three other pilgrims agreed to go, and Felix, as usual,
gives the list of their names with appropriate descriptive
epithets.

"My lord Heinrich von Schaumburg, a noble knight and a brave man.

"John the Priest, an archdeacon of Transylvania, a devout and learned man.

"Caspar Siculi, knight, a daring and vigorous youth.

"Burchard von Nusdorf, knight, a good and cheerful man.

"One Rudolf, a Swiss of Zurich, a tall and honest man.

"One John, a merchant of Flanders, a very thirsty soul." [17]

It is interesting to note that the first three among these indefatigable sight-seers were to be members, along with Felix, of one of the three parties in the Sinai pilgrimage. Whether the "thirsty soul" was that grass widower whose wife had been left behind, we can only wonder.

It was after sunset and already growing dark when they started. The guide whom Felix had hired led them first to the house of a friend where they had a supper of bread, cheese, and wine. By the time they had eaten and were ready to mount the mules which the guide had provided, the moon had risen, and by that light they "set out joyously. . . . for we, the chosen eight, were all comrades. The weather was fine, the country beautiful, the road good, and besides all this the shrubs of that land breathed forth the sweetest fragrance, for almost all the herbs of that isle are spices of divers sorts, which smell by far sweetest in the night time, when they are moist with dew." [18]

They reached the village of St. Croix just before daybreak, and there rested, lit a fire, and breakfasted—all but Felix who as usual intended to say Mass in that holy and interesting place. As soon as it was light, they went on again, up "a delicious valley, through the midst of which ran a clear sweet stream of living water, whose banks were full of most beauteous flowers, whose names we did not know, and sweet smelling shrubs." The last bit of the climb, so steep that they must do it on foot, brought them, hot and blown, to the gates of the church.

Of the relic which they had come to see strange and curious tales were told. "The miracle which is noised abroad about the cross is that it hangs in the air without any fastening . . . as firm as though it were fixed with the strongest nails," but it is clear that Felix approached the sight with an open mind. He took care to warn his lay companions that they had no right to expect to behold a miracle, and cautioned them that they should not be overinquisitive when they viewed it.

He was, therefore, himself unable to make the thorough investigation which he clearly yearned to undertake. "I might indeed," he says regretfully, "I might indeed have searched this thing more narrowly than I did, but I feared God, and had no right to do that which I had forbidden others to do." So he must content himself with kissing the cross upon the silver-gilt plates which covered the front, thrusting his head into the opening, and peering round, by the light of the candle he carried, to see the bare wood behind, and groping with his hand in the holes into which the arms and foot of the cross projected, to "perceive by touch that there is no fastening there." But what he longed to do, and felt restrained by his company from doing, must have been to lay his hand upon the cross, as d'Anglure had done nearly a hundred years before, who found that "when one touches it, it shakes much."

So, leaving the tantalizing problem unsolved, he and the others went out, to stroll for a while outside the church, where there were not only the ruins of ancient walls to examine, reputed to have been part of a temple to Venus, but also a very fine and extensive view.

"In whichever direction we looked, whether along or across the island, we could see the sea," which, on this perfect morning must have displayed that celestial milky blue which is the color of the early morning, sunlit sea round about Cyprus, though unfortunately the heat haze hid from them the Armenian coast and the mountains of Galilee. After this, and a farewell visit to kiss once more the holy cross, "we . . . hurried down . . . to where our beasts stood, and rode to the village of Holy Cross, where we found our much longed-for dinner ready," the party having providently ordered it on their way up. Later in the day, when the heat had abated, they made their way back to the coast, reaching the ship in the cool of the evening to find those they had left behind in a very ill temper, and "sorry that they had not gone with us." [19]

During the rest of the voyage, in which contrary winds once set the ship back as far west as Limasol, the pilgrims were preoccupied with their watch for the first sight of the Holy Land. Now one, now another would claim to see it, arguing together "in pious dispute," or betting glasses of malvoisie, and appealing to the lookout in the maintop as an arbitrator. With Felix himself the unrest went very deep. He lost, he says, appetite and sleep. "My only pleasure was to sit at the prow of the galley up on the horns thereof, and from thence to look out ceaselessly across the wide sea . . . On all these days I was seated on the prow before the dawn, whose rays I welcomed with joy, and then awaited the rising of the sun, and most diligently cast my sight over the surface of the sea . . . Wherefore I did not look aloft, but fixed my gaze unflinchingly upon that part of the sky which seemed to join the sea . . . and as the sun rose I used to look earnestly whether I could see any impediment or opaque body between the bright body of the sun and the clear body of the water. . . . For when a galley is floating on the high seas, and the sun rises, it seems as though he rose out of the water . . . But when the galley is within about twenty or thirty German miles of the land, the sun seems to come forth from the mountains of that land, so that in the brightness of the dawn the mountains can be seen before the sun, because they are between the sun and the sea. But as soon as the sun has risen above the mountains . . . those mountains will be invisible." [20]

It was soon after sunrise on July 1 that the pilgrims heard the watch in the maintop hail them:

" 'My lords pilgrims, rise up and come on deck; behold, the land which you long to see is in sight.' "

Yet not for another hour could the eyes of the landsmen on deck distinguish "peaks and mountain-tops rising as it were out of the sea," and the sailors themselves held divergent views as to what land they saw, for some maintained that they were yet in sight of the Cilician or Cappadocian coast. Only when it became certain that they saw the mountains of Israel, was the landfall announced by the captain's herald and celebrated by a Te Deum sung by men of many tongues, "Latin priests, Sclavonians, Italians . . . Franks, Germans, Englishmen, Irishmen, Hungarians, Scots, Dacians, Bohemians, and Spaniards," while the ship's trumpeters blew, and Bogadellus, the jongleur, played his drum and sackbut. Dinner followed immediately, and after that all spent the afternoon leaning against the ship's side and staring at the coastline, Felix being in the happy position of one not only able to rehearse to his companions recollections of biblical history, but, as an experienced traveler, to impart local information and point out remembered landmarks.[21]

Jaffa was, during the whole of the fifteenth century, the regular port of call for the pilgrim galleys, and here the pilgrims were taken in charge by a system so reminiscent of that which obtains today at any port at which foreign tourists disembark, that the writer is tempted to drop into the use of modern terms, to speak of quarantine, customs, immigration officers, passports, and the rest of it.

In the earlier part of the century entry into Palestine had been a comparatively simple matter. In those days Venice and Genoa each kept at least one consul at Jerusalem, for the sake of the pilgrim traffic, and de Caumont received his safe-conduct, on board ship, at the hands of one of these, and of "the Father Guardian of Mount Sion," that is to say, the prior of the Franciscan house at Jerusalem. The pilgrim sometimes known as Claude de Mirebel, who probably made the journey a little earlier than de Caumont,[22] gives the procedure as follows: the "patron" sent the galley's clerk to Ramle where the emir at once issued a safe-conduct "for all by name, making one or two of the greatest of the pilgrims head over the rest." (The writer of the narrative acidly suggests that the reason for the emir's promptitude lay in the conviction that the transaction was "for their profit.") The pilgrims then disembarked, each man was registered, "and to each is given a ticket (*bullette*) which they must carry with them wherever they go." [23]

By the time Felix made his pilgrimage the arrangements were in some respects different. For a few years there had been no Genoese or Venetian consuls, or indeed consuls of any Christian state, at Jerusalem. What they had done for the pilgrims was now left to the Father Guardian of Mount Sion, who, without the power of any sovereign state at his back, must depend for his influence upon the prestige of his character and office. Probably as a consequence of this lack of consular representation, which in fact reflected the changed political equilibrium of the Levant, the whole business of the entry of the pilgrims was the subject of prolonged and acrimonious negotiations between the galley captains and the Saracens, the captains endeavoring to keep for themselves as much as they could of the pilgrims' contract money, the Saracens trying to exact as high a price as possible.

With the Moslem conquerors in control of the Holy Places the plight of the pilgrims was, even at the best, one of uncertainty and discomfort. But this year the embittered quarrel which existed between the two Venetian captains was added to their other disabilities. Each captain, Felix says, aimed at leading his own pilgrim passengers through the Holy Land independently of the others. Lando, who at first had done his utmost not to be left behind in the voyage by Contarini, seems later to have decided that if he loitered long enough at Crete and at Cyprus, the other captain would have made his bargain with the Saracens, and moved away from Jaffa with his batch of pilgrims, before the arrival of the second galley. Contarini, equally anxious to avoid Lando's company, did, in fact, try to do that very thing, and it was only the blank refusal of the Saracens to treat with one galley captain before the arrival of the other that prevented him. If he had succeeded the second galley would have been forced to retire to Cyprus, there to wait till the first party of pilgrims had been passed through the machinery of the tourist organization and deposited once more in their galley for the homeward voyage.[24] Felix and his company were, therefore, proportionately delighted, when, on coming to anchor beside the Contarini galley at Jaffa, they saw that the other pilgrims were still on board, since they themselves were "all of one mind, and wished . . . to be taken to see the Holy Places together."

The second galley having arrived, the usual preliminaries could now go forward. Next day the two captains sent off messengers, not only, as in the past, to the emir of Ramle but also to the governor of Jerusalem and the Father Guardian of Mount Sion. Only when these were all gathered at Jaffa, would negotiations begin.

Meanwhile, the pilgrims, as yet without safe-conduct, must remain in the galleys, not close in shore, for the artificial harbor was too shallow for ships of draft, but beyond what were called Andromeda's rocks.[25] They were near enough, however, to learn to know the appearance of the town, set on a hill with flat country beyond, and to see that, though once great, it now lay mostly in ruins. Doubtless they had pointed out to them those caves, or half-ruined vaults, known as St. Peter's Cellars, and the knowledge that they themselves would be lodged in these made them watch with interest the coming and going of Saracens about the caves.

Other diversions helped to pass the time. Mamelukes

*Pilgrim Galley in the Harbor of Jaffa*

came on board to drink forbidden wine in the privacy of
the captain's cabin, and to give news, true or false, in return. Strange fish appeared sometimes alongside: early one
morning Felix observed among these a variety of extraordinary shapes—"some were large and quite round, like a
winnowing-fan. Some had heads like dogs, with long ears
hanging down . . ." [26] There might be dolphins to watch,
or a big turtle, or "certain long slender fish which went in
great numbers and seemed like a great sea-wave when they
were pursued by some large fish." Or there might even be
the excitement of seeing the sailors angle for and catch a
shark, which, when skinned—"the hide was like iron"—a
few, but only a few, of the poor pilgrims sampled for dinner.[27]

On the other hand the pilgrim galleys provided an interesting spectacle for the inhabitants of Jaffa and the neighborhood; there might be, of an evening, twenty to thirty
riders on camels, drawn up in line along the edge of the
sea, staring out toward the ships.[28]

On July 5 the Saracen emirs arrived to take possession
of those tents which the pilgrims had seen pitched by their
servants, and now at nighttime the camp was lit by hanging
clusters of glass lanterns, set up on poles among the tents.
After the arrival of the emirs a new host was seen coming
down toward the shore, but this turned out to be, not more
horsemen, but the donkeys and donkey boys assembled from
the surrounding country in order to provide transport for
the pilgrims. With them came the greater Calinus and the
lesser Calinus, as Felix calls the two official Saracen dragomans.*

* The title "Calinus" is used by Felix, von Breydenbach, and Paul
Walther, but by no other pilgrim among those upon whose accounts I
have drawn. Walther, p. 214, once writes it "Callilus," and de Rochechouart, who was in Palestine twenty years before Felix, refers to "the
head dragoman of the Soldan, which means interpreter, whose name is
Callilus, in the vulgar tongue, Kali. (Magni truchemanus Soldani, qui

Already the captains had gone ashore, and now the pilgrims in Lando's galley were told to get ready to land. They dined hastily, and while at dinner were confronted by that last embarassing trial which the modern ocean liner's passenger also knows—namely tipping. The Venetian galley's crew employed, however, more forcible methods than any usual nowadays. As the pilgrims sat at dinner the men came "one after another . . . with silver cups, asking for gratuities . . . and if anyone refused . . . they said they would not set him on shore in the boat." [29] But, at last, with what food they could carry in their scrips—cheese and smoked meat—and the rest of their gear, the pilgrims went over the side and were rowed ashore.

The first business on landing was that of registration, as at the present day, of passports. Each man, severally, must pass before the Saracen officials, who, when they had scrutinized him with care, inquired and registered his own name and that of his father.[*] In the earlier part of the century it had been possible for pilgrims, by payment of a fee, to wear their swords while in the Holy Land,[30] but when Felix made his pilgrimage, they were warned before they left the ship that swords must be left behind; there was no option, and no purpose would have been served by smuggling in weapons which could not be worn. It was otherwise with wine. From the guidebooks pilgrims had learnt that it was well to carry wine with them; but the bottles must be hidden in innocent-seeming sacks, or they would be broken by the Saracens. The pilgrims must therefore have experienced, upon landing,

proprie dicitur interpres, cui nomen Callilus, vulgariter Kali.)" Rochechouart, p. 237. This official met the pilgrims at Jaffa.

Khalil is a common Arabic name meaning "friend," and might have become a designation for a guide if borne by a family which for generations had acted as guide to the Holy Places, but no such family is known.

"Dalîl" is the ordinary word for a guide. (See Acknowledgments)

[*] Röhricht, p. 16, says that noblemen sometimes tried to pass themselves off as servants of the captain in the hope of evading extortionate charges.

just those sensations known to so many travelers of today as they anxiously watch the facial expression or the groping hands of a zealous customs official.

Once registered they were seized and bundled into one of those dark, dripping, and ruinous vaults or caves which they had seen from the galley's deck, and which now they discovered to be as Sir Richard Guylforde's chaplain described them: "bare, stinking stable ground." [31] Indulgences were obtained by any pilgrim entering these in the right spirit, and to endure the filth would, Felix points out, provide salutary spiritual discipline; but if the Saracens had done their best, as the pilgrims believed they had, to foul the place for the strangers' reception, they had done so less from a hostile than a commercial motive. No sooner were the pilgrims all herded into the caves than they were followed by poor men selling rushes and branches of trees to lay on the ground, and merchants with "water of roses from Damascus, in glass bottles, very precious . . . Some of them had balsam, some musk, some soap . . . some rolls of the whitest muslin . . . and many other precious and sweet-scented things were brought in to us, while both the merchants and the Saracens were anointed with aromatic unguents and distilled perfumes, so that they spread scent far around them. Moreover, the merchants . . . burned frankincense and Arabian gums . . ." with the result that the cave became "a storehouse of sweet perfume." Nor was it only the elegances of life which were catered for. Some Saracens "cooked eggs in a frying-pan with oil, and some of them brought loaves of bread, some cool water, some fruit, some salads, and some hot cakes made of eggs . . ." [32]

Yet "amenities," to use that obnoxious and pervasive word of today, cannot be had for nothing, and besides what they spent on such things, the pilgrims were constantly finding themselves forced to pay to unauthorized persons here a penny and there a penny—now for their lodging in the cave, now for permission to leave it. Young Saracens too, with

schoolboy malice, delighted to enrage the visitors by pil-
fering, or snatching what they might, and, when the Christian tempers rose, demanding money as compensation for
any retaliation. When the pilgrims were driven to hire
watchmen to keep intruders out of the cave at night, these
young men, with the ingenuity of their kind, continued to
annoy and disturb their victims by sitting down outside and
conducting a singsong, "howling, barking, and grunting like
beasts, dogs, and pigs. For all Easterns have harsh voices;
nor can they form any melody, but their singing is like the
noise of goats or calves." [33] Meanwhile the Father Guardian
lodged, aloof and in comfort, in his tent on the hillside,
and, what must have been even more exasperating for those
confined in the caves, Contarini's passengers remained on
board their galley.[34]

Yet the imprisonment of the pilgrims was not very rigor-
ous. One day some of them "plucked up their spirits and
were bold enough to come out of their cave down to the
sea-shore, and to the place where the asses stood with their
drivers, and they went to and fro among the Saracen host
. . . and made friends with them." [35] Felix himself, the experienced globe-trotter, fared even better. The lesser Calinus paid him a visit, and took not only the Friar but also
the knights of his party on a sight-seeing tour of Jaffa. On
another occasion when most of the pilgrims were cautiously
exploring in the vicinity of the caves, Felix and some friends
enjoyed a long and pleasant walk by the seashore, "to a
fountain of living water which ran down a gorge in the
hills, and there we drank of that water without payment,
though for many days we had drunk no water save what
we had bought and paid for." Even when they were in the
caves there was always the sea to watch as it dashed itself
into spray upon the rocks of that harbor which, Felix believed, must be the most "abominable . . . to be found in
the whole circuit of the sea." And there were the curious
beasts of this strange land: buffaloes, more than a hundred

of which would come down to the shore at evening, and stand "all night up to their necks in the sea for the sake of coolness . . ." [36] or stranger still, there were the camels of those who brought bread, grapes, melons, and other fruits to sell to the Christians. Brother Paul had watched those camels with absorbed attention. "The camel," he says, "is a very ill-shapen creature, large, taller than a big horse, and ordinarily all camels are of one colour, a ruddy colour," and here the Franciscan lapses into his own homely German— "ruddy as a roan horse, 'als eyn rotfalbe.' " "But it is a very strong creature, with a hump on its back to which burdens are attached; it can easily carry the third part of a cartload of wine for thirty miles and more. It has a great belly, a long neck, a small head, short ears, eyes like a goat, it keeps its head stretched out and up like a crane; its legs are long, the feet soft, divided, and without nails, its tail like a cow's. . . . It makes a horrid roaring, eats straw and dry thorns in the fields. And this is its habit; when it is to be loaded or un-loaded, it lays itself down completely on its belly and legs, and so rises up, unladen. But if when it rises loaded it knows that the load is too much for its powers, then it lays itself down again, and rises not until its load is such that it can bear it . . ." [37]

It was not until July 8 that the two captains could be brought to an agreement to combine their respective parties of pilgrims for the journey to Jerusalem. The persuasions of the Father Guardian, and of "some respectable and peace-able Saracens" had failed utterly to move them. Only the threat that they themselves should be thrown into prison, and the pilgrims returned to Venice under the care of a new pair of captains, broke their resistance.

Next day, while it was still dark, the pilgrims were roused and told to come out of the caves. By torch and lantern light they passed once more between Saracen officers, and were checked off upon the lists drawn up on their arrival.

Only then were they allowed to go on to where the donkeys waited.

Those who knew no better may now have hoped that for the moment their troubles were over. But this was not so, for at the news of the arrival of the pilgrim galleys the countrymen might bring to Jaffa twice as many donkeys as there were pilgrims to ride them, and if so, "as soon as a pilgrim came down to the level ground the nearest driver laid hold of him, and led him to his asses. Wherefore it not seldom happened that two or three drivers were dragging one pilgrim, one in one direction, another in another . . . for one Saracen brought seven or eight asses, of a sort, and hence it happens that when there are not above two hundred pilgrims there will be four hundred asses, wherefore the drivers fight for the pilgrims . . ."

As a newcomer, and ignorant of the economics of the situation, Felix had suffered a sad fright at this point in his first pilgrimage. "A black Moor ran up to me and snatched me violently away, trying to drag me towards the crowd of asses, round which a wondrous riot was going on. I, fearing that he meant to rob me, hung back all the harder, and by great force shook myself free of him . . ." and retreated to where, serene above the turmoil, the Father Guardian and the Saracen emirs stood among torches and lanterns. But the Father Guardian, when appealed to, sent Felix back: " 'Go down quick, quick, and go willingly with whosoever leads you away.' "

Down once more Felix went, and was met by a Saracen, a man with "a very cruel look," who "caught me by the right hand with his right hand. He began to run very swiftly, because by this time all were ready mounted on their asses. Now as he ran I was forced to run sideways and awkwardly, because, as I have told you, he held my right hand hard with his own, and so he ran holding me, over stones against which I struck several times as I ran sideways, and fell."

The connection, inauspiciously begun, proved to be so

satisfactory that Felix was determined, on his second pilgrimage, to have if he might the same "good little ass, black all over," and the same man, for whom indeed he had bought with him from Ulm a pair of iron stirrups as a gift. And this time, as an experienced traveler, he knew what he must do to find his man, for "whenever the pilgrim has to start for any place he must run among the crowd of asses to seek for his own driver, loudly calling for him by name." So now he went toward the donkeys, crying, as he had learnt, "Galela Cassa."

At first no one answered his call, though, on the other hand, no other driver molested him. Then "a kinglike Saracen noble, seated on horseback, rode up to me and touched me gently with a staff which he held in his hand, signing to me to hold my peace, and stand quietly by his side."

Felix obeyed, but after a little while, the disorder and hurry of the business round the donkeys infected him with anxiety. He began to think that the Saracen might have forgotten him, and at last tried to slip away.

"When he saw this, he said something to me in the Chaldee tongue which I did not understand, but I have since guessed that he said: 'Stand still here by my side; I am Galela, and my slave Cassa will presently come to me, and will furnish you with a beast.' " *

This, indeed, was what happened. The donkey man arrived. "As soon as he saw me he recognised me . . . and he ran to kiss me . . . with a most joyous countenance . . . and he laughed and said much to me that I did not understand . . ." 38 With such a friendly donkey man Felix suffered none of the annoyances which some pilgrims experienced.39 On the contrary, he enjoyed privileges which none of the others had. The man "often changed my asses that I might have one that pleased me better; when the ass was climbing a hill he supported me; when going down a steep and rough road he held me . . . gave me drink from

* See footnote on p. 189.

his water-skin, and shared his biscuits with me: he would climb over the stone walls of gardens and bring me figs, grapes, and other fruits . . . He gave me the goad which he used for his ass, albeit none of the other drivers will suffer pilgrims to have goads . . ." Such preferential treatment provoked comment among Felix's companions, who supposed that the Friar must have done as Casola advised, and given the man "much money in secret." Felix, knowing that this was not so, wondered, with a touching and innocent snobbery, whether the donkey driver took him for some great lord in disguise, "and this was why he served me so zealously."

It was still early in the day when the pilgrims, on foot and carrying their own baggage, for the Saracens would not suffer any Christian to ride into a Moslem city,[40] reached Ramle, and entered the hospice provided by the pious generosity of Philip the Good, Duke of Burgundy, where it was customary for the pilgrims to halt, sometimes for a matter of days.* Entering by a long and narrow door they found themselves in what even Brother Paul describes as "a large and beautiful court, with many chambers and vaulted rooms . . . and a fountain full of good and wholesome water." It is true that the rooms were bare of furniture, a fact which the more critical Casola viewed with disfavor [41] but it was possible to buy or hire mats, and Felix's party installed themselves in one of the empty rooms very cheerfully. Meanwhile an altar had been set up in the inner courtyard of the hospice, under "a great palm tree . . . loaded with dates," and the pilgrims were soon called to attend their first Mass upon the holy soil of Palestine. A sermon followed Mass, and instructions, delivered by the Father Guardian in Latin, and translated into German by Felix,

* Röhricht, p. 17, says that this was built in 1420. He states also that it was at Ramle that the pilgrims received their safe-conducts. But Fabri, I, 259–260, says that in 1480 Contarini was imprisoned and the pilgrims threatened with deportation on the ground that they had arrived at Ramle without the safe-conduct.

as to the correct behavior to be observed while on pilgrimage. This harangue, beginning with a reminder that the pope's dispensation or the Father Guardian's absolution was necessary for every one entering the profaned land of Palestine, proceeded to give advice in the ticklish business of dealings with the Moslem inhabitants, and warned the pilgrims against those same bad habits which are displayed even yet by their tourist successors, such as the carving of names upon walls, the chipping off of fragments from notable monuments; and concluded with an exhortation that the visitors should pay cheerfully what was demanded of them, and not forget "the poor convent of the brethren of Mount Zion in Jerusalem." [42]

It was close on noon when they came back into the outer court, and found it crowded with those of every race and religion, who had come to sell, and especially to sell food, to the pilgrims. To Felix the temptation to record the strange and delicious food which he ate was as irresistible as it is to most travelers. At the hospice at Ramle you could buy "cooked chickens and fowls, cooked milk . . . most excellent loaves of bread, eggs, bunches of the sweetest grapes, pomegranates, apples, oranges, watermelons, lemons, figs both great and small, confections of almonds and honey, dried figs, some confections of sugar, almonds and dates, and cold water. One man likewise brought leather bottles full of an artificial drink used by great Saracen lords instead of wine." [43]

The pilgrims had already, at Jaffa, learnt something of the malice and ingenuity in torment of the Saracen street-corner boys. Here at the hospice, though otherwise much better off, they had to endure more of the same, so that they had need of all the wise exhortations to patience which had been addressed to them in the Father Guardian's sermon. Sometimes, indeed, retaliation succeeded in quelling the tormentors without causing further trouble. A pilgrim noble, "a great and respectable man," sitting upon the ground, found that one of his feet was being pulled by a youth who squatted in front of him. When he withdrew it, the boy seized and tugged at the other. "But while he was pulling hard at the knight's legs, the latter became angry, and with the foot he had drawn back kicked the Saracen so violently in the belly that the youth let go . . . and fell head over heels, rolling like a ball into the very middle of the paved court. He then arose in confusion and left the place. At this we were much alarmed, fearing that he might stir up the people to attack us; but no harm came of it."

With such exasperations and anxieties, it was no wonder if the pilgrims longed to be gone out of Ramle, whose population had the reputation of being one of the most hostile to Christians, and the naughty boys, according to Felix, worse than at any other place. Yet the captains, the dragomans, the governors would not move. They were "shut up in a chamber together holding a secret council," but it became known that they feared an encounter with Bedouin tribes who were reported to be across the road to Jerusalem.[44] Once preparations for a start were ordered: the pilgrims made ready, and with all their bags packed sat near the door of the hospice; but the order was canceled, and when they returned to the rooms they had left, they found that the mats which they had bought had been taken away. At that the Christian worm turned, and would pay no more; the Saracen who owned the mats "was exceeding furious, and often times spat at us, while wrangling with us . . . He would have let us have them for a few pence, but we bade him begone." Tempers were rising so high that the wiser among the pilgrims importuned the captains "to lead us out of that fiery furnace. They promised that we should start in an hour's time."[45]

The departure that evening was not to be without unpleasantness. The pilgrims must go out, as they came, on foot, and soon they found themselves mobbed. In the narrow, stifling streets the dust rose "so . . . that a man could

scarce see the comrade by his side, and if he could see him
. . . could not recognise him, so thick was the dust. My
black hood was so covered with dust that it looked not
black, but grey." In all the press Felix found himself
crushed against the wall of a house and looking through a
window into a room where stood several women with little
children, all of whom "made crosses with their fingers, and
kissed them, thereby giving me to know that they were
followers of the Crucified . . ."—a sight which moved and
saddened the Friar.[46]

Clear of the town the donkeys and the Saracen escort
were waiting. But the pilgrims were not yet out of the wood.
They passed through an Arab encampment—empty but for
the wretched-looking women and black and naked children.
The men, mounted on camels, asses, and horses, lurked
further on, at the opening of a valley. For all their warlike
show however it was not difficult for the Saracen escort to
clear the way; only for a while the wild folk followed,
hustling the pilgrims, trying to shoulder them from their
saddles; if they fell, snatching at scrip or cloak, and sometimes throwing stones; yet, "when they saw that they could
get nothing from us by force, they ran after us and humbly
and tamely begged us to give them something; but they did
not," says Felix, "get much." [47]

So the pilgrims went on, up into the hills in the darkness,
forbidden by the escort to camp, for fear the Arabs should
pursue, until at last, by starlight, they came to "a small
village where there was a fountain of good and cool water."
There they waited, picnicking by torchlight upon the food
they had brought from Ramle, and upon the bread, fruit,
and water which the villagers, late as it was, brought to them.
The place was a rough hillside, "full of stones, like those
Alps which are between Ulm and Weissensteig." There was
an alarm when someone discovered a scorpion under the
stones, but the escort was emphatic that scorpions met out-
of-doors never stung. So the pilgrims rested a while, saw the

moon rise, and waited for the dawn which would set them upon their last day's journey to Jerusalem.

They started before sunrise, and had gone some way before the day broke; when they could see the country through which they were passing, they found it to be rugged, barren, and inhospitable, and altogether so contrary to the expectations of some of the devout, that an argument developed between two of the pilgrims which almost ended in blows. But the way grew more pleasant. They came to a cultivated valley with olive trees; then went up again to the crest of a hill from which they saw to the east, not Jerusalem indeed, but the Church of the Ascension on the Mount of Olives beyond the city.

On they went, with a pause to look at "a castle which is the holy Emmaus"; through mountainous country where there were yet to be seen many ruins of crusading castles,[48] down to the Valley of Elah, "the valley of the Terebinth," and up once more, going southward this time between "gardens of fruit trees, pot-herbs, and figs . . . among dry stone walls."

And now at last, "like a flash of lightning" Jerusalem appeared, not the whole city, but that part of it "which adjoins the Mount Sion, and we saw the holy Mount Sion itself, with all its buildings and ruins. Above all we saw the citadel of Sion . . . in such a clear light that the lofty walls and towers . . . seemed to enclose the whole city . . ." [49]

The pilgrims did what pilgrims before and since have done, those, that is to say, who are not inhibited by the Protestant or Victorian shyness which, at the same place, kept Robert Curzon uneasy and self-conscious in his saddle. They dismounted and knelt in the road, bowing their faces to the stones, though whether any one of them, even Felix himself, addressed to the Holy City that long and ornate apostrophe which he records, may well be doubted. Then, mounted once more, they moved on, the priests among them singing Te Deum, but in voices discreetly subdued lest they should annoy their escort.[50]

## CHAPTER V

# JERUSALEM—THE HOLY PLACES

THE pilgrims entered Jerusalem by the Fish Gate, now the Jaffa Gate, going two by two, in silent and reverent procession; all were on foot, some had cast off their shoes and walked barefoot. They came, says Felix, "through a long street to a great closed church, before which was a fair, large courtyard, paved with polished marble of exceeding whiteness." When all were gathered together in the court one of the Franciscans announced to them what that church was: the Church of the Holy Sepulcher itself, the chief aim of all their pilgrimage, whose walls, none doubted, contained that very hill, that very tomb, where Christ had died, and from which Christ had risen; scene of those events from which, as water from the smitten rock, Christianity had sprung.

The announcement caused frantic excitement. There were tears, groans, wailing, sighs, and sobs from the men; the women shrieked as though in labor. Felix declared it a sight "pleasant to behold," and considered it above the average level of such displays of sensibility. "As a rule those who visit the holy places are . . . merely roused to unusual devotion and piety"; he had even seen some "dull and unprofitable pilgrims" who, witnessing similar manifestations of emotion, had been moved to smile.[1]

It would be a great mistake to imagine from this that the Friar was one who cultivated or admired hysterical emotion. "Those weepings and sobbings," he acutely remarks, "which are common at the holy places arise for the most part from the fact that when one pilgrim weeps another cannot refrain from tears, and so sometimes all of them lament

together; or because some people have the art of working
themselves up to weep even in matters unconnected with
religion. Such people as these shed many futile tears at the
holy places, and make a howling at almost all of them, not

*The Church of the Holy Sepulcher*

because of the power which the place exercises over them,
albeit the places do certainly tend to devotion, but because
of the ease with which they weep." [2]

In Felix's account of the scene in the courtyard a little
must probably be allowed for his undeniable fondness of
rhetoric, and a little more, when we compare it with the
passage just quoted, for the inconsistency which is not surprising in a writer so spontaneous and so profuse. Yet it is

obvious that he himself was profoundly and painfully moved. With all his cheerfulness, shrewd sense, humor, and enjoyment of physical comforts and sensations—qualities which break down the barrier of time, and show common humanity the same then as now—he was still a man of his age, and that age one which in every emotion, religious or secular, found free and vehement expression as natural as the emotion itself.

Nothing however is so hard to communicate as that emotion which is the result of religious experience, though it is one which every believer craves, above all others, to communicate. It can be communicated, but rarely, naked as in the tremendous prose of Augustine: "If . . . He himself should speak, alone . . . by himself, so that we should hear his word, not through any tongue of flesh, nor Angel's voice, nor echo of thunder, nor in the dark riddle of a similitude, but might hear indeed him, whom in these things we love, himself without these . . ." or wrapped around by the fantasies and images of poetry:

> "In a valley of this restless mind
> I sought in mountain and in mead,
> Trusting a true love for to find.
> Upon a hill then took I heed;
> A voice I heard, and near I yede [went]
> In great dolour complaining tho:
> See, dear soul, how my sides bleed
> Quia amore langueo."

But the ordinary man, however sincerely devout, is only too likely to transmit a travesty, which will move others to laughter—even to disgust. For that reason, in all which follows, we must be content to deal with what is superficial, leaving hidden beneath the childish, the comic, even, to us, the grotesque, that secret place and moment in which the finite finds itself in the presence of the infinite.

From the closed doors of the church the pilgrims were

led to their various lodgings, for in Jerusalem Italians might lodge apart from "Ultramontane" barbarians, and priests did not always share the quarters of the laymen. The latter went on this occasion, and usually, to the ancient Hospital of St. John,[3] ruinous now, and habitable only in parts, so that early in the century one disdainful pilgrim had dismissed it as "a very poor place." [4] As in the hospice at Ramle there was no furniture, but the friars provided carpets for the pilgrims to sleep on,[5] and Felix's party were able to appropriate a place for themselves "at the end of the house, where there is a kind of chamber apart from the rest, in a place which was shut in, fair and respectable," instead of sharing with the other pilgrims that vaulted building, "squalid and ruinous," which reminded Felix of the refectory of a large monastery, and may have been the refectory of the knights, or perhaps the infirmary of the Hospital which had given the order its name and origin.[6]

On Felix's first pilgrimage the laymen had not lodged here, but in a house "with a beautiful garden," in that district of Jerusalem known as Millo.* This, Felix says, was an unusual arrangement, though from the number of paintings and drawings of German coats of arms upon the walls, he deduced that in times past the building had served as a hospice for pilgrims.[7]

Right up to the time of Casola's pilgrimage the galley captains had the right of quarters at the Franciscan house of Mount Sion, and might take with them there two other guests; it was thus that Brasca, who had eaten at the captain's table while on board, came to know so well that "most delicious wine in the world" which the friars provided.[8]

---

* This in Old Testament times was in the northeast corner of the city. Felix seems to locate it between Mount Sion and the Church of the Holy Sepulcher; as he says in Fabri, IX, 103, that the house of Elphahallo, the lesser Calinus, was "on the hill as one goeth down to the holy sepulchre" from Mount Sion; and in Fabri, IX, 154, that he went "from Sion to Millo, to the house of Elphahallo." Breydenbach describes the house of Elphahallo as "close to the Hospital."

The Franciscans however had strong objections to this custom; whether in 1483 Lando and Contarini took advantage of it we do not know, but certainly the friars politely but flatly refused to accept as guests those lay pilgrims who, in that year, remained behind after the departure of the rest in order to make the Sinai journey.[9] Just ten years later they petitioned the Venetian Senate against the continuance of the custom, and the Senate forbade any captain in the future to impose himself upon the friars as their guest, "in contempt of the divine worship, and to the no small detriment of that Holy Place." As a result Agostino Contarini, in the year of Casola's pilgrimage, must, to his disgust, stay within the city, instead of in the fresher air outside the walls, at a house which the prior of Mount Sion had taken for him.[10] This did not mean however that the friars entirely shut their doors to lay boarders, at any rate outside the pilgrimage season, for von Harff a few years later, traveling as a merchant, and with merchants, stayed in the convent.[11]

To members of other religious orders the Franciscans were very ready to show hospitality. Felix was their guest on both of his visits to Jerusalem; during his second stay in the house he shared a cell there with two other pilgrims, Dominican friars both, one from the Ile de France, the other a Neapolitan, living with the Minorite brethren, and enjoying "perfect peace and excellent treatment."

Since not only those who stayed with the friars, but all our pilgrims must have come to know well the Franciscan house on Mount Sion, we may pause to gather together from their various narratives the information which they give us as to the priory and its inhabitants.

For eighty-one years, according to Paul, but in fact for a century and a half, the friars had occupied what remained of a convent of Canons Regular of the crusading period, having been installed there by Robert, king of Sicily, in 1333.

In addition to the twenty-four brethren in the convent on Mount Sion there were two always stationed in quarters within the Church of the Holy Sepulcher, to tend the lamps and serve the altars reserved there to the Latin Church. At Bethlehem lived another half-dozen friars and did the like in the church there.[12]

Besides these responsibilities, and their seasonal duty to the pilgrims, to whom they acted as guides in all the expeditions within and in the near neighborhood of Jerusalem, the friars kept up, so far as they might, the celebrations of those great festivals of the Church which, in the time of the Christian kingdom, had been held at such places as the Church of the Ascension, Bethany, or on the banks of the Jordan.

Close by the friars' house, under their care, and dependent upon them for direction and maintenance, stood the house of those Italian ladies, five in number,[13] whom Felix called the Marthas. These "elderly women, very grave and respectable," lived according to the Third Rule of St. Francis, and doubtless did what they could for the friars, as they did for Felix, washing his tunic and scapular, with "other works of charity," which may with probability be interpreted as doing his mending.[14] He had made the acquaintance of one of the five on board Lando's galley, for at Larnaca a lady of Queen Caterina Cornaro's court took her passage to Jaffa, on her way to join the little community at Jerusalem.[15]

For maintenance the friars depended, apart from the legacy left to them by Philip the Good, Duke of Burgundy, upon the voluntary alms of pilgrims, and, in spite of the splendor of the same Philip's tapestries, made especially for their church, woven with gold and showing scenes of the life and death of Christ, in spite of the crowd of gilded monstrances and reliquaries which they could set out upon the altar when pilgrims came to Jerusalem, the friars lived in true poverty; for all their work and their journeyings they had, besides the Father Guardian's mule, only three donkeys between them, and it was an event to be chronicled when a new one was bought.[16]

Even for their small numbers the convent was "very cramped, the church small, the cloister narrow, the cells little." The church, which contained the Chapel of the Last Supper, was only a fragment of the far greater church which had once stood there, of which part of the east wall and the broken vault above could still be seen. In the conventual buildings there were visible traces of more recent destruction; the friars' dormitory, "where there were once fair cells built with arched roofs," had been gutted by fire in some riot of the Saracen population of Jerusalem.

Small though their quarters were, and narrow their means, the Franciscan house at Jerusalem was yet a pleasant place. It stood high, with a fresher air than was to be found within the walls of the city. In the little cloister, reached by a covered passage leading from the low-browed, iron-bound door upon the street, one found, in front of the kitchen and refectory, a cistern, from which, Felix was convinced, was to be drawn water purer and colder than any in Jerusalem. Beyond the cloister there was an inner garden, and besides that the friars had just bought another and larger one on a spur of the hill. Here they had cleaned out the old disused cisterns, and these, now filled with rain water, were sufficient to keep the garden, designed to serve as graveyard, orchard, and pleasance, irrigated throughout the whole year, so that even in July, when the pilgrims arrived, it was a green place, with beds for the brothers' potherbs, and fig, pomegranate, and other fruit trees.[17]

Of the inhabitants of the Franciscan house we know a few by name, and two of these a little more intimately. In 1480 the prior was a Neapolitan of noble birth, Giovanni de Tomacelli.[18] By 1483 he had been succeeded by Paulo de Caneto, of whom Felix remarks only that he knew no German. The prior at the time of Casola's visit was Francesco Surian, a Venetian, and member, like the galley captains, of that caste of princely merchants who turned from seafaring to statecraft or diplomacy as occasion demanded. He had begun the usual apprenticeship to the sea at twelve years old in one of his father's ships, and till he was twenty-five took part in the regular Levantine trade, making something like two voyages a year. Then he turned his back on wealth and the world's cares, to become a Franciscan. He was prior of the convent at Beirut at the time of Felix's first pilgrimage, returned to Italy in 1484, and in 1493 was elected prior of the house on Mount Sion. Casola disliked him; so did Agostino Contarini, though the sentiment of the galley captain may have been due partly to annoyance at the new order which forbade him to take up his quarters at the convent while at Jerusalem, and partly to professional jealousy of the man who ten years earlier, while a passenger in Contarini's galley, had trussed up his friar's gown in a storm, and taken command of the navigation.[19]

The Infirmarius of the house was a German of Lubeck, known among the Italian friars as Brother Baptista. He had been chosen for this office by no less a person than Pope Pius himself,[20] and he had, as one would expect in a man selected by Aeneas Silvius Piccolomini, a variety of gifts. As well as performing the duties of Infirmarius, in which capacity he had occasion to dose both Felix and Brother Paul, he was also the architect in charge of the works at the church of Bethlehem.[21]

But in 1483 there was a greater personality in the house on Mount Sion than either the Father Guardian or the Infirmarius. Brother John of Prussia, a layman, lived with the friars according to the Third Rule of St. Francis, and acted as their business man. Himself noble by birth, it was he who conferred upon pilgrim noblemen the knighthood of the Holy Sepulcher. But besides all this he was one of those Europeans who, by something of force and sympathy within themselves, become a power among the eastern races; a man "wise, and of great experience, of quiet habits, conscientious and God-fearing," he was counted by Felix to be one of the chief bulwarks of the pilgrims in the Holy Land. A bearded and venerable figure (he had been procurator or bursar of the Franciscans for nearly forty years already, and it was to be from his hands that von Harff received knighthood in 1498), even Saracens and Jews, said Felix, feared him, and children (as a result, one hopes, of his beard, rather than his character), hid from him.[22]

Another, a temporary inhabitant of the house on Mount Sion, we have already encountered. Brother Paul Walther was still a guest of his fellow Franciscans, though Brother John Wild had long gone home. A year ago, on the conclusion of the "conducted tour," by which the seasonal influx of pilgrims was regularly disposed of, Paul had experienced one of his spiritual crises. He could not, having failed of the pope's approval, proceed to the missionary expedition to India. He did not wish to go home. "My spirit was stirred within me, and I considered within myself what I was to do." The conclusion he reached was, that finding himself safe in the Holy Land, in good health and a welcome guest of the Franciscans, he should remain, with the devout intention of washing, in a spiritual sense, by "meditations, prayers, fasts, abstinences, discipline, Masses, obedience, and other good works," his own feet, and those of his hosts, in that very place where Christ had washed the feet of the disciples.

John Wild, however, the chosen companion of his pilgrimage, proved to be as unstable as Reuben, and as water. In Italy, as we have seen, he had shown himself a querulous companion. "In the hazards of the sea, he began to change his mind about staying in the Holy Land, although he had previously promised to stay with me; for I had intended to journey to India, and he asked me that I should content myself with the Holy Land, and so I postponed India on his account."

Now he proved himself discontented and tetchy. " 'There is nothing for me to do here,' " he would say, " 'Every office is filled. I can do nothing.' "

With a display of dignity and forbearance Brother Paul gave him free leave to return, and the two said farewell, "with much weeping, confessing our faults, and reconciled one to the other." All on Brother Paul's side was "peace and charity," though he "strongly suspected him [Brother John] of that same inconstancy which I had observed in him on our journey," and did not fail to record, with a corroded pen, the quarrel, the forgiveness, and the hoarded grudge.

So Brother John departed, and Brother Paul remained "as an orphan, alone in a distant land, among strange brethren and the hosts of the infidel, hearing about me alien tongues which I did not understand." [23]

Not that Paul was dissatisfied with his position. He was able to find plenty of interesting and varied occupations, for in addition to spiritual exercises he washed up for the brethren, dug and planted in their vegetable garden, went about with them when any stray pilgrims arrived who needed to be shown round the Holy Places, and besides all this collected in the friars' library material for treatises upon such subjects as "the genealogy of Christ from Adam to Christ, the whole life and work of Mohammed, all nations dwelling in the Holy Land, the errors and sects of the same . . . the wonders of the world and of divers men." In fact, if anyone found the arrangement disadvantageous, it was not Brother Paul, but, as we shall see, his hosts.

Wherever their lodging might be,* the pilgrims were allowed, during their first day in Jerusalem, to remain in it and to rest. It was a merciful dispensation, for after all their excitements and discomforts at Jaffa and Ramle, after a march either by night, or worse still in the heat of the day, even the bald narrative of the chamberlain of Mainz betrays the weariness of the pilgrims, and Casola describes them as "almost dead of heat and thirst." Yet perhaps more eloquent than either of these notices, is the blank silence in which

* Röhricht, p. 19, gives instances of individual pilgrims who lodged in private houses with Jews or Syrian Christians.

Felix, the all but tireless sight-seer, allows the rest of this day to pass.

Their labors began again betimes next morning, and were to be "no light task" indeed. During the next ten days or so the pilgrims must endure "the intense heat of the sun, the walking from place to place, kneeling and prostration; above all . . . the strain which everyone puts on himself in striving with all his might to rouse himself to earnest piety and comprehension of what is shown him . . . and to devout prayer and meditation. . . . To struggle after mental abstraction whilst bodily walking from place to place is exceeding toilsome." [24]

The actual quantity of sight-seeing crammed into the short time allowed to the pilgrims was immense. In Jerusalem, whose memories range in time from the prehistoric, through Jewish, Roman, Arab, crusading, Saracen, and Turkish history; whose Holy Places are shared by three great religions; story overlays story in every corner of the city, and association crowds on association. Much of what the medieval pilgrim was shown can be still found by running a finger down the index of a modern guidebook—"The House of Caiphas . . . of Dives . . . of Lazarus . . . of St. Veronica . . ." and so on. And if the visitor is not, today, directed to the pillar on which stood the cock whose crowing reminded St. Peter of his boast, yet, when Robert Curzon was in Jerusalem the guide could not be sure, when questioned, whether the dogs in the street near the House of Dives were descendents of those who licked the sores of Lazarus; on the whole he inclined to think that they might be.

In the later Middle Ages, when the tide of tradition ran highest and to every conceivable moment in biblical history and later legend was allotted some particular rock or well, some point on a road, some field, some tree, some bit of ruinous wall, the pilgrim's task might have seemed impossible of fulfillment, had it not been for the contemporary love of type and congruity, which rejoiced to bunch together at one place a number of events exemplifying one theme. This process, when applied to the thronging memories of Jerusalem, resulted in very compendious concentrations of association. Through that same gate by which Christ was led on his way to Calvary, Abel, so the pilgrims were told, had passed out to the place of his death, and Isaac had borne the wood prepared for his own sacrifice. At no place did the memories press so thick as in the Church of the Holy Sepulcher, in which were, and still are, preserved not only the traditional sites of the Crucifixion and Resurrection, as well as the Invention of the Cross and many more, but where also, for the fifteenth-century pilgrim, the rock of Calvary "was from the beginning very worthy of respect, because," as Felix succinctly records:

"Adam, our first parent, died here;
    Abraham was blessed here by Melchisedech;
    Isaac was brought hither by his father to be sacrificed,
    The brazen serpent was set up here;
    The Lord Jesus was crucified here." [25]

Even with such feats of cumulative association the pilgrims must live strenuously. Three nights they passed locked up in the Church of the Holy Sepulcher from dusk to dawn.* The better part of two days—and one of these followed without pause upon a vigil in the Church of the Holy Sepulcher—they spent in viewing sights within Jerusalem itself; longer expeditions to the valleys, and the heights near by must also be made. Besides these "half-day excursions," a night and part of a day would be spent at Bethlehem. The expedition to Jordan, with Jericho, the Dead Sea, and the Mount of Fasting generally thrown in, took at least two days and sometimes meant two nights in the open, and in

---

* Fabri, VIII, 429, says that until recently the arrangement had been different, and the pilgrims spent the day in the church. But de Caumont earlier, and Casola and Guylforde later, all mention the visits as taking place at night.

this excursion the descent into the tropical climate of the Dead Sea basin subjected the pilgrims to a good deal of suffering from the heat.

The order in which expeditions were arranged was not constant, liable as they were to interruption or postponement from causes beyond the control of the pilgrims. This was especially so in the time of Casola's pilgrimage, when the Moslem officials were in a bullying and hostile mood; now a doorkeeper would be missing with his keys; now the demands of a rapacious governor must be beaten down by prolonged haggling; now more serious trouble threatened, so that no Christian dared show himself out-of-doors.[26] Even in the friendlier atmosphere at the time of Felix's pilgrimages an expedition to Bethlehem would have to be put off at the news of Arab bands prowling in the neighborhood; or on account of a great Moslem festival, the pilgrims must regard a certain Friday as a day upon which no sight-seeing might be done.[27]

The pilgrims of 1483 began their first day with Mass at the friars' church at Mount Sion. A Latin sermon followed, translated this time by Brother Paul Walther. After Mass the tour of the sights of the convent itself began, for besides showing in their church the exact spot where Christ washed the disciples' feet and ate the Last Supper, the friars led the pilgrims up and out to "a high place in the open air," from which the sound of their chanting "rang out all over the Mount Sion and the city of Jerusalem"; for this was the site of the upper room to which the Holy Spirit had come with the sound of wind and the brightness of fire.[28]

These, and other places less sacred and connected with less authentic events, were visited with appropriate hymn singing and devotions, collected in that "little book" called *Processional for Pilgrims in the Holy Land*, a copy of which Felix contrived to obtain, and presumably to retain, for himself, and which perhaps Brasca reproduced in his pilgrim narrative.[29]

By the time the tour had been completed it was close on midday, and the pilgrims, who, in Brother Paul's phrase, went about "devoutly and on an empty stomach," were probably glad to sit down to dine at the table laid for them in the friars' inner garden, shaded from the heat of the sun by a canopy embroidered with the symbols of Pentecost.[30]

After dinner, with a perseverance and enthusiasm which drew commendation from the Father Guardian, the pilgrims, or rather some of the pilgrims, asked for more sightseeing. Others, indeed more than half their number, defeated by the fatigues of the morning, preferred to return to the Hospital to rest. Those who persisted, and no one will be surprised to hear that Felix was among them, were then led out, not processionally now, nor with singing, but more in the manner of secular tourists, though they took their *Processional* with them, and read the appropriate extracts at various points.

They visited first, beyond the small compass of the convent, the ruins of the greater church outside. In this peregrination they dipped not only into memories of the New Testament but into those of the Old as well, so that a visit to the Oratory of the Virgin was followed by one to the place where David had set up the ark of the covenant; the pilgrims were also able to stare at the "small door . . . iron-bound and most carefully shut," which led into the mosque built over the burial place of David and Solomon. The mere sight of the door must content them, for a mosque, to the Christian pilgrim, was forbidden ground, unless either he were ready to risk martyrdom in the cause of "tourisme," or like von Harff, he could find and bribe a Mameluke willing to smuggle him in,[31] or, like Felix, his noticing eye and persistent curiosity were rewarded by a chance of entering alone and unobserved. For Felix, passing one day, realized that the Saracen custodian had jammed the lock "so that the key would not move the iron bolt; so he went away leaving the mosque open: and it remained open as long

as I was in Jerusalem . . ." to be visited stealthily and fear-
fully by the Friar "more than ten times," so that he could
describe its appearance and contents: the vaulted roof, the
marble tomb, the paved floor strewn with mats, the two
hanging lamps, but "no altar, no painting, no carved work,
only bare whitewashed walls," for so, Felix adds, "are all
Saracen mosques, empty and void." [32]

On this day, however, the pilgrims must console themselves for the lack of that forbidden interior by visits to a
variety of other places of interest, including the burial place
of St. Stephen, the House of Annas, the High Priest, inhabited now by "Armenian monks . . . black and respectable men," the House of Caiaphas, "the kitchen where the
Paschal lamb was roasted and the water heated for the
Lord's Supper"; a sight, Felix is careful to remark, "not
without holiness or edification, for the cooks in that kitchen
were holy men." [33] There were other points along the route
equally worthy of reverence in the Friar's opinion, such as
"the corner where the Blessed Virgin stood looking towards
the House of Caiaphas," and the crossroads where the
apostles separated "at the bidding of the Blessed Virgin"
to preach the Gospel throughout the world.

The pilgrims came at last to that new garden of the Franciscans, bounded upon one side by the wall of the church
and convent, but "on the other three sides it has valleys and
it is surrounded by a dry stone wall," set at the edge of "steep
stone cliffs." Upon the broad, sun-warmed top of this wall
they lay down, to rest and to look about them upon one
of those views which Felix loved to remember and record,
and in the descriptions of which we seem to see, as if with
a bird's eye, stage after stage of his pilgrimage. For from this
place the pilgrims could look south into the Valley of
Aceldama, on the east to the Valley of Siloam, and beyond
that across the Valley of Jehosaphat to the Mount of Olives.
But nearer still, and far more impressive to the eyes of Felix's
lay companions, stood the Dome of the Rock, than which,

they protested, there was "nothing more glorious or more beauteous within sight." Felix rebuked them, disabused their minds of the mistaken idea that what they saw was the Temple of Solomon, or indeed anything but an "abominable and desecrated church . . . [in which] Mahomet the accursed is praised," and directed their attention toward the many genuinely holy sights spread out before them.[34]

After lounging on the wall for a while the pilgrims separated to take what rest they might, since that evening they were to be admitted for the first time to the Church of the Holy Sepulcher. For the moment however we shall not follow them there, but will rejoin them for their second day of general sight-seeing, which was to lead them beyond the gates, into the Valley of Jehosaphat, up the Mount of Olives, and then, descending again and continuing southward by way of the Valley of Siloam, to "the hill Aceldama," and the Mount of Offense.

The expedition began early. The sun was not yet up when the tireless Felix, and one or both of the other Dominican visitors, left the Franciscan house, to awaken the sleeping lay pilgrims at the Hospital. When they were ready the whole party set off, led by some of the Franciscan brothers, and escorted by the lesser Calinus "with his stick, who . . . kept the boys from throwing stones at us." On their way along the Via Dolorosa to the Porta Judiciaria most of the sights to which their attention was called were connected with the events of Good Friday; they were shown such memorials of that day as those actual stones, "square stones as big as the bottom of a wine cask," [35] upon which Christ himself and Pilate had stood, or the arch stones, carved "with wheels, squares and triangles," of Pilate's house.

From time to time, as was natural in this Moslem city, they encountered difficulties. Herod's house, which at the time of Felix's first pilgrimage had been used as a school for Saracen boys, now contained the harem of the governor of Jerusalem; in both uses it was inaccessible. Pilate's house also was closed to pilgrims on account of the surly temperament of its owner; but here again Felix's pertinacity as a sight-seer was later to be rewarded. He and a few other pilgrims having learnt, he does not say how, that the owner was from home, ". . . we knocked, and were let in by his daughters . . . two good-looking, rather tall girls, and, when we came in, they laid aside their veils, and spoke to us with smiling countenances, a thing they would not have dared to do with Saracens." Obligingly they exhibited the vaulted chapel, traditionally the scene of the scourging of Christ. A small gift at parting produced a promise that the pilgrims would be welcome any time that the father was absent, an invitation of which Felix, at least, took advantage.[36]

Another halt was made by the pilgrims on their way through the city to view the exterior, "ancient yet beautiful," of "the house of the rich glutton, whose proper name was Dodrux, though," Felix explains, "the Lord was loath to pronounce it in the Gospels." Felix was confident that owing to the merits of the beggar Lazarus, the pilgrims received indulgences at this point; von Harff, equally positive, warns his readers that "there is no absolution here." [37]

Having looked in upon "the Pool of Bethsaida [sic]," and "the Inner Pool," the pilgrims left the city by the Gate of St. Stephen, pausing to kneel and show reverence, though at a distance, to the blocked and forbidden Golden Gate. From here, having noted the stone upon which were laid the garments of those who stoned St. Stephen, they came to the underground Church of the Sepulcher of the Blessed Virgin, "very deep and dark," [38] but possessing an echo more "sweet and musical" than any except that in the cave of the Invention of the Cross.[39]

Here, to their surprise, they found the hereditary Saracen janitor ready to admit them without a fee, an occurrence of such rarity as to call for a miraculous explanation, which was supplied by the story of a dream in which the Blessed Virgin had appeared to the janitor's father. At parting, the pilgrims, impressed by the legend, and gratified by the Saracen's politeness, administered a tip, "to encourage him to let Christian pilgrims enter." [40]

They were now in that Valley of Jehosaphat, in which, according to tradition, the Last Judgment would take place. For this event many considered it desirable to make sure of a seat, and pilgrims would do this, for themselves and their friends, piling stones "whereon they may sit on the day of judgment." Simple and stay-at-home folk were much interested in the valley and would earnestly inquire of returning pilgrims how big it was. Felix was a little puzzled how to answer this question. The valley was small. ". . . in its present form it would hardly be able to take in one nation, for all the Swabians who are now actually alive could barely find standing room in it." The best he could do was to supply alternative explanations. Either the valley would be enlarged for the occasion, or the good "will have altogether unmolested places to stand in . . . But the vicious and wicked will have very . . . wretched places . . ." [41]

Their tour of the Mount of Olives, with all its Holy Places, the Church of the Ascension, the Garden of Gethsemane, the "Mount of Galilee," the tomb of St. Pelagia, "the place where the Blessed Virgin used to take breath," and many others, filled up the rest of the morning. In the afternoon there was another expedition, but, as on the first day, this was optional. Only "those of the pilgrims who were strong, met together," and started off once more. By now we have learned to expect that Felix will be of the party, but it is interesting to hear that among the band of determined sight-seers were at least some of "our companions, the pilgrim ladies."

The first place which they visited was the fountain of the Virgin at the foot of Mount Sion. But here, as they were descending into the cave, "walking on sand without any

stairs," they were met by a Saracen, who, "running swiftly
up from the depths below," tried to turn the pilgrims back.
Had the man, Felix admits, carried a stick, they would have
retreated; as he was unarmed and alone they simply walked
on, preceded by the enraged Moslem. At the fountain's edge
he tried to prevent them from drinking, by pushing, striking,
and shoving them back. But now a Lombard knight, losing
patience, grappled with him; there was a fight, of such
ferocity that Felix thought if the two had not been separated
by the other pilgrims "they would have torn each other in
pieces." The next danger was that the Saracen should make
off, and bring his friends down upon the Christians, "but
we caught him and held him fast, though he shouted and
struggled exceedingly." At last the softening power of a
tip was suggested. It worked wonders. The Saracen
"changed into a different man, for his countenance became
calm, his voice sounded more gentle . . ." and he now
hastened to oblige the pilgrims by drawing water for them
from the well.[42]

From here the party went on up the course of the brook
of Siloam, making for its source, and visiting on the way the
old "Pool of Siloam," dry now, and serving as a Saracen's
kitchen garden. Above the tannery, which had till this point
fouled all the water beside them, they entered "the cleft in
the mount, which is deep and high but not wide, and from
whence water flows from the innermost parts of the earth."

The pilgrims found it a very awkward place to scramble
along without spoiling the "costly shoes," which, says Felix
smugly, all were wearing, for the only way to walk was "by
straddling our legs, and walking with one foot on one side
of the water, and the other on the other side." In the narrow
gill tempers began to fray as the pilgrims crowded forward.
"Those in front cried out against the impatience of those
behind, and those who were last cried out at the slowness of
those who were in front, and those in the middle because
they were squeezed by both the others." Only the pilgrim

ladies, wisely taking advantage of the conventional belief
that theirs is the weaker sex, allowed the men to fill "basins
and bottles" for them with the holy water, and themselves
"sat quietly and peaceably saying their prayers outside." [43]

After resting awhile in the shade of a tree upon the side
of Mount Sion, which marked the place of the prophet
Isaiah's execution, the party went on to visit the Mount
of Offense, climbing up from the valley through "orchards
of figs, pomegranates, and other fruit-trees," to the caves
which were shown as having been the refuge of the apostles
when they had fled from Gethsemane. The personal associations of this place made a strong appeal to the pilgrims, who
rambled about, each appropriating some cave to his favorite
saint, so that it was: " 'Lo, my brother, in this cavern
perchance sat the beloved Apostle Andrew,' " or " 'And
here sate the Apostle Bartholemew,' " or " 'Here is a seat
whereon it may be Thomas sat . . .' "

After this harmless and devout fooling the pilgrims continued to climb, "scorched by a most blazingly hot sun,"
which wrung complaints neither from ladies nor churchmen,
but from the "tenderly nurtured and luxurious knights."
Their efforts were, however, rewarded, not only by the
sight of the field of Aceldama, the potter's field, but by a
timely meeting with a young Saracen, who carried a basket
of grapes, "some of which we bought, and so sat and ate them
there in the field, and enjoyed ourselves well."

It was not in Felix to leave unexplored the possibilities
of any interesting locality. While, doubtless, the others sat
resting, he examined and measured the charnel house which
had existed there from the thirteenth century. He counted
the openings in the vault, which on one side was level with
the hill. There were nine, and peering through one of them
he was able to enjoy the piquant if gruesome spectacle of
"five fresh human corpses among dry bones."

Unexpectedly, this place exercised a peculiar attraction
upon the cheerful Friar. He made his Franciscan hosts prom-

ise that if he died in the Holy Land they would "cast my body through these holes." He made a practice, too, of coming down from Mount Sion to read his hours on the hillside. From Ludolph von Suchem's book he had learnt that the site had once been bought by his own Dominican order, for the purpose of building a convent here. The idea of this convent fascinated Felix. He played with it, as Dr. Johnson, stalking "like a giant among the luxuriant thistles and nettles" upon Inchkeith, played with the idea of a house there. " 'I'd have this island,' " said the Doctor. " 'I'd build a house, make a good landing-place, have a garden, and vines, and all sorts of trees.' " So, in the same vein, Felix. He weighed the advantages of the site against that of the house of Mount Sion. This, but for the danger of its remote position, was the better. Here "the brethren would plant gardens, vineyards, and fig-orchards, and the place is pleasant, looking as it does towards . . . the valley of Siloam, and it could get its water from the fountain of Siloam . . . There is also a view." [44]

We have now followed the pilgrims throughout their tours of Jerusalem and the near neighborhood. But between these two days of sight-seeing came the night of their first solemn vigil in the Church of the Holy Sepulcher. At sunset upon their second night in Jerusalem the pilgrims were told to hurry over supper, for already the Moslem officials waited to admit them to the church.

They assembled in that courtyard outside the south doors of the church to which they had been brought on their arrival in Jerusalem. By now they knew it well: the cloister of marble columns; the "lofty tower built of white marble-stone," once the bell tower, but voiceless now though the beams from which the bells had swung were still to be seen; the doors, divided into an upper and lower half, with the sultan's arms "carved in wax and wood upon the upper," and with a wicket by which the friars' food might be handed in; [45] the sculptured lintels which, though partly defaced, showed, and still show, the entry of Christ into Jerusalem, the driving out of the money-changers, and the raising of Lazarus.

The courtyard was crammed. Besides the pilgrims—and there were one hundred and fifty or so of them—besides the high Moslem officials sitting cross-legged like tailors, yet stately and aloof, upon their marble bench, besides a nondescript crowd of men, women, and children, there were the usual hucksters of food, selling "loaves of bread, eggs, and grapes . . . whereof we bought some," and the usual regiment of merchants who would enter the church with the pilgrims.[46]

When the time came for the Christians to be admitted they must pass two by two between the Moslem officers and endure the same piercing scrutiny to which they had been subjected at Jaffa, before they found themselves at last within the church.

Here for a few minutes they were half blinded by the gloom, for most of the stained windows had been blocked, and what light there was came chiefly from above, where the painted cedar roof beams converged above the Chapel of the Sepulcher in a great circle so as to form a round opening, in the manner, Casola notes, of Santa Maria Rotonda in Rome, or rather, he corrects himself, of San Lorenzo the Greater at Milan, because of the two-storied gallery which surrounded the dome in that church.[47]

It was during those few minutes, in which the pilgrims were allowed to scatter about the church as they chose, that Felix, three years before, had from ignorance made a most regrettable mistake. Once inside the church, he says, "I did not hurry, but went with a slow step towards the middle of the church, walking without any set purpose, and after I had gone about seventeen paces I stopped, and, lifting my face, looked at the vault above me. I cast my eyes upon the upper windows with curiosity, as ill-bred men stare about in strange places and houses."

He was recalled to himself by finding two of the women pilgrims—one of them a German of rank—lying at his feet, sobbing and kissing the stone on which he stood.

"I was surprised . . . and said in German to her, 'What is the matter, Lady Hildegarde, that you should do so?' " He was told that he stood upon the stone where Christ's dead body had been laid for anointing.

It was, in every sense of the word, a religious faux pas of the first magnitude. But as parsons have jokes among themselves which they would not share with a skeptic, so Felix, writing the promised account of his adventures for the brothers at Ulm, could tell the story demurely, yet with a smile only half concealed.

It was not long before the pilgrims were once more collected together to receive instructions as to their behavior while in the church. These instructions, Felix says, the Father Guardian "reduced" under thirteen heads; passing over the usual exhortations to devotion we may notice that while the pilgrims were told to buy candles for the procession, they should not "sit and waste time trafficking with the . . . merchants," who had followed them into the church; that they should prefer, in their almsgiving, Catholic to schismatic altars; that they should not leave about any of their personal property lest this should be stolen.[48]

The procession started, the pilgrims each carrying a candle, the Franciscans vested, all singing hymns apt to the Holy Places which they visited. *Salve Regina* brought them as far as the Chapel of the Virgin; to the sound of the ancient and magnificent music of *Vexilla Regis* they climbed the eighteen steps to the marble-encrusted Chapel of Calvary, with its three altars, its many lamps, its central column supporting the pictured vault, though the walls were so darkened by time that de Rochechouart, even with the help of a candle, could only make out upon them prophecies of Christ, of David, and of Daniel.[49] Here, as well as the tears, prostrations, and kisses, there was the business of thrusting heads into the fissure beside the socket hole of the Cross. This was a thing to boast about, in pious fashion, at home: it was one of the few personal experiences recorded in von Breydenbach's book.[50]

ffo̜ma et di̜po̜fitio dominci ̜fepuld̜ri

*The Chapel of the Holy Sepulcher*

So the pilgrims made their rounds, "with much pushing and disorder, and disturbance, and singing and weeping," till at last to the sound of Easter hymns, they reached, at about eleven o'clock, the Chapel of the Sepulcher itself, which stood, as Felix explained to his untraveled brethren at home, "just as the sepulchre is placed in the parish church at Ulm on Good Friday."

Von Breydenbach's artist drew a picture of the outside of the building; Brasca made a plan of it; many pilgrims gave descriptions, more or less coherent. Externally "a fine round tabernacle," or more precisely a duodecagon surmounted by a hexagonal "tabernacle or tower," the pilgrims approached it from the east by a small open outer court which was enclosed within a wall "so low that a man standing within it can lean his stomach upon it and look round the church. I have," said Felix, "often sat upon that wall, and have looked down upon the goods of the merchants lying upon the pavement below." This outer court led into the first chamber of the building, the so-called "Angel Chapel," from the stone shown there, upon which the angel had sat. From this, half crawling through "a hole, as there is no door," the pilgrims entered the tomb chamber, so small that there was room only for three or four of them at once. "This cave has no window, nor is there any light in it save what comes from nineteen lamps which burn in it . . . and inasmuch as the cave is small, the fire of the lamps makes a smoke and a stench, which greatly troubles those who enter the place . . . Besides the lamps there are many lighted candles . . . Thus, by the smoke of the lamps and the candles together the whole inside surface has been completely blackened . . . throughout, both the pavement, the walls, and the vault." [51] Along the northern wall of this chamber was the altar which occupied the place of the sepulcher itself.

But Felix was not content with describing, nor with collating the diverse and contradictory descriptions of other pilgrims, nor with referring the reader to Rewich's woodcut. He set out to investigate for himself whether beneath the marble casing the original tomb existed entire, or in part, or not at all. During one of his vigils in the church he took a candle and "examined most carefully to see whether I could find any part that was not covered with marble." The outside was "cased in marble all the way round." So were the side walls of the Angel Chapel, ". . . but I found that the wall before my face . . . in which is the door leading into the Lord's sepulchre, was bare; and on holding my light near it I saw a wall cut out of the rock, not made of ashlar work, but all of one piece . . ." though, "in the upper part there seemed to have been a fracture, which had been mended with stones and cement." From this he deduced that the tomb had once been partly destroyed, but afterward restored.[52]

For about an hour after their visit to the sepulcher, the end and climax of the solemn procession, the pilgrims were left to themselves, to eat, to rest, or to wander about the Holy Places, till at midnight Masses began, culminating in the High Mass upon Mount Calvary.

At eight o'clock in the morning the doors of the church were flung open by the Saracens, and the Christians ordered to leave. Instead, scattering like so many hens, the pilgrims "ran round from one Holy Place to another, kissing them," before parting, to the fury of the Moslems, who "banged the doors of the church so violently that the hinges creaked, and ran with frightful yells among the Holy Places, from which they drove the pilgrims by force." [53] So ended the first night in the Church of the Holy Sepulcher.

The second visit took place two days later, and followed a night of vigil at Bethlehem, and a long morning's sightseeing; only between dinner and vespers had the pilgrims snatched what rest they might.

During this second visit the noble laymen among the company were to be dubbed Knights of the Holy Sepulcher, and admitted to that order, the surpassing excellencies of which Felix celebrates even to "Fortiethly and lastly . . ." The ceremony took place during the hour before midnight, while the rest of the pilgrims roamed at will about the church, and Felix went up to the holy hill of Calvary, and "lighted a candle, and sat down with ink in front of me . . . and . . . wrote down the names of all . . . for whom I was in duty bound to pray," and after laid the paper on the various Holy Places.

Of the ceremony itself, which took place in the innermost chamber of the tomb, we have three separate and conflicting accounts, which, if accurate—and de Caumont and von Harff are describing each his own experience—show, that for all the antiquity which is claimed for the order by Felix, there was yet no set ritual of conferment.

De Caumont, who arrived alone, and not by the ordinary pilgrim galley, had brought with him a Knight Hospitaler from Rhodes to perform the ceremony. After Mass at midnight the Hospitaler gave de Caumont the accolade, five times in memory of the Five Wounds of Christ, and once in honor of St. George, and then, assisted by the celebrant friar, still vested, delivered into the new knight's hand the naked sword, bidding him receive it "in honor and reverence of God and of my lord St. George." De Caumont, having sheathed the sword, took an oath of six clauses: to guard Holy Church, to help in the recovery of the Holy Land, to defend his folk and keep justice, to keep his marriage holy, to do no treason, and to protect widows and orphans.[54]

In 1480, and again in 1483, it was Brother John of Prussia, himself a knight and of noble birth, who conferred knighthood on the pilgrims. In the first of these years he dubbed all the knights, since all were of equal rank; in the second he dubbed the count of Solms, as highest in the feudal hierarchy, who in his turn knighted his next in rank and so on to the last. Felix, who as we have seen, was, at least on the second occasion, otherwise engaged, described the ceremony as though he had watched it. The count stood before the tomb while Brother John girded him with the sword and buckled on the spurs. He was then bidden to kneel, and to bow himself so that his breast and arms rested upon the top of the tomb. Thus kneeling he received, in the name of the Trinity, a threefold accolade. This done Brother John "raised up the count, loosed the sword and spurs from him, kissed him, and respectfully said: 'May it be for thy good.' "[55]

Fifteen years later von Harff received knighthood from the same Brother John. He was led into the innermost chamber of the sepulcher, where lay a golden sword and a pair of golden spurs. He was bidden, he says, to put first one foot, then another, upon the tomb, while the spurs were buckled on. When he had been girded with the sword he knelt down, partly drew it from the sheath, and, laying two fingers of his right hand on the blade, swore to be "God's knight," to protect widows, orphans, churches, and the poor, to keep justice, to right wrongs, " 'so help me God and the holy sepulchre.' " After this Brother John, drawing his sword, struck von Harff's shoulder, saying " 'Arise, knight, in honor of the holy sepulchre and the Knight St. George." [56]

In 1483 the pilgrims' third vigil in the Church of the Holy Sepulcher was timed for that night which would be, for all except those making the Sinai pilgrimage, their last night in Jerusalem. Many devout souls would doubtless be moved on this occasion to visit the Holy Places "with the more zeal and devotion because we reckoned it for the last time that we should see them in all our lives." [57] Unfortunately it was not so with all. This visit lacked the poignancy of excitement of the first sight of the Holy Places: for the crowd of young laymen it lacked the concentration and purpose of the vigil which had preceded their knighthood. Even on the pilgrims' first entrance into the church petty jealousies had mingled with ecstatic devotion. In the purchase of candles for the procession "there was no lack of vainglory . . . for some had candles twisted and decorated with gilding and painting, which they carried with ostentation, and looked with scorn on those who carried plain candles, blaming them for closefistedness." Even the priests, spurred by professional enthusiasm, disgraced themselves on that night by fighting among themselves for their turn to celebrate Mass on the altar of the Holy Sepulcher, struggling for the vestments of the last celebrant, and so shamefully abusing each other that the scandalized lay pilgrims were forced to intervene.[58]

On the night of the last visit behavior degenerated still

further. There were indeed many distractions in the church, which made devotion difficult. For one thing the place so swarmed with fleas, "jumping all about the pavement," that Felix was driven to suppose that they might be "bred naturally from the marble." [59] For another, as well as the noise of "unbroken throng of pilgrims" who moved about the Holy Places, the church resounded with the clanging of the hammers of the Jacobite priests * as they beat upon their "pieces of thin, polished iron," [60] and with "the yells and strange outcries of the Eastern Christians," whose ritual of worship, including leaping, singing, and clapping of hands, was practiced fasting, and with such fervor that it was a marvel "how they could perform such profound reverences, such high jumps, such cries, such efforts." [61]

In addition to these disturbing factors there were the merchants, who having paid a handsome fee for the privilege of entrance, quickly spread their cloths upon the pavement, and displayed their wares: "not only Pater noster beads and precious stones, but also cloth of damask, of camlet, and of silk," so that some of the pilgrims forgot not only the holiness of the place, but even their own worldly dignity, to an extent which shocked Felix. "I saw there," he says, "some nobly born and illustrious pilgrims, who on their own estates would have thought bargaining with tradesmen . . . to be a thing unbecoming to them . . . yet here . . . they never ceased making bargains, and buying precious stuffs and jewels." [62]

And during the long night there was time for many other lapses from the behavior proper to the devout worshiper. Some of the pilgrims, tired out by their arduous days, slept "as though they had been lying in their bed chambers." Some, after making a perfunctory tour of the Holy Places, "sat down, ate and drank what was in their scrips, which they had brought in stuffed with food," while others, having brought in good, strong wine, "sat down together swilling

* These are priests of the Syrian Monophysite Church.

. . . till the bottles were empty." Others, who neither slept nor swilled, still showed less than a proper reverence for their surroundings, and strolled about, talking, not of spiritual but of worldly things, "about princes and quarrels, about the campaigns which they had served, and the comparison of warriors one with another."

Besides these exhibitions of foibles common to humanity, some pilgrims indulged that weakness to which the tourist in particular, and those who visit historical monuments, have been prone since the time when Caesar's legionary scratched his name upon the stone of the Egyptian quarries. They had been warned at Ramle, and in the Church of the Holy Sepulcher they had been warned again, that they must not carve or paint their coats of arms upon the Holy Places. But the warnings were disregarded. Felix knew one pilgrim "who always had a red stone in his purse, with which he used to write his name in every place, on every wall." So consuming was this passion, that he would scrawl his name upon altar stones, upon the margins of "antiphonals, graduals, missals, and psalters, as though he were the author of the book." Others when apparently bowed in devotion at the socket hole of the cross in the Calvary Chapel, "within the circle of their arms would secretly scratch with exceeding sharp tools their shields, with the marks—I cannot say," observes Felix with justifiable severity, "of their noble birth—but rather of their silliness . . ." And the practice, "wrong, foolish, and criminal," was catching. Following the example of their betters, "some simple labouring men take charcoal and write their own unknown names and the names of their rustic calling on the walls." [63] It would have amazed the Friar to know how, by the mere passage of time, the few remaining results of this deplorable habit have become precious to archaeologist and historian.

## CHAPTER VI

# ROUND ABOUT JERUSALEM

THE first expedition which Felix and his companions made beyond the immediate surroundings of Jerusalem was to Bethlehem, in order that the pilgrims might keep their vigil in the Church of the Nativity there. In the pilgrimage of 1480 there had been time for no more than this; the pilgrims arrived at vespers, and were hustled away at daybreak in order to make the tour of the hill country of Judea.[1] This year however there was to be leisure for them to explore Bethlehem and the country nearby.

The pilgrims left Jerusalem in a cheerful mood, to take that road which even Casola, cool in judgment and chary of praise, found "very gay and beautiful . . . the most beautiful we saw in those parts . . ."[2] Felix was more enthusiastic. He "never saw pilgrims so merry as on that road," and even thought that he could detect, in the demeanor of the Moslem escort as they listened to the pilgrims singing their Christmas hymns, a cheerfulness beyond the normal.[3]

But they were not to reach Bethlehem without trouble. As they drew near a crowd of Arabs met them. The pilgrims, bunching together, sent their escort ahead, but the Arabs would not make way, and after an hour's wrangling the pilgrims must resign themselves to paying 24 ducats, or return to Jerusalem. They paid, and passed on, but that was not the end of it. Yet another mob of Arabs came out from Bethlehem, servants, says Felix, of the first; these were not bandits but mere hooligans who "charged into the column of the pilgrims, and with much jeering and shouting passed through the midst of us, dragging and pushing us about, and discomposing us much with their rough jokes."

Felix, at the height of all the confusion, had what he mildly refers to as an "adventure." As he rode upon his donkey among the rest of the pilgrims, he found himself facing an Arab, who, mounted on a horse, bore down on him, his lance couched, and "pointed . . . straight in my face; but because of the press I was not able to make way for him, nor yet to fall off my ass, which" says Felix, with his usual candor, "I would willingly have done . . ." The Arab however only "tore my cap off my head with a strong blow of the sharp steel, and passed by me with a laugh." The Friar's comment on the episode is surprisingly temperate. "I was well contented that the Arab knew so well the art of touching things just as he pleased with the point of his spear, for had he held it pointed the thickness of one finger lower, he would have run it through my skull." [4]

The sun was setting and inside the church at Bethlehem it was nearly dark when the pilgrims entered. They were accompanied by the same flock of merchants which had attended them into the Church of the Holy Sepulcher, so that they had hardly risen from their knees when they found themselves offered an assortment of candles for the procession which, led by the friars, would soon begin a perambulation of the Holy Places.

Pilgrims who visited Bethlehem twenty years or so before Felix had found the church in a state of mournful disrepair, with the cedar beams of the ceiling gradually collapsing, especially over the choir. In those days the soldan, obdurate as any governmental department in a modern bureaucracy, was steadily refusing to issue the necessary license for its repair, but by the time Felix made his first pilgrimage Qâ'it Bey ruled at Cairo, and showed his friendliness for the Franciscans by giving them permission to begin the work. It was high time, for the ceiling, borne down by the weight of the wooden roof above, would already have fallen if it had not been for the great beams which shored it up.

But already in 1480 the wood for the new roof lay

stacked in one of the courtyards of the convent at Bethlehem, pine wood from the German mountains, says Felix,
prepared in Venice to Brother Baptista's measurements,
shipped to Jaffa in Venetian galleys, and from there brought
on camel back to Bethlehem,[5] so that when Felix returned
three years later the work was already completed.* Not only
was there a new ceiling, but the pavement of the church was
no longer fouled by the droppings of the pigeons and sparrows which had once nested in the roof, and the birds did
not now dare to return on account of a colony of pine
martens which had taken up their quarters among the timbers; Felix had cause to remember those animals, for in
one of his solitary vigils in the church the unaccountable
sound of their scamperings overhead gave him a sad fright.[6]

Even in the days of its disrepair the bishop of Saintes had
declared of the church at Bethlehem that "for a little church
I never saw fairer." [7] More than thirty years later Casola
judged it to be "the most beautiful between Venice and
Bethlehem," with "most beautiful mosaics that look quite
new"; he was, he says, "never tired of looking at the many
beautiful pillars." [8] To a later and far more simple-minded

* The writer of the *Voyage de la Saincte Cyté*, p. 81, says that Philip,
Duke of Burgundy, gave the wood. M. Ch. Schefer in a note repeats this,
and adds that permission for the repairs was obtained in 1481, "on condition
that the new ceiling was recovered with the old strips of lead."

Surian, quoted by M. M. Newett, *Casola*, pp. 389–390, n. 83, does not
mention any duke of Burgundy but says that Giovanni Tomacelli (who
according to the editor of Paul Walther, p. 128 n., was prior at Mount
Sion from 1478 to 1481) got the sultan's permission, and "sent for two
shiploads of prepared wood from Venice, and new lead that the King
of England had sent."

Philip the Good died in 1467, his son Charles the Bold, last Duke of
Burgundy, in 1477. If either, then, gave the wood or money to provide
it, the gift must have been made some time before the sultan's permission
was obtained.

In 1468 Charles the Bold had married Margaret, sister of Edward IV
of England, and friendly relations existed between England and Burgundy
till 1475. It is tempting to suggest that if Charles the Bold were the donor
of the wood, it may have been his influence which induced his brother-in-
law to provide the lead.

pilgrim those forty-four monolithic limestone pillars seemed to be "of the finest marble . . . [and] not only marvelous for the number, but for the outrageous greatness, length, and fairness thereof." [9]

As usual in his narrative Felix offers us all the ordinary information supplied by pilgrims about the beauty and holiness of the church at Bethlehem, and in addition a great many curious and amusing observations of his own. He describes the general plan of the church; the narthex leading into a basilican type of building but with an apse at the east; the flights of steps from nave to choir and from choir to sanctuary; the "costly columns . . . polished with oil so that a man can see his face in them as in a mirror"; the mirrorlike marble facing of the lower walls, the mosaics above. Below the choir, reached by a flight of sixteen steps, was the Chapel of the Nativity itself. There, under "vaults adorned with gold and blue,"—two of the most costly colors used by the medieval craftsmen—upon a pavement of marble, the color of which reminded Felix of vellum, stood the manger, of white marble, "curiously polished."

The Friar, recalling the words of St. Chrysostom, felt a qualm as to the propriety of the splendor which had here replaced the original and most holy simplicity. But he was obviously pleased at one of those trivialities, so dear to guides and tourists of all ages. In the Cathedral of Oxford today they will point out to you the profile of a man, delineated upon the plaster of the wall by a creeping stain of damp, and tell you that it strangely resembles that of the unloved Dr. Fell. Upon the front of the manger at Bethlehem one of the friars showed Felix "the figure of an old bearded man, lying on his back on a mat, in the dress of a dead monk, and beside him the figure of a lion." A divinely ordained memorial, so the Franciscan said, of St. Jerome, and "not produced by art or work, but by simple polishing . . ." Felix, who had at first thought the friar to be joking, could, when the outline had been traced out for him by the other's finger, see it "distinctly . . . just as though it had been delicately painted." [10]

As if the central sanctuary of the Chapel of the Nativity were a magnet, around it, as around the Holy Sepulcher and Golgotha, clustered a whole galaxy of places of lesser sanctity and, to us, of very dubious authenticity. With a fair show of reason the friars displayed the study of St. Jerome in an underground chapel opening off the cloister, and his empty sepulcher nearby. But the pilgrims were also led to a chapel beside the choir, and told that this was the place of the circumcision of the Holy Child, which ceremony, Felix explains somewhat anxiously, could not have taken place "in the cave where He was born . . . because of the darkness, and it may be that the circumcisers disliked the smell of the stable." No further away than the other side of the choir, the Magi had dismounted from their camels and dromedaries, and had drawn water from the well close by. Into a second well had fallen that star which had led them hither. In a cave not far off the whitish liquid oozing from the rocks had been caused by a drop of milk which fell from the Virgin's breast. Into another cave had been cast "many thousand bodies of the Holy Innocents," and here the German nobles poked about in the dust by candlelight in the hope of finding at least a portion of one of these—a hope which Felix could not share, as he considered how many churches in the west possessed the whole or part of a Holy Innocent. [11]

It was late at night, with good appetite and a great thirst, that the pilgrims came out again into the cloister, and sat down here to eat the food which they had brought with them, washing it down with draughts of Bethlehem water, which, besides costing nothing, was, Felix declared, "cooler, clearer, wholesomer, and sweeter than any . . . in parts beyond the sea." The pilgrims had already drunk of it on their way into the village, for outside the gate they had been shown the famous well of David, "a large, deep and wide grotto" with a triple opening, and had stopped to draw up and to drink of the water there, contemptuous of the squeamishness of Bethlehem residents, who "now look with disgust upon this water, because a few days before our visit a Saracen woman, trying to draw water . . . fell through the mouth of the well, and was drawn out dead." [12]

After their nocturnal meal they were free for a while to rest, or, if they would, to keep vigil in the church. But at midnight all were roused by that beating on a board which must, in Moslem countries, take the place of a bell, and the Mass which then began lasted "till it was bright day."

When that was done the pilgrims, weary doubtless, but undaunted, took their donkeys and rode out and down through the olive yards to visit that place in the valley where, it was said, the shepherds had heard the angels' "Gloria in Excelsis." Though the church which marked the place was roofless, and its altar desecrated, the pilgrims could see round about, less subject to desuetude and decay than any work of stone, the common, homely spectacle of flocks of sheep and goats in the place which had, according to the Venerable Bede, "from of old been called 'the land of the flocks.'" [13] But the whole countryside was, in fact, over-laid with memory upon memory. Near a pleasant farm the ruins of great walls were said to be the remains of the con-vent of St. Paula, the friend and disciple of St. Jerome, and Ruth had gleaned in the field of Boaz below the walls of that village which had been the city of David before it became the birthplace of Christ.

During this expedition the pilgrims were, for once, un-accompanied by their Saracen escort, which had remained in Bethlehem, and they made the most of their freedom from supervision. Felix had read somewhere "in a very ancient book of pilgrimage written by some saint," of a cave which was reputed miraculously to conserve the water which St. Joseph had emptied out after the washing of the Holy Child. The pilgrims, fortified by the consciousness that they were not only enjoying themselves, but were assisting in a pious and laudable investigation, joined with him in a painstaking search for this cave, but without success.[14]

When at last they returned to the church they found the Moslem dragomans waiting, "quietly," says Felix, but with tempers rising at the delay. So it was in haste that the pilgrims must "run to the grotto," there to pay a last reverence to the place and to make their oblations. Then they set off on the return journey to Jerusalem, having little time left for dinner and a brief rest before the time came for them to enter the Church of the Holy Sepulcher for their second night of vigil.

Two days later, early in the morning, they "rode out of Jerusalem to the southward in a great hurry," to visit places of note among the hills of Judea. The early start and the hurry were not surprising, for into a long half day was to be packed a great deal of sight-seeing, and many miles of riding over steep and stony roads.

First in order among the sights came the house of Simeon, "great and tall, but in ruins," standing on a hill in a rugged but fertile country "full of fruit-trees, figs, and olives." It would not have been Felix if he had not discovered and remarked that from an upper room "there is a view of Jerusalem and of Bethlehem." They came next to what was known as the fountain of the Blessed Virgin, where the pilgrims drank, but did not break their fast. The fountain lay between two small hills, upon which had stood, so Felix reports, the upper and lower houses of that "rich priest," Zacharias, who, "had a farm in that place, with gardens of olive-trees, fig-trees, and vineyards . . . and servants to wait on him and to feed his cattle; so he used to live now in one of these houses, and now in the other, according to the time of the year, and the fountain stood in the midst, and was used by both of the houses." After such a wealth of precise domestic detail it is not surprising to find Felix

equally positive that it was at the lower house that the
Blessed Virgin came to visit Elizabeth; but that the birth of
St. John, the Forerunner, took place in the upper house.[15]

The honors being equally divided between the two habi-
tations the pilgrims could not leave either unvisited. Yet at
first it seemed that they could not enter the lower house. The
door was assaulted with "stones, clubs and staves, but no one
answered us." Only when the young Saracens of the escort
began to roam round looking for a way to break in, did the
owner, "a Saracen . . . a beast rather than a man," open
the door, and even then stood in the way, himself armed
with a club, his wife with a firebrand, though, after money
had changed hands he did consent to let in the horde of
pilgrims.

Once inside these took care to see everything in the half-
ruined buildings which had been hallowed for them by such
great events. They were shown the very rooms in which the
Blessed Virgin and St. Elizabeth met, where Zacharias sat
dumb, where the infant John was hidden from Herod's
soldiers. When their devotions were over they "viewed the
place" more at large. It had been, in the time of the crusading
kingdom, a convent of Religious, and in a barn there were
"broken altars and ruined vaults," upon which now shrubs
and grasses grew. Felix noticed also "some pods of a blue
colour, like beans," which were to be found there but nowhere else.[16]

The upper house proved to be deserted, except for camels,
oxen, and donkeys stabled in a building whose flaking wall
paintings, and vaulted though tumble-down roof showed
that it also had been a Christian church. The pilgrims had to
climb on each other's shoulders in order to make their way
into that "grotto beneath a rock, wherein it is believed that
the most holy Baptist was born," but were rewarded there
by "the sweet and wholesome odour" engendered by the
sanctity of the place. And here Felix was able, as so often,
to amplify his own observation and adorn his narrative by

reference to one of those many authorities which he had studied in the library at Ulm. Albertus Magnus, he reports, following the Gospel of the Nazarenes, had said that the soldiers, in their search for the children condemned to death by Herod, killed Zacharias, though his wife and child escaped. As a consequence, so it was said, the blood of Zacharias, collected and preserved by priests in the temple, would, perhaps not unnaturally, "boil whenever anyone of the family of Herod appeared in the temple." [17]

By now the sun was high and the heat great. The pilgrims, turning back toward Jerusalem, climbed up into a delightful and fertile valley to reach a small convent of Georgian monks, in whose church the high altar was said to stand upon the very spot where grew the tree of the holy cross. After kissing the earth here, and the arm of St. Barbara which these monks possessed, the pilgrims sat down to rest and to eat in the cloister. Some of them, not content with what they carried in their scrips, asked the Georgians for cooked food, but in vain, nor could they discover, in the poor hovels where the monks lived, so much as a kitchen or a cooking pot. However a passing Moslem sold them grapes, and these, with water from the cistern, must do; the place itself was pleasant enough, for there were many olive trees round about, and a little wood of figs and olives. Looking around at the trees well-read pilgrims such as Felix could recall that King Solomon had had a garden in this place, and would sometimes drive out from Jerusalem, "in his golden chariot," to take his pleasure here.[18]

Far more arduous than either of these outings was the two-day expedition to the river Jordan. This, though stipulated for in the pilgrims' agreement, frequently proved a bone of contention between them and the "magnificent captains," intent as these were upon cutting down expenses wherever they could. Three years before, the pilgrims and Agostino Contarini had "passed one entire day in wrangling

. . . and the pilgrims and the captain became so bitterly enraged one with another, that they ground their teeth, insulted one another with evil words and bandied to and fro reproaches and foul and outrageous imputations, to the great scandal of the Saracens." The dispute almost reached the pitch of an international situation, when some hot-tempered Frenchmen threatened war between their king and the Venetian State.

Contarini had based his refusal upon a report that a band of armed Arabs waited near the river in order to attack pilgrims; in this he was backed up by the Calini, who said that if the pilgrims went they must have an armed escort. Contarini had no objection, so long as the pilgrims paid for what was, he said, no part of the ordinary expenses of the pilgrimage. Neither side would yield. The captain refused to go or to pay. The pilgrims, equally resolute, and putting their trust in God and the Calini, demanded that the latter should conduct them as they were bound to do, though without an armed escort. The Moslems proved more sympathetic toward the Christians' aspiration than the Venetian captain, and the pilgrims finally set off with the dragomans, accompanied also by the prior of Mount Sion and some of the Franciscan brethren.[19]

After such an experience Felix was not surprised to hear, on the very day of their trip to the house of Zacharias, that the captains were again preparing to bilk their clients. This time, however, the pilgrims brought up the matter themselves, demanding to be taken to the Jordan. The captains at once produced a variety of excuses: they feared the Arabs; they feared for the health of the Christians at this hottest season of the year. They objected, as an argument against the pilgrims' desire to see the river, that in the direction of Jordan lay "no church, no place of prayer, no indulgences."

Although Felix dismissed as groundless all the captains' objections we may suspect that there was something in each of them. In the summer of 1480, only a fortnight after the

pilgrims' expedition to Jordan, the governor of Jerusalem
had, at Jericho, pounced upon one of the Arab chiefs and
had killed many of his people.[20] In 1483, at Easter time,
Brother Paul, going down to the Jordan with the friars upon
one of those traditional ecumenical outings, in which Christians of all sects participated, had suffered great inconveniences at the hands of the Arabs. The huge Christian company
of three hundred or so had camped in the Jordan valley, the
friars in their tent "in the midst of all the nations." But at
dawn came a rumor that the Arabs were upon them; the
pilgrims seized their donkeys and fled. At the fountain of
Elisha, below the Mount of Fasting, where they intended
to breakfast, they were waylaid by Arabs who demanded
money. The Armenians, in the majority among the Christians, and more stout-hearted than the rest, refused. But the
Arabs would not allow them to climb the Mount, and after
long dispute the pilgrims "still fasting" fled once more. Again
they were held up; this time they had to pay what was demanded, and got nothing for it, except freedom to return
to Jerusalem.[21]

To the heat of the Jordan valley in that season of the year,
and the cruel hardships of the hurried journey, the pilgrims
themselves bear witness. Brasca, looking round at his fellows, could be ruefully amused at the sight as he and they
went "with mouths open and panting like tired hounds," in
the scorching heat which was so great that they could hardly
bear to dismount and put foot to the ground.[22] Brother Paul
endured, heroically of course, great suffering on the return
journey of his first visit to Jordan. Roused all too soon
from rest in the pleasant shade by the fountain of Elisha,
"we took the road to Jerusalem in the hottest part of the
whole day. And such great heat of the sun fell upon the
heads of the pilgrims"—(a literal translation of Paul's very
literal Latin "*Et cecididit tantus fervor solis super capita
peregrinorum*")—"that many began to fail, and we left them
behind here and there along the road, in the charge of the

Moors; my companion Brother John Wild even stayed behind ill till it was evening. I however, though I thought I should breathe my last for weakness, yet by the help of divine grace, kept on and on, though with difficulty."[23] Casola, who never pretended to heroism, had had enough even before the pilgrims left Jerusalem. For two hours, sitting on their donkeys "in the blazing sun," they must wait for their escort, which when it finally was mobilized, consisted of a Mameluke, "with certain bare-footed soldiers; it is true," adds the Milanese with bitter sarcasm, "that they had a bow apiece."[24]

And Casola too would have endorsed the third argument by which the captains tried to discourage Felix and his companions. He undertook the expedition against his will, because the delicate and ailing Fra Trivulzio's determination to go at all costs shamed him into it, but he was convinced that many were prompted to make the trip "rather by curiosity to see the country than by any sentiment of devotion."[25]

Yet, whether sustained by faith or urged by curiosity, Felix and his company persisted. After long argument the captains yielded and promised that they would go next day. The pilgrims then prepared themselves, filling their scrips with food, and taking the wise precaution of depositing their money with Brother John of Prussia.[26]

Next day they heard Mass at the friars' church and were entertained at dinner there. Then they gathered in the courtyard, to wait, much as Casola was to wait, through the heat of the afternoon, till, about the time of vespers, donkey boys, donkeys, and guides appeared. Tempers by this time had grown short, and the decorum of the start was upset by a quarrel between one of the knights and a priest who both claimed the same donkey. Fortunately for the pilgrims the first place of interest which was pointed out to them, as they went between the Mount of Olives and the Mount of Offense, was a ruined house, which, they were told, had belonged to the archtraitor, Judas. They need not, for this, as for some place of holy associations, stifle or transmute their feelings of ire and exasperation. Instead the sight offered them a safety valve; fiercely and with gusto they might "view and scorn this house," as they passed on.

Night came soon after they had gone through Bethany, and till the moon rose their guides would have allowed them to rest, though in the open field, had not a brawl arisen which, begun by some ill-conditioned youths soon embroiled the pilgrims with their own Saracen escort, and looked like becoming so serious that the two Calini ordered all to mount and ride on.

The moon rose and made their journey easier. Felix at any rate was by now sufficiently serene in mind to notice and appreciate the cunning of the donkeys, which, though they went "at a great pace . . . down the dangerous road, down glades and steep rocks," knew how to "travel easily and without falling, and how to let themselves down rocks with their fore-feet with wondrous cleverness, in a way which is impossible for a horse." [27]

Another matter which interested the Friar during this moonlight ride was the presence, which he does not account for, of a young Saracen woman among the troop of pilgrims. She came with them as far as Jericho, riding so boldly as to astonish him, "seeing that a woman is timid by nature." He summed her up as "young and well-dressed after their fashion; but no one could see her face, because of a black transparent cloth, though she could see us."

Going through Jericho "at a run" they rode on for another three hours, until, a little before dawn, they at last reached the banks of the river. Till day came all rested, the Saracens "among the bushes," the pilgrims, after they had cooled their hands in the water, upon the sand beside the river.

Our pilgrims are not usually, with the exception of Felix, given to describing natural features, but some remarks they do let fall upon the subject of the famous river which they had suffered so many discomforts to reach. It was, according to von Harff, "a noble but muddy stream." [28] Brasca describes the water as "very thick, and when I went into it I was above my knees in the mud of the bottom." [29] Casola reckoned that the river was not wider than the canal which passed through Milan; it was deep, "and the mud is high and sticky, almost like bath mud * and the water is muddy like that of the Po. . . . Many drank it from devotion, and I let them drink." Felix, less fastidious, as well as **more devout** and more curious than the Milanese, did not **refrain from** sampling the water, but even he was unable to commend it. "It was not," he says, "very pleasant to drink, being warm, and as muddy as a swamp." As for the general appearance of the river the Friar as usual gives more detailed information than any one else. It was no more than sixty paces in width, yet very deep; where the pilgrims bathed it had a sandy botton and high clay banks set back from the sandy shore; though its current was strong it flowed silently. In his anecdotes of the pilgrims' many agitating experiences at the Jordan he mentions incidentally bushes along the upper banks and reeds close beside the river.[30]

As soon as the sun rose those among the company who were priests moved down in procession to the edge of the water, rousing all, both Christian and Moslem, by their lusty chanting. The pilgrims followed them, and joined in the hymns and prayers, which were however, for most of them, only the preface to what was both the pious duty and the pleasure of the day, namely their bath in the sacred river.

But as soon as the Saracens on the higher banks, watching like so many nursemaids the antics of their charges, saw the pilgrims stripping to enter the water, they intervened with anxious directions and prohibitions; no one, they said, must try to swim across; no one must dive under the water.

At this point pilgrims often seem to have been taken possession of by a frivolous holiday spirit. Even Brother Paul does not except himself from the hilarious behavior

---

* *Casola*, p. 268. The editor suggests that Casola was probably thinking of such mud baths as that at Abano.

of his companions as they went into the river, "bobbing up and down, washing and cooling themselves." And such an exalted and venerable ecclesiastic as Casola, would, if he were a swimmer, take off his clothes and prepare to enjoy a dip.[31]

It is not surprising that on his first pilgrimage the cheerful Felix, infected with the irresponsible gaiety which had seized upon the rest, and disregarding the warnings of the Saracens, stripped and swam across the river with a number of the knights. But as they "were sporting merrily in the water on the further side . . . lo! of a sudden there were loud shouts . . . and they who were on the other bank uttered piteous cries. Moreover, the Saracens . . . ran along the top of the bank and shouted to us with horrible angry cries, cursing and threatening us. At this we stood astounded, and by reason of the number of people shouting we could not make out what had happened, until a pilgrim swam over to us . . . and when he was near us shouted: 'Ho! one of our brethren the pilgrims has sunk in the midst of the waters, and cannot be seen.' Straightway, when we heard this, we swam to the place where he had sunk, and, swimming round about it, waited for him to appear," when he did so laying hold of him by the hair and dragging him to the bank, alive, but trembling and unable to stand.

"Now, the Saracens were standing on the other bank, and crying out to us to make an end of this, and swim back again; so we encouraged that pilgrim, and went into the water with him, but after he had swum a little way he again began to sink, and we held him by the hair, and had some trouble to drag him out, the Saracens, meanwhile, standing over against us very impatiently and shouting to us."

The next attempt to get the unfortunate man over was no more successful; ". . . two strong pilgrims, who well knew how to swim, took him between them . . . hanging on their necks," but now all three sank, and the two rescuers had difficulty in freeing themselves from the frantic grappling of the drowning man. It was long before he rose again to the surface, and they could once more lug him back to shore, "almost dead."

By this time the Saracens had decided to send a rider across the river by a ford higher up, who should bring back the unfortunate man; they therefore ordered the other pilgrims to swim across without further delay. Those who were with Felix obeyed, but the Friar remained, suddenly overwhelmed by fear and compunction. He was there, contrary to orders, for no better purpose than to indulge in mere frivolity, he, a son of St. Dominic, without his habit, in "irreligious nakedness"; should he drown as he swam over, would not the pit of hell receive him? "It seemed to me unbearable that I should sink in the water without my dress [habit], but with my dress I should not have minded it so much." At last, fortified by the sign of the cross and a prayer, "I . . . leaped exceeding lustily into the water, forced myself along with my feet and hands over the middle of the river, and reached the other bank without hindrance." *

His fright and the fit of remorse which it engendered led him to give a list of the bathing accidents in the Jordan, only one of them fatal,[32] of which he knew, and to devote some space to an inquiry into the cause of the danger, which could not be due to the width of the river or its rapid current. "Unnatural and hellish beasts" from the Dead Sea which drew the swimmer under, or the more insidious venom of the Dead Sea waters themselves, or "strong imagination" in the victim—all might be put forward in explanation, but Felix himself was inclined to find the cause in the judgment of Heaven, "because swimming across is a sign of wantonness and dissoluteness . . . in so holy a place . . ." [33]

On his second visit to Jordan he was taking no chances,

---

* It is difficult to reconcile the above eventful narrative with Brasca's brief notice, Brasca [f. 39a], of the visit to the Jordan in 1480. At the river, he says, the pilgrims drank, bathed, washed their hands, and filled their water flasks, but did not stay long for fear of the Arabs reported to be in the neighborhood.

either physical or spiritual, and instead of swimming, "sat down on sand in the water up to my neck, wearing my shirt and scapular," as decorous as the old ladies of the company, "who bathed among the reeds above us with modesty, silence, and devotion, and far more sedately" than the rowdy and merry party of male pilgrims below, although it seems that he joined with the latter while they "jestingly baptized one another."

Apart from the refreshment and the fun, to bathe in Jordan was credited, at least by ignorant laymen, with all sorts of potent influences for good. By common report whoever had dipped himself in the holy waters would grow no older; some even went further than this and declared that whatever length of time the pilgrim spent in the water, by just so much was he rejuvenated—a belief upon which Felix cracks a mild, parsonical joke. For he could, he says, have wished this to be true in the case of the estimable old ladies, "our women comrades," but they, alas, "would have needed a bath of sixty years to restore their youth, for they were of eighty years of age and upwards"—and he leaves the reader to marvel at the stamina of such pilgrims.[34]

Not only their persons, but the pilgrims' belongings, were the better for immersion. Some of the knights went into the water fully dressed, "saying that they would always be lucky in those clothes hereafter"; at home those garments, Felix says, would be laid up "like treasures," to be worn for their lucky properties, whenever there was fighting toward. Some, as a more convenient and comfortable means of attaining the same object, laid in the river lengths of linen or wool which could be made up into clothes afterward. Others dipped and baptized little bells which were on sale for this purpose at Venice; their note would, as a result, give protection against storms and thunder. Many busied themselves in filling "jars, flasks, and glass bottles" with Jordan water, reputed to be of great efficacy against warlocks and witches. Unfortunately the presence of this water in the galleys was vehemently objected to by every sailor and pilgrims were warned not to bring it on board. If the ship were becalmed or ran into storms they would be ordered to throw it away; if the bad weather continued, search would be made, the officers rushing about the ship, insolently rummaging in the pilgrims' lockers, and threatening "that whosover is found with any of this water belonging to him, they will throw him and all his baggage into the sea." [35]

When at last the Saracens had contrived to collect and remount all their party, the pilgrims, many of whom now had their faces set toward home, rode briskly up through a wilderness in which "there is not a fruit-tree to be seen, nor any other plant save abominable thorns." Thus, with feeling, Casola describes the place, having suffered severely from those same thorns when his mule ran away with him here.[36]

Through this wilderness Felix and his companions had not proceeded more than a mile, when they were startled by a sudden "crying and shrieking" from the women pilgrims, a disturbance all the more alarming because of the uniformly irreproachable behavior of these ladies. The men turned back at once to inquire the cause, and heard that it had just been realized that one of the venerable females was missing. At once a search party was sent off, composed of Christians and Moslems. The rest waited under a burning sun, and full of a variety of fears; the old lady "might have been drowned in the water of the Jordan, or be lying faint for want of food in the wilderness, or perhaps be stuck fast in the mud by the river-side, and unable to get out, or perchance seized, robbed and outraged by some Saracen . . ." The Saracen escort added their quota to this catalogue of possible disasters—"some Arab or Midianite shepherd" might have kidnapped, or some lion eaten her. Happily none of these catastrophes had occurred. The search party "roamed shouting along the road through the wilderness, and went down even to the bank of the Jordan, to the place where the women had bathed, and there they found her lying asleep in a bed of reeds." [37]

All these alarms and excursions the pilgrims had endured upon that "fasting stomach" to which Brother Paul, for all his austerity, so frequently refers. When they had left behind them the thorn and scrub, and come to "a bare land, whereon grew neither grass nor trees, and . . . made uneven by sandy hills and swellings of the ground," they were allowed a short rest in the shade at the Church of St. John the Baptist, but not till they had reached Jericho could they hope for their Sunday breakfast.

And Jericho, as to so many pilgrims, proved itself inhospitable. They entered that poor relic of a city, which Casola was to dismiss as containing nothing left but ruins, a tower "and a hut or two propped up against the ruins," [38] but in which more credulous and romantic pilgrims looked with interest at the house of Rahab the harlot, and the impressive remains of the house of Zacchaeus. Well might the fasting Christians wish that Zacchaeus had still been in residence, to show them hospitality, for now their guides began "with horrible cries" to drive them out of Jericho, and away from the promised hope of rest and food. The reason of this change of plan was only too clear. The inhabitants of Jericho, described even by a modern guide book as "obtrusive," and in those days a rough lot, "the women . . . as strong as labouring men," "not black," according to Casola, "but . . . burnt and dried up by the sun," these ill-favored inhabitants were already gathered, intending to mob the pilgrims and extort toll. The armed and mounted Saracens rode into the press, trying to open a way for their charges; in retaliation those ungovernables, the women and boys, "ran up and pelted our host with stones; and while they did this many were dragged from their asses, and robbed of their hats and . . . hurt with the stones." With all the trampling "the dust was stirred up from the ground so thickly that it seemed as though Jericho were wrapped in a dark cloud." [39]

At last the Saracen guides were able to lead the pilgrims out and away, soothing them with promises of food to follow them out from Jericho, toward that famous fountain of Elisha, the beneficent effects of which they very soon began to see. They had been riding through country "like a sea beach . . . as barren and untilled," but now, hardly had they left Jericho when they found themselves in the shade of sycamores, among stone-walled orchards and gardens, in which grew "scented grape-vines and many fig-trees, bearing exceeding sweet fruit, and . . . sundry kinds of flowers and roses . . . and we smelt delicious and fragrant scents . . ." [40] The roses of Jericho, which had been known to the son of Sirach, and which still flourished, are celebrated by Felix in his most stilted and ornate rhetorical style. Yet he contrives to preserve and communicate something of his delight if the reader cares to strip his phrases to the bare bone: "the roses . . . their beauty . . . their scent . . . their softness . . . their color . . . one rose has more than a hundred petals." [41]

Climbing higher the pilgrims left the gardens behind them. They were not far from the fountain now, but they were to find yet two obstacles in their way. The first was a deep bog, as if it had been Christian's Slough of Despond, but made more difficult by hazards of "exceeding sharp thorns: for all the . . . bushes in that country bristle with thorns"; the second was an unfriendly Saracen miller who would have prevented the pilgrims' passage, had not the Saracen escort forced a way for them through the house.

At last, however, a little beyond and a little higher than the mill, they came to a place gratefully remembered by many a pilgrim, "a shady place full of trees and bushes, through the midst of which the water rushed at a great pace. Here we dismounted . . . and went down under the green leaves, each company by itself. We brought forth what was left in our scrips and ate it, and we drank of the water, which fell down among the rocks, and was clear, bright, fresh, and wholesome," drank of it, says Felix, "like cows, without stint." And here came to them men and women "bringing great baskets full of grapes and loaves of bread," there being some, fortunately even in Jericho, who were swayed rather by the profit motive than by ideological or national sentiment.[42]

It would be satisfactory to think that the pilgrims were able to dally long among the green bushes and sweet-scented shrubs, listening to the sound of the water, which "as it coursed eagerly along over the stones, made a noise which invited a weary man to sleep; moreover the leaves . . . rustled . . . as the wind blew upon them, and the sound sweetened our slumbers." Those slumbers, however, for the more stout-hearted, must be short, for not the pleasant fountain of Elisha, but the arid and sun-scorched Mount of Fasting was their real object.

It was not long before Felix and some others, as a sort of appetizer before climbing the mountain, tried to make their way up stream to the source of the water, to be foiled by a stone-throwing Saracen. They next "left the cool refreshing shade, came out from among the goodly trees into the excessive glowing heat of the sun," and addressed themselves to the main task of the day.

They had not gone far when they found that others were as resistant to the temptations of ease as themselves, for they overtook the valiant old ladies who had already begun the climb, but who, their powers surely, rather than their spirit, failing them, had stopped and could go no further. For here the path led along a narrow ledge between a sheer drop into the valley below and a cliff, toward which a man "must needs turn his face, lest he should be made dizzy with fear at the abyss below, and also that he may cling to the wall with both his hands, and having found places whereby to hold on, may look at his feet to see where he shall put one after the other and one hand after the other."

In spite of all difficulties Felix and some of the others held on, clawing their way upward to the top, to find there, waiting, as one might say, to take the gate money, an Arab armed with a club. The charge—a Venetian mark apiece—admitted them to what was held to be the cave in which Christ had endured the forty days' fasting. After prayers and meditations the pilgrims roamed about it, noting two altars, some wall paintings, and from the mouth of the cave "a way up to the top . . . over exceeding sharp rocks, an ascent too perilous for anyone to make . . . . I climbed up," says Felix, "into the window, but did not dare to adventure upon the ascent . . . Many of the other pilgrims stood watching me; if I had gone out many would have followed me." It was grievous to leave that track unexplored, since by it the Devil had led Christ up to the top of the exceeding high mountain.

Yet, failing this experience there were many other caves to investigate, in which long-dead anchorites had lived. The pilgrims climbed from one to another, identifying "the places for prayer, for sleep, for the dressing of food, for the keeping of necessaries, and in the walls square recesses for books."

They had still to reach the top of the mountain. Chance sent them a guide—a young Saracen who passed by on the slope above. They began the climb, when the guides, far below, but on the watch, rushed out from the shade, shouting threats and commands. The pilgrims too, who had stayed below, "stood endeavouring to call us back, and pretended to be getting ready to go away." The climbers, resolute sight-seers to a man, turned their backs, continued the ascent, and were soon beyond sight and call.

That climb, which led them from crest to higher crest until at last they reached the top, but always over sharp rocks and crags, landed them panting and "glowing with the heat" at a little deserted chapel, in whose shade they sat down, "fanning their faces with their hats and their clothes," and no doubt drinking in what a later pilgrim described as "a fine cool air." All were in need of rest, but two were utterly spent. One of these dropped as if dead; he was a priest, but they all knew that in fulfillment of a vow he wore a coat of mail next his skin. The other, a knight, had accomplished the terrible climb upon his knees. These two desperate feats of endurance moved Felix deeply to a sense of joyful devotion. If the modern mind, on the contrary, recoils from the thought of such self-imposed torture, it must at least be admitted that the resolution necessary for such performances is a quality of soul that any might envy.

Having got their breath, finished their prayers, and admired a view of mountains, wildernesses, and the Jordan far below, a view described by Baedeker as "a noble prospect," every part of which recalled for Felix some incident of Old or New Testament history, the pilgrims began the descent, in high spirits, some of the young knights going on before "running and leaping down, but we followed them sedately over the rocks and crags, the slopes and steep places."

The dignified, but doubtless cheerful descent of the elders was interrupted by shouts and angry cries from below, and among these "we could hear someone calling out 'Robbery!' in German words, *'Mordjo! Mordjo!'* On hearing this we straightway understood that those knights who had gone down before us were in trouble, and we hurriedly slipped down the hillside . . . till we came to the place of strife. Here five pilgrim noblemen were standing in a hollow cave . . . holding stones in their hands, ready to cast them; four Arabs stood in front of the cave, also with stones . . ."

The trouble was the usual Arab demand for money; this time, since "those five pilgrims would have eaten up the four Arabs if they had come to blows," it had been refused. Felix, however, and the rest of the elders, realized only too well the troubles that a brawl might bring upon all the pilgrims. With difficulty they persuaded the young men to drop their stones; the Arabs were told that they would get nothing unless in the presence of the captains, and so the two parties separated, neither satisfied, and the Arabs threatening revenge. That revenge they took when, after sunset, the pilgrims had set off to ride through the cool of the evening. They had not gone far when they found their way barred by armed Arabs demanding a fine because certain pilgrims had trespassed upon the mountains, and had threatened violence. After the usual long debate the Calini decided that the fine must be paid, and, the guilty pilgrims being unknown, that the captains must pay it. So they paid, but, says Felix, "with the most furious anger, and they cursed us, and wanted to know who the culprits were . . . but no one would tell them . . ." [43]

That night the pilgrims spent at the inn known as the Red House, a poor and foul place, where they must push and jostle to draw water at the small wellhead with their thirsty guides, and content themselves for supper with what remained in their scrips. Little however they cared for the discomforts of the place; oblivious to any danger, whether from ruinous walls, scorpions, thievish Saracens, or vermin, they lay down and "fell into a deep and mighty slumber." [44]

It had been the intention of the guides to start before daybreak, but mercifully for the pilgrims, all overslept. "The risen sun," says Felix, "had bathed the peaks and tops of the rugged rocks with golden splendour," before the Saracens began to rouse the pilgrims, shouting to them in a variety of tongues; "some in our own language, whereof they had learned some few words cried '*Uff, uff! Rita, rita!*' "

After the fatigues of the expedition it might have been expected that the one desire of every pilgrim would be to reach Jerusalem as quickly as possible, especially since that night they would be keeping their third and last vigil in the Church of the Holy Sepulcher. Some indeed "were in a hurry to get some cooked food and a place to rest in," but

Felix planned to add yet another experience to the day's total, and persuaded some of his fellows to share it. While the donkey boys and the less-determined pilgrims went on by the high road to Jerusalem, he and those other choice souls turned aside to see the sights of Bethany, whence they intended to proceed, "walking devoutly on foot, along the holy way whereby the Lord Jesus came from Bethany on Palm Sunday . . ."

With such a pious intention in mind they were unfortunate in having twice to suffer from the unfriendly Moslem habit of throwing stones, though it must be confessed that both times they brought trouble upon themselves. First they were beaten back by a woman from an attempt to cross a Saracen graveyard. Then, going "in devotion, silence, and prayer, through orchards of fig-trees," they saw in one of the walled closes trees bearing ". . . large ripe figs of a dark purple hue." Prayer and devotion were interrupted while two of the company broke into the orchard, climbed the trees, and began to pick the fruit. They were driven off by another old woman with a volley of stones and abuse, but Felix remarks with satisfaction that they brought enough away to provide themselves and their friends with a very welcome breakfast.

So the little company went on, always upward now, expectant of the sight of Jerusalem, hidden from them by the shoulder of the hill. At last they saw the bell tower of the Church of the Holy Sepulcher, then the "entire Holy City, glittering joyously in the sunlight, at the sight of which we were gladdened . . . for this most sweet city hath an exceeding delightful aspect . . ." [45]

That, for the pilgrims who tomorrow would start for home, was the last sight of Jerusalem, except as they would see it, turning to look over their shoulders on their way to Ramle and the sea. It is the last also of those glimpses of the city, seen from the neighboring hills or from the friars' garden on Mount Sion, which Felix describes. In these descriptions the Holy City appears, bright, distant, and minutely clear as the clustered towers framed in some great initial letter of a manuscript—a city which is not only the earthly Jerusalem, seen in the perpetual remembered morning brightness of the returned traveler's recollection, but also the Heavenly City of which Hildebert sang:

"In hac urbe lux solennis
   Ver aeternum, pax perennis;
In hac odor implens caelos,
In hac semper festum melos!
Urbs caelestis, urbs beata
Supra petram collocata,
Urbs in portu satis tuto—
De longinquo te saluto,
Te saluto, te suspiro,
Te affecto, te requiro."

But though the soul of Felix might share with the simplest pilgrim the joyful ardors of devotion, his mind, as he went about the Holy Land, was busy with matters which were no concern of the layman, and which interested by no means every priest. From the first he had avowed, as motive and justification for his obstinate desire to make the Jerusalem pilgrimage, the need of the preacher to understand, and thus be able to expound the Scriptures, though we may doubt whether he did not oversimplify the motive and overestimate the justification. But he was certainly sincere in his claim, and when in the Holy Land he pursued his end with enthusiasm, investigating on the spot the evidence for doubtful and conflicting statements, and eagerly acquiring knowledge which would enable him to make that gloss upon the text which could only be made by one who was familiar with the land itself, its ancient monuments, its towns and countryside, and who had besides seen in practice there customs older than the Saracen domination, as being, in fact, indigenous and oriental, rather than either Jewish or Moslem.

*Jerusalem*

*in 1483*

In all his discussions of such subjects, as in the account of his inquiry into the form and authenticity of the Holy Sepulcher, we can hear the wheels of the cumbrous mechanism of his scholarship groan as they slowly revolve, yet it is the chariot of archaeological and historical research which has begun to move.

Thus he will consider the much-debated question: What was the true nature of the food, the locusts and wild honey, eaten by the Baptist in the wilderness? First, following the tradition of medieval scholarship, he offers to his readers without an attempt at discrimination, a wide selection of the theories advanced by his predecessors; but his comments by the way are very much his own. Locusts, "tiny animals, which fly in a jumping fashion" are even now, he says, when fried in oil, eaten by the poor in Palestine. Some rejected this identification on the grounds that the Baptist's austerity of diet would not have admitted even such a slight deviation from vegetarianism, and that in the text the word had been *longusta*, the name of an herb; this had been corrupted into *locusta*, and thus mistranslated. Another view was that the text referred to the pod of a certain bean which grew plentifully in the desert, but Felix had experimented with these and discovered that the beans "were hard, like stones, and I could not split any of them with my teeth." Others, and the Friar seems on the whole to incline to their belief, argued in favor of carob beans, "which are oblong black pods, and when taken out of the pod are good to eat. This fruit is everywhere called St. John's bread, and they that deal in spices sell them in their shops. In the East they are thought to be worth nothing, and poor men gather them, tear off the skin with their teeth, and dress and eat the sweet juice with the substance between it. I have," he concludes, with a very characteristic remark, "often eaten of these for pastime, but could never satiate myself with them." [46]

Not only Felix but de Rochechouart too recognized that similarity between the Holy Sepulcher of the Bible narrative, and the ancient tombs to be seen round about Jerusalem, a similarity of which painters like Carpaccio were also conscious.[47] But Felix also, on his way down to Jordan pauses to describe the Syrian khans, "great houses beside the highways, with many stables below and chambers above, for man and beast to rest in, and the house stands with its gate open, without any inhabitant or furniture, and when strangers are passing by, they can enter therein, and rest in the shade, and eat whatever food they bring with them . . . In the East a man will find no inns beside these empty rest-houses . . . Moreover it was in an inn of this sort that the Lord was born." [48]

Again, he rejects the tradition by which the Roman soldiers crowned the Christ with "sea-thorns." They would use, he says, "thorns from the nearest bushes, or perhaps [they] found them in the kitchen of the house (of Pilate) among the faggots of wood for the fire, for I have seen with my own eyes that even at the present day they have no firewood save thorns, and their kitchens are full of exceeding sharp thorns for burning in the fire." [49]

A few of the pilgrims were conscious not only of the ancient and holy past of the land, but also of the times, not so distant, when Christian kings ruled in Jerusalem. Curiously enough but for de Lannoy, whose purpose led him to notice any place strategically strong, and who consequently mentions the ruined crusading castles still to be seen in Palestine, it is not the French pilgrims who find time to notice relics of that great colonial adventure of the West. It is Casola, Ludolph von Suchem, von Breydenbach, and Felix Fabri who, among the older and more august sanctities of the Church of the Holy Sepulcher, mention the tombs— "very humble," says Casola—of Duke Godfrey and King Baldwin I, the preservation of which by the Moslem gives Ludolph a text for a reflection upon the sadly different behavior of Christians in Lombardy, who violate the graves of

their dead enemies and brother Christians.[50] Casola, with his
eye for the aesthetic, comments also upon the "letters in
the ancient style, beautiful still and legible," of the inscrip-
tion upon King Baldwin's tomb.[51]

Close beside the Church of the Holy Sepulcher, separated
only by a garden "planted with orange-trees and pomegranates," stood what had been the palace of the Latin kings, "a
great house with many rooms," says Felix, but now half in
ruins, and inhabited by "a few poor Greeks . . . who . . .
in this royal palace can hardly exist through poverty." [52] It
is the Friar who, when giving an account of a walk round
about the walls of Jerusalem, remembered to have read that
near the Gate of St. Stephen Saladin had stormed the wall
at its weakest point and entered the city. So too, in tracing
the history of the temple site, from its first mention as a
threshing floor until his own day, Felix does not forget
that period during which the Knights Templars had it for
their own, when, in the words of the fiery saint, their
founder, it was "gay with arms, not with gems or ancient
crowns of gold; the wall . . . covered with shields slung
thereon instead of chandeliers, censers, and flagons;
the whole house . . . fenced about with bridles and
lances . . ." since there dwelt "the knights of Christ . . .
in the holy house together with their horses and their
arms." [53]

As well as these secular and military glories of the Christian kingdom he remembers those public, solemn, and
triumphant celebrations of worship which had been possible
when the whole land was in the hands of the crusader
kings. It is Felix who notices the custom, beautiful both in
itself and its symbolism, by which "when any hour was
struck in the Church of the Lord's Resurrection, at once
the Canons Regular of Mount Sion also struck it. After them
struck the monks of the Mount of Olives, through all the
churches. When this was heard in Bethany it was struck
there also . . . and the sound of these bells reached as far

as St. Saba, whose bells also were heard in the places round about." [54] That ancient custom Felix had only from hearsay, and from hearsay too the ritual visits, still in his day kept up, though with much curtailed solemnities, to the Jordan on the Sunday after Easter, and to Bethany on Palm Sunday.

But Brother Paul had shared in both of these, and in the second had played the chief part. After Mass at Mount Sion, and Paul adds, breakfast, he and twelve of the friars, thus making up the number of the Christ with his twelve apostles, set out for Bethany with one of the convent donkeys. At Bethany Paul was chosen to act as Christ in that strange traditional pageant of the triumphal ride to Jerusalem. It was for the egotist a great experience. He rode, with branches of palm and sprigs of olive in his hand, the chanting friars going before and after. On the Mount of Olives a great crowd waited; Christians of all nations were there, and even some curious Moslems. From the Church of the Ascension the procession went down the hillside toward Jerusalem, clergy and people spreading their garments in the way for Paul to pass over, trying to kiss him or even the donkey he rode on, and scrambling to catch the palm leaves which he scattered among them.[55]

## CHAPTER VII

# THE LAND AND THE PEOPLE

WHILE following our pilgrims in their tour of the prescribed sights of the Holy Land, we have observed, except when recording some experiences of theirs by the way, the concentration, proper to pilgrimage, upon the past of the places which they visited, whether the ancient Jewish past, or those few but stupendous years which began the Christian era, or the period of the Latin kingdom of Jerusalem.

But the land had also its present; the pilgrims were also travelers moving among strange scenes, and not only among strange scenes but among strange people. Some of our pilgrims ignored that present. Brother Paul and Margery Kempe were each the central figure of a drama which might with justice have been entitled "Ego et Deus meus"; it is therefore not to be wondered at if the back cloth of their stage is painted but cloudily, nor if their fellow men—except for such individuals who virtuously assisted or perversely resisted the principal character—have little more than walking-on parts. Other pilgrims: de Caumont, William Wey, the author of the *Informacōn for Pylgrymes*, and the two sixteenth-century Englishmen, Parson Torkington and the chaplain of Sir Richard Guylforde, are equally silent, though for a different reason. All of these, whatever their date of birth, belong to the Middle Ages, that period during which Europe was at work upon the clearings in the dark forest of its barbarian inheritance, during which the vigor of the human spirit threw itself into the impersonal, the corporate, the traditional, finding in these not only strength but freedom. Such writers will as little obtrude their personality as the architects of the Gothic cathedral or the artists of the illuminated manuscript.

But in others among our pilgrims the new impulse of the Renaissance was at work, causing them to look inward upon themselves, or outward upon the world around, and to find in both a novelty as absorbing, almost, as that which the first days in Eden must have offered to Adam. Subjectively a new territory was opened up in literature. It became worth while for a man to record those trivialities which so nearly concern the individual, as old Cardan found it worth while to record, not only that he still retained his faith in God, but also fifteen teeth; from which appetite to impart, and confidence and alacrity in imparting the personal and intimate, were to spring the diary, the autobiography, and the familiar letter. Objectively too men looked with quickened consciousness at their surroundings, so that travelers, even if also the devoutest of pilgrims, could not refrain their pens from descriptions of places, peoples, customs, and must look about them, even though it were in the holy city of Jerusalem and see it as a city, strange, even as Venice and Cairo were strange. So de La Brocquière, a member of that brilliant Burgundian court in which, but for the distastrous rivalry between the dukes and the king of France, the Renaissance might have flowered sooner and more richly than anywhere north of the Alps, writes hardly at all as a pilgrim, and with his characteristic soldierly brevity dismisses the Holy Land as too well known for him to describe, but has much to say about the Mecca caravan. De Lannoy's brief confines his narrative strictly to the secular and military aspect of places; de Rochechouart turns from his keen and curious examination of the Holy Places to observe the contemporary scene; Brasca and Casola—the one sincerely if conventionally pious, the other perhaps only politely so—each makes an attempt at a brief but systematic description of Palestine and its modern inhabitants. But it is in the German-Swiss Felix that we find most abundantly the energies of the new spirit, and alongside them, in equal abundance, the prejudices, enthusiasms, and devotions of the medieval past. A traditionalist, indeed a militant traditionalist, if it is true that he was an ardent defender of indulgences, he had a nature capacious enough to comprehend varied and even opposite habits of thought in a disorderly profusion. No other pilgrim was more truly devout, or more conscious of the romance of the Christian belief, a romance at once intimate and tremendous; no other pilgrim was more earnest to note the bearing of oriental customs upon the Gospel narrative; and no other pilgrim had such an inexhaustible appetite for observing and recording secular, human, and trivial things. So we find him moved by emotion at one improbable and apocryphal religious tradition, or commenting with crushing common sense upon the impossibility of another. Or he will pry curiously into the habits and beliefs of those fascinating enemies, the Moslems; or with equal gusto he will pause to tell of some amusing or exciting or even uncomfortable experience of his own. So, in trying to reconstruct some sort of picture of what our pilgrims noticed of contemporary Palestine, we shall find ourselves relying upon Felix Fabri's quick and curious observation more often than upon the experience of any other. He does not attempt Brasca's coherent description of Moslem habits, but instead adheres to the orthodox and traditional in giving a voluminous account of their beliefs. He does not, like Casola, criticize and discriminate, but bustles eagerly through his pilgrimage, moved and uplifted at every place where the pilgrim was expected to feel emotion. Yet for all that there is no pilgrim who gives the reader, as Fabri gives in the haphazard confusion of his narrative, such a sense of having traveled with a company of men, through a strange country and among strange people.

Of the city of Jerusalem itself we can glean a good deal from the pilgrim narratives. De Lannoy saw it as an ill-fortified place, with walls neither high nor in good repair, a moat shallow and in places altogether filled up; "the greatest strength it has is its strong position"; Brasca, who thought it a fine city, "as big as Pavia," agreed with de Lannoy on its military weakness.[1] Brasca's admiration was not, as we have already seen, shared by Casola, whose disparaging conclusion was that the more a man tries to say about this city the less he has to say, except that such a famous city, called by the Christians the Holy Place, is a great *cavagniaza*, and whatever the precise point of comparing Jerusalem to a rush market basket, the intention was clearly not flattering.[2]

Very different is the enthusiasm of the devout "Ultramontanes." "I saw never city nor other place have so fair a prospect," says the chaplain of Sir Richard Guylforde, and proceeds to copy from von Breydenbach a few lines on the views to be seen from there. But Felix Fabri, as well as breaking out into those ecstatic descriptions which we have already noticed, makes an effort to convey the general character of contemporary Jerusalem. It stood upon a site which was "hilly and uneven," so that "one goes up and down everywhere throughout the city." Like Brasca, he compared, for the sake of his readers at home, the unknown with the known. Felix was reminded of Basel: "As the city of Basel is hilly, even so is this city; for in Basel St. Leonard's Hill answers to Mount Sion, St. Peter's Hill to Mount Calvary, and St. Martin's Hill to Mount Moriah . . ." Then, to prevent any misconceptions, he adds that there is, notwithstanding, "much difference between the one and the other."[3] He also noticed, as de Rochechouart did, the number of areas with the walls filled with ruined and deserted houses, in which waste places the inhabitants found a handy dumping ground for their dead animals. "Yet," says Felix, "in the parts where men dwell there are many people gathered together from every nation under heaven . . ."[4]

The houses, mostly "of fair white freestone all built terrace wise,"[5] though poor men's hovels might be of mud,[6] were "not covered with tiles, nor have they sloping roofs like ours, but are covered with hard plaster." [7] They appeared "to be vaulted and have vaults above vaults," said Casola; he did not admire their appearance though he admitted to there being "some very honourable dwellings" among them.[8]

All the pilgrims, even Casola, were impressed by the bazaars of Jerusalem, where the long straight streets were vaulted over "with windows so set in the vaults as to give a very clear light, while neither rain nor sun can cause annoyance," and where there were low walls running along either side of the roadway which anyone might use as a bench if he wished to sit. Each trade kept to itself: shoemakers here, tailors who sold "ready-mades" there, jewel merchants, merchants who sold silk or cotton or sugar, all were to be found in their separate streets.[9]

But it was the Dome of the Rock (the Haram ashsharîf, or Noble Sanctuary), the Moslem center of Jerusalem, which, like a magnet, most often wrenched the attention of the pilgrims from the Holy Places of the Christian faith. Casola rated it as the only beautiful building in the city; Felix's lay companions, seeing it from the wall of the friars' garden, could find "nothing more glorious or more beauteous within sight"; [10] the simple English chaplain of Sir Richard Guylforde thought it "in largeness, height, and sumptuousness building far above and beyond any work that ever we saw in our lives." [11]

For Christians and Jews it was out of bounds, though they might look at it from the friars' garden on Mount Sion, or going further off, see from the top of the Mount of Olives, the mosque surrounded by its white marble pavement, seeming "to stand in a pool of quiet whitish water." [12] From here Felix watched it one night when those lamps were lit whose number varies from the five hundred of von Harff's account to the twelve thousand vouched for by d'Anglure's dragoman.[13] In the darkness Felix "saw through the windows of the temple as bright a fire therein as though it were a lantern filled with clear flame." [14]

"Although I am myself fond of seeing strange and curious sights," the Friar remarks—and one seems to catch in the words a tone of surprise—"yet I was never tempted to enter the temple . . ." [15] But now and again among the pilgrims there would be one who could not be contented unless he did. A knight of Felix's company bribed a Mameluke to smuggle him into the forbidden courtyard, but seized with panic, and suspecting the renegade's good faith, turned tail at the last moment.[16] Von Harff was more resolute. Having found the necessary venial Mameluke and bribed him to the tune of 4 ducats, he was fetched one evening by this man from the convent of Mount Sion, and brought to the Mameluke's house within the walls, as though to spend the night there. Instead, when von Harff had been rigged up in the dress of a Mameluke, and instructed how to act and speak if he were questioned, they proceeded to the mosque and were admitted. The German knight was able to make a leisurely survey of the place, to pace out the dimensions of the Dome of the Rock itself, to count the pillars, to visit the Aqṣa Mosque, and even to appropriate a number of pieces of wood and copper from the Golden Gate.[17]

It was possible for less adventurous pilgrims, by persistent dodging about in the streets leading to its gates, to catch glimpses of the wide court with its marble paving, though they were always liable to be shooed off by the jealous Moslems of the neighborhood.

This, in fact, was what the Friar and his companions did one day. They had gone out, with the lesser Calinus as guide and escort, and found themselves so near to the great mosque that they could see "in the courtyard thereof . . . many Saracens standing with pails, pots, and pitchers to draw water, which here bursts forth abundantly from a water-pipe . . ." Explanations were necessary before the Moslems in the street reluctantly allowed the Christians to kneel and pray with the courtyard in view; yet the pilgrims were not satisfied with this. They insisted on making their way to another gate, and from there, fetching a circuit, to yet another, by this insubordinate behavior greatly embarrassing the unfortunate Elphahallo, who was abused by his fellow Moslems for allowing the Christians to approach so near the mosque.[18]

At last however the party found itself at the southeastern corner of the Haram enclosure, at a place close to the Mosque al-Aqṣa where workmen were busy upon a building. This, which Felix, like von Harff, took for another mosque, was in fact the Madrasah al'ashrafîyah, a work of the reigning Mameluke sultan, Qâ'it Bey, which, begun in the autumn of 1480, and by this time completed constructionally, had been handed over to the workers in marble for its interior decoration.[19] The pilgrims asked if they might enter. This time they were not hustled away, but told that permission must be obtained from "Thadi." This "grave and ancient man, reverend and bearded," whom Felix took for a bishop, not only gave the Christians permission, but sent a friend to show them over the madrasah.

Here they found the artificers at work "making wondrous thin panelling out of polished marble of divers colours and adorning both the pavement and the walls." Much of that marble, so Casola was told, had been dug from the ruins of Jaffa, or salvaged from the sea itself; Agostino Contarini could confirm this, for the Saracens, exacting a sort of corvée, had used his boats and sailors to help in raising columns from the harbor at Jaffa for the building of this madrasah.[20] Above the heads of the pilgrims were ceilings, "glowing with gold and costly colors," being fashioned, according to Moudjîr, of polished wood, adorned with leaf gold and lapis lazuli, while the cupola which crowned the building was counted by the Saracens one of "the three jewels" of the Haram.[21]

But not only was the madrasah worth visiting for itself.

On its inner or northern side "there were great and tall windows, not as yet glazed . . . through which," says Felix, "we saw the court of the temple and the temple itself," and beyond it "a delightful grove of olive-trees planted to supply oil to the temple lamps . . ." [22] The great mosque as the Friar describes it was "a noble and exceeding costly building, great and round, after the fashion of a great and wide tower . . . . built high up in the air," from what he calls "[a] wide surrounding aisle," in which were "great oblong glazed windows" and mosaics where "the field of the picture gleams with gold, while the picture itself consists of palm-trees, or olive-trees, or figures of cherubim . . ." Above all soared the leaden dome, showing traces of gilding upon it, and bearing at its apex "a horned moon, with the horns uppermost . . . a moon on its back like a boat." [23]

The visit ended with satisfaction no doubt to all, for the Christians had been able to see far more than they could have hoped to see, and the workmen profited by the pourboire which the visitors administered on leaving. [24]

While Bellini was painting the portrait of the Ottoman sultan, Pisanello making his exquisite drawings of Tartar faces, and Erhard Rewich sketching groups of the various races of Palestine for von Breydenbach's handsome volume, many pilgrims attempted descriptions, haphazard or coherent, of the inhabitants of Palestine, their habits and customs, appearance, psychology, and language.

Moslem cooking arrangements come in for frequent notice. The pilgrims found it strange to see how all food was bought ready-cooked in those three streets described by Brasca, "cooked fowls, cooked meat, eggs and all other eatables . . . very cheap." [25] The business of cooking too—carried on in open kitchens and always by men, with the result that "no woman knows how to bake a cake"—impressed the western visitors by its scrupulous cleanliness. [26] Only bread was made at home in flat, unleavened cakes; in-

cidentally, this bread, "not cooked at all, but soft like paste,"
played Old Harry with the digestion of the pilgrims, and
was, so the clerk of Paris believed, one of the great causes
of illness among them.[27]

Equally strange was the oriental use of the flat house
roof. "When the sun has set men ascend thither to enjoy
the coolness, and there they work, eat, make their beds, and
sleep . . ." [28] They entertained friends there too; Brasca
watched the women dancing on one of the roofs to the
sound of "drums and other instruments very different from
ours." He noticed that though men were of the party, and
looked on, not one joined with the women in the dance.[29]

"They always and everywhere," said de Rochechouart,
describing the evening occupations of Saracens, "sit like
tailors, laying carpets under them, which are brought to
them by slaves." [30] Casola was surprised to note how dignified the Saracen grandees could look, as they sat cross-
legged on their marble bench outside the Church of the Holy
Sepulcher, waiting to pass the Christian tourists in.[31] De La
Brocquière, who shared, instead of looking on at, the life of
the East, learnt from his Mameluke friend, among many
other oriental habits, this, "which," he says, "I found rather
difficult at first . . ." [32]

Santo Brasca, accustomed to the fantastic and opulent
variety of Italian Renaissance costume, observed tritely but
truly of the Moslems that "their dress and clothes are very
different from ours." Men wore the turban of white linen,
and "clothes, most often of white, half way down the leg,
and quilted like our blankets." They wore no stockings,
but "gloves and slippers after their fashion . . . down at
heel," which they took off in the house or when entering a
mosque, as a man of the west would take off his cap.[33] The
women, who wore breeches down to their feet," like sailor's
breeches," also dressed commonly in white,[34] and wore on
their heads a confection which the masculine pilgrim's pen
labors heavily to describe but which can be seen in von

Harff's illustration. There is "a frill on top, covered with white and shaped like a box; the neck and back of the head are swathed in white material; on each side hangs down a long cloth like the white towels in Italy . . . the face is quite hidden by a black veil . . . In fact they look like devils from hell." [35]

*Saracens*

Brasca attempted to give a systematic though brief account of Moslem habit and custom. The information which Felix supplies, and it is copious and interesting, is conveyed haphazard in reflections upon or explanations of experiences of his own which would otherwise be incomprehensible to the circle of his friendly readers at home. Freely as he will serve up solid slabs of book learning, in the hope, perhaps, that this should give respectability and ballast to a narrative which would else be considered too frolic, he is as free to impart this other knowledge, picked up as he went about, listening, staring, a little fearful but far more curious, and we must suppose, with a good nature and simplicity so patent to all as to explain why he never, as he himself remarks, was "ill-treated in any way by any Saracen, Arab, Midianite or Mameluke with whom I had to do . . ." [36]

*A Moslem Woman*

Thus he will tell how one day, as he went down alone from Mount Sion toward the Church of the Holy Sepulcher, he passed the door of the Moslem boys' school near the old house of the Teutonic Knights, where "the heathen children are instructed in the law of Mahomet, and there they shout all day long, making a surprising noise . . .

They were sitting in rows upon the ground, and all of them were repeating the same words in unison in a shrill voice, bowing down their heads and their backs, even as the Jews . . . do when saying their prayers. They repeated the same words so many times, that I remembered both the words and the notes, which sounded thus:

Ha y la Halyl la lach Ha y la Ha lylla lach Ha y la Halyllalach

In the same way he mentions, just as he came across them during the pilgrims' outings, various oriental customs. One day they were returning to Jerusalem from a sight-seeing expedition when they met a great company, armed and mounted, with outriders, who warned them that an emir was approaching; ". . . we straightway jumped off our asses, and so stood by the wayside until they had all gone by. . . . for the custom of this country is that poor men, countrymen, pilgrims, and mean people should thus give place to nobles and rich men when they meet them." There were refinements upon this code: of two rich men meeting, he who wished to be most polite would draw aside; a rich man meeting an armed noble or a Mameluke, says Felix, "draws his feet out of the stirrups, and lets them hang down." [38]

Brasca will succinctly note that the Moors "worship mad folk as saints and hold them in great reverence." But Felix tells a story of how the pilgrims were held up at a narrow place because "a black and half-naked Saracen" stood in the way beside a pile of stones which he threatened to throw if any came on. For a half hour the Saracen guides argued and shouted but to no purpose; in the end the whole company, Moslem officials, pilgrim noblemen, and all, must turn aside and go round about, for the easterns, with their strange dislike of violence, would do nothing against "that poor, unarmed, naked man." And " 'Oh!' " said Felix to himself, thinking of the hasty, testy, turbulent Germany which he knew, " 'if you were thus to stand in the road unarmed in our part of the world, and stop the way of one of the least of these nobles, how quickly would you have a sword or an arrow in your side!' " 39

In several pilgrim narratives, in those for instance of von Breydenbach, Wey, the *Informacōn for Pylgrymes,* and von Harff, we find reproductions, more or less faithful, of Arabic script, and lists of Arabic words and phrases which might be thought to be useful to pilgrims, though some of these indicate concerns hardly proper to those under a vow of pilgrimage.40

Felix's tastes did not run to lists or to tabulation; nor had he in mind any vague and impersonal public, but the friendly readers at Ulm, and at Basel; consequently, instead of alphabets and lists of phrases, such scraps of Arabic as he transmits, come, according to his custom as a writer, through the medium of anecdote.

He was, like many more sophisticated travelers, pleased to air his knowledge of tongues, and felt himself well qualified to pronounce on the comparative difficulty of pronouncing the German and other languages, although he admits that German was "the only one familiar to me, and which I know thoroughly." German was, he was sure, "the noblest, clearest, most rational language," but it was also, for the less fortunate peoples of inferior speech, the most difficult to master. Felix had experience of this with a Saracen "with whom I made friends, and to whom I would repeat our words, which he could not pronounce, though he were to die for it." On the other hand Felix was comfortably persuaded that "I could say anything in his language without difficulty." [41] Unfortunately there was more in Arabic than he thought. Now and then his phonetic version of the names or words which he heard in use around him, is recognizable, but often his ear seems to have failed him, and what he writes defies identification.*

But when the Christian pilgrim came to Palestine he did not only find himself in a strange land, and among people of an alien race. He found himself also in a country ruled over by infidels, and in which the Latin Christian must rub shoulders, in the holiest places of Christian tradition, with members of sects whose varying faiths and practices he rated, in greater or less degree, as heretical. Heretics, of course, he had heard of at home, but they were few and proscribed, and it cannot be said that he took kindly to the experience of finding them in the majority. A man of a just mind and charitable heart, like Brother Burchard of Mount Sion, might, after living for years in Palestine, acknowledge with humility the "austerity of life and wondrous virtue" of the prelates of the Greek Church, speak with reverence of the catholicus of the Armenians, and roundly declare that "our own people, the Latins, are worse than all the other people of the land," [42] but such impartial judgment was rare. De Rochechouart indeed, in his account

* The following are a few of Felix's versions of Arabic words or names, with suggested interpretations: (See Acknowledgments)
A Kossa. Alquds. Jerusalem.
Albaroch. Al Burâq. The beast on which Mohammed rode.
Halachibis. Allah Kabīr. The Dome of the Rock, so called according to Felix because built "in nomine Summi Dei."
Rucholla. Rih'allah. The Breath, or Word of God, i.e., Christ.
Galela Cassa. Jalil al-Khāssa. Jaleel, the (private) servant.
Elphahallo. El-pahlawān.
Ameth. Hamid or Ahmed.
Ha y la Halyl la lach. La ilala illa llah. "There is no God but Allah."

of the various Christian sects, confines himself to externals:
the Georgians grow immense beards; the Syrians pronounce
"y" as "u," and therefore should rightly be known as
Surians; the Nestorians make the sign of the cross with one
finger; the Indians howl like wolves at the Christie eleison;
the Christians of the Girdle dress in Saracen fashion except

*Syrians*

that, instead of the white turban, they wear one of bright
or dark blue; the Armenians are of all the most friendly to
Latins; "they kiss our hands and respect us highly." [43]

But most pilgrims are content with a graded condemnation of all their fellow Christians of the East. Hardly any
had a good word to say for the Greeks. Surian held them
"our worst and most atrocious enemies." [44] Felix, inevi-
tably intolerant, but a candid and openhearted man all the
same, hated them as he hated members of no other sect
or faith, and entirely concurred with the judgment of the
kindly Saracen, Ameth, who assured him that "these Eastern

Christians are the least to be trusted of any men." [45] Felix openly declared that he preferred, and would more readily trust, a Moslem than a Greek Christian, and the one ill-tasting anecdote in his huge book is that, recounted with pride, in which he warned the church people at Ulm against giving alms to an old Greek monk who had undertaken the journey to the West in order to beg for the sake of the convent on Mount Sinai.[46]

It was not to be wondered at if such ill feeling was reciprocated. The Greeks, says de Rochechouart, called Latin Christians "dogs," and if the opportunity offered, were delighted to score off them; it was the custom of western pilgrims, when spending the night on the Church of the Holy Sepulcher, to sleep in the choir, a part of the church which belonged to the Greeks; these found a simple means of preventing the practice by swilling water over the pavement.[47]

Moslems, of course, as followers of Mohammed—apostate, antichrist—were "befouled with the dregs of all heresies, worse than idolaters, more loathsome than Jews." [48] Yet it was the unpleasant duty of Christian theologians to study their shocking creed, and as long ago as 1143 Peter the Venerable, abbot of Cluny, had inspired a team of scholars to translate the Koran. That translation was, perhaps, felt to be outmoded by the time de La Brocquière made his journey, for he thought it worth while to bring back with him from Damascus an account of the life of Mohammed and of the Koran, written at his request by the chaplain of the Venetian consul there.[49] Brother Paul's treatise on the same subject is lost. That supplied by Master Roth, who "ghosted" for von Breydenbach, remains, but he borrowed its various sections from writers of the thirteenth, the twelfth, and even of the eleventh centuries.[50] Felix in this matter was much more up to date. He had read the *Cribrationum Alcorani*, in which Cardinal Nicholas of Cusa, a churchman at once mystical and progressive, endeavored so to refute Moslem doctrine that its believers should be led to realize that, taken at its highest and noblest, it did but lead upward to Christianity.

So, though Felix's attitude toward Mohammedanism is one of orthodox condemnation, he will, even when discussing it in the vacuum of theological argument, admit that "this execrable and profane law derives its authority from a tincture of both the Old and the New Testaments and hath within it some truths, mixed with matter utterly absurd . . ." [51] He will even go further, and assert that though the Mohammedan faith "remains dark, being turned away from the light of Christ, yet [it] has light on the other side, for in many respects the law of the Alcoran bears splendid testimony to the truth, more especially with regard to the blessed Virgin Mary. They call Christ Rucholla, which means the 'Word of God,' the 'Breath of God,' or the 'Spirit of God,' words which, when well and piously interpreted, are full of holy awe." [52]

When it came to the Moslem practice of religion Felix made no attempt to conceal his admiration. At Ramle, where he and a few pilgrims, copying the Moslem habit, had slept upon the roof of the hospice, they had heard throughout the night the voice of the muezzin from a mosque nearby, who, as the pilgrim clerk from Paris described it, "cried out aloud and held his arms up as if he would embrace something. We could not understand him at all because he spoke all the time in Hebrew." [53] In the morning Felix, waking early, went up "on a higher vault than that whereon I had slept, sitting upon the convex roof of a loftier chamber . . ." and thence was able to look down upon the stir that took place at dawn. As it grew light he saw how the Saracens got up from their beds on other housetops, and at once "bent their knees in devotion, and prayed very seriously, saying their prayers in a kind of roaring tone, with their hands clasped together and raised on high. Several times they would bow their heads and bodies to the very earth, and remain awhile in that posture, and then would raise themselves up again and look upwards towards the heavens. All of them prayed at the same time, and in the same fashion, just as though they had all been monks of the same rule. . . . Now, after the sun had risen, our pilgrims rose, and straightway, without any previous prayer, began to talk and laugh with one another." [54]

One of the first expeditions which pilgrims made after their arrival in the Holy Land was to the place of St. George's martyrdom at Lydda. There, from the ruins of the Christian church, Felix looked through the open doors of the courtyard into the mosque, "and," he says, "it was like Paradise for cleanliness and beauty." That same scrupulosity and care impressed him in the Dome of the Rock, "for the Saracens . . . treat the temple with great respect, and are wondrous diligent to keep it clean and well-ordered with all external care, washing it daily both within and without, and it is all splendidly polished, so that it is a marvel to behold." The ceremonial cleansings of the worshipers impressed him too, and their behavior, as they "approach . . . with gravity and decorum, not in troops, but each man walks alone, even though he be a great lord; and they do not talk with one another, or bring children or dogs with them . . ." [55] (Nor did they, de Rochechouart remarks, either speak or spit in their mosques.) [56] Felix does not limit himself to the above implied criticism of Christian practice, but goes on to drive the point home with all the vehemence of the medieval preacher, citing as an example of western practice, the condition of that most holy Church of St. John Lateran in Rome, where "the courtyards are filthy, the chapels . . . desecrated," and then, sweeping into his net all lesser sanctuaries more likely to be familiar to his readers, denounces their condition in terms, the mildest of which describes "the filthy churches, misuse and neglect of fabrics, vessels, books, vestments, altar-cloths, churchyards, burial-grounds, and out-buildings." "Our churches," he cries indignantly, "stand all dirty, with people walking through them as though they were inns, and befouled with filth . . ." [57]

The Friar found other things besides cleanliness and religious decorum to admire in Moslem life. He was impressed, as even Casola was impressed, by the dignity of the "Saracen lords" who sat at the door of the Church of the Holy Sepulcher when the pilgrims were let in, "men of a fine presence, well stricken in years, handsome, wearing long beards, and of solemn manners, dressed in linen clothes, and with their heads wrapped round . . . with countless folds of very fine linen." [58] He could, on occasion, account for their otherwise unaccountable behavior by declaring roundly that "the Easterns are men of a different kind to us . . . they have other passions, other ways of thinking, other ideas . . . they are influenced by other stars and a different climate." [59] But their dignity and calm he believed to be due to the fact that their religion forbade them to drink wine. It is true that he gave Mohammed no credit for this prohibition, which he suspected to have been devilishly devised in order that converts should be attracted by its admirable effects upon the followers of the Prophet, since abstention from wine made them "outwardly very sober and composed, tranquil, benign, given to peace among themselves, patient . . . unostentatious in dress . . ." [60]

Notwithstanding such feelings of respect in the Christians, and in the Moslems a toleration for, and even a sympathy with any demonstration of religion, so that Margery Kempe could claim that they "made much of her and conveyed her and led her about the country as she would go," [61] relations between members of the two religions were not always happy. De La Brocquière reported that the friars of Mount Sion had to endure much bullying from the Saracens. "I am speaking of what I know," he says in his positive way, "since for two months I saw it for myself." Merchants suffered as well as the friars; at Damascus de La Brocquière's host, a Genoese, was arrested with others as a reprisal for damage done to one of the sultan's ships.[62] When de Roche-chouart was in Jerusalem he was told of the "very grand and lofty chapel called the Chapel of the Holy Spirit," which had been begun, by order of the duke of Burgundy, at the convent on Mount Sion, but which had been destroyed by the Saracens.[63] Surian, looking back at this period, during which he was still voyaging between Italy and the Levant, could remember how the Franciscans had been subject to periodical visitations by Saracen officials who ransacked the house and appropriated whatever happened to please them; it appears that the fancy of these marauders ran especially to the friars' bedcovers of coarse wool. They also "poked their noses into the cooking-pots in the kitchen, and if there was a piece of meat that pleased them they took it . . ." Besides these official visitations, the mob would sometimes break in and spill all the wine.[64]

When Surian wrote down his recollections, for the sake of his sister in her convent at Foligno, everything was changed. "The friars," said he, "live in blessed peace; and happy the Moor . . . who is considered their friend."[65] Felix, conscious of this happy state of things, thought that it depended upon the influence of two men: Brother John of Prussia, and Elphahallo, the lesser Calinus.[66] The Franciscans themselves knew better, and even a hundred years later, remembering that time of peace, gave the credit of it to the Emir Yeshbeck al-faqîh (Yeshbek the lawyer or schoolmaster). He, so they told, had once been an exile in Syria, where the prior of Mount Sion had been one of the few who had dared to show him friendship. The emir never forgot the debt, but when he became Qâ'it Bey's trusted councilor, "gave the religious into the charge of a great friend of his among the nobles of Jerusalem,"[67] namely, Fakhreddin, whom the pilgrims knew as Vaccardinus.

To have such a protector did not mean that all the Chris-

tians in Jerusalem, or even the friars themselves, lived completely secure. It did mean, however, that there was someone to whom they could appeal for redress of grievances or
for protection. In 1482 Arab robbers broke into the house
of the blameless Marthas or Poor Clares, threatened the
ladies with death if they screamed for help, and so pillaged
the place and made off. The news of this unpleasantness
reached the prior of Mount Sion at Bethlehem, whither he
had gone with several of the friars and their visitor Brother
Paul, to show the Holy Places there to two Flemish pilgrims. The prior at once returned, with such haste that
Brother Paul, forgotten in the excitement, had hard work
to catch up with him, even though he was mounted upon
that "strong and very new donkey of the convent" which
the friars had lent him to ride. At Jerusalem the prior at
once appealed to Fakhreddin, who, warning the brethren
to keep night watch in their own house, set his servants to
guard the house of the Marthas till the robbers should be
taken.[68]

The pilgrims naturally took note of such incidents as
these and of the special benignity with which the sultan
seemed to regard Christians. They saw how he had recently undertaken the construction of a "watercourse
through the hollows of many mountains, through cuttings
in the rock and clearances of stones, for a distance of eight
German miles . . ." in order to bring water from the
Hebron district to Jerusalem, repairing the old water
courses, and building storage tanks in the city. The more
optimistic among the pilgrims, discussing such matters
among themselves, put two and two together, and made five,
suggesting that Qâ'it Bey's purpose was "to resume the faith
of Christ which he has renounced, and to restore to . . .
[the Christians] the city of Jerusalem . . . May Almighty
God," Felix concludes, reporting these suppositions, "put
it into his heart to do this thing . . ." It is clear that the
Friar did not build upon the hope, yet he recommends that

the sultan should be prayed for, as a second Cyrus, inspired by the spirit of God, "albeit he knows nothing thereof." [69]

By the time Casola came to Jerusalem the sultan and his minister were old men; two years later, the year in which von Harff began his pilgrimage, Qâ'it Bey abdicated. This was enough to account for the exactions and tyranny which Casola and his companions had to suffer, not only from the poor and ignorant, but from such high officials as the governors of Gaza and of Ramle. At Ramle on their return journey, the pilgrims were held for five days upon one pretext or another. First it was "a fine parrot" which one of the knights had bought in Jerusalem, and which now was denounced as stolen property. Then it was a question of some sailors of Cyprus, ransomed by the pilgrims on their arrival, but now reclaimed as slaves. The parrot, after a costly transaction, was allowed to pass; the sailors, to the rage and grief of the pilgrims, were led away, chained once more and weeping, to captivity. Even at the last moment "Abrayno Grosso," as Casola calls the official who had accompanied the pilgrims from Jerusalem, found opportunity for extortion in their request to bury a dead comrade before they sailed. Nobleman though he was, the best grave they were permitted was upon the seashore, and that cost them 10 ducats.[70]

Even in the days of Felix's two pilgrimages, when Christians had the good will of sultan and emir, pilgrims must school themselves, in order to avoid friction with the Moslem populace, to adopt a humble and inoffensive demeanor, which must have put a strain upon the self-control of knights and nobles. At Ramle, on the way up to Jerusalem, it was the custom for the prior of Mount Sion to embody in his sermon to the assembled pilgrims a code of behavior consisting largely of a series of prohibitions. The newly arrived travelers were warned not to wander alone without a Saracen guide; not to trust even friendly Saracens too far; not to laugh at them when at prayer; not to enter a mosque

or walk over Saracen graves; not to wear white; not to touch
a Saracen's beard or those "balls of cloth," their turbans; not
to joke with boys; nor stare at women. They were also
exhorted to observe sobriety of deportment, because the
infidels "are always suspicious about laughter and merriment
among pilgrims"; to drink wine only in private; and to
endure blows patiently, appealing to the Calinus for redress.[71]

Even if they maintained the utmost propriety of behavior
the Christian visitors might find themselves in trouble. Apart
from the ungovernable Arab wanderers, women and lads
were the most likely sources of trouble. Women might be
too friendly; at Ramle some waved provocatively to the
younger pilgrims from a roof near the hospice; others even
went so far as to bore through the wall in order that they
might stare at the pilgrims through the peephole. This advance, and the response it got from the young knights,
caused the Minorite friars the greatest alarm; they hastily
closed the hole, and lectured the lay pilgrims upon the furious jealousy of Moslem husbands.[72] On the other hand pilgrims might find women joining in the stone-throwing of
the naughty boys.

Wine, unless carefully concealed, might easily cause
trouble. The bottles would be snatched at and broken by
the more rigid Moslems; others, less correct, would drink the
contents;[73] the pilgrims felt a certain sour satisfaction
when they saw the thieves "drink so greedily that they
make themselves sick."[74] Sometimes the theft was on a grand
scale: when Brother Paul was going up from the coast to
Jerusalem the captains arranged that wine should be carried
after them on six camels, but Saracens or Arabs, raiding the
caravan, made off with four camels and their load of wine.[75]

The last days in the Holy Land were the worst, even in
the comparatively easy times of Felix's pilgrimages. Those
pilgrims who left Jerusalem in 1483 to go down to the coast,

while their fellows remained for the setting out of the Sinai caravan, were "detained for many days, and grievously tormented" at Ramle. At Jaffa they must suffer from delay, oppression, and provocation, "so that the pilgrims were wrought up to such a pitch of rage and bitterness . . . that, when they were going on board ship, they meant to cut the throats of all the Saracens whom they met, both old and young . . ." They relinquished this plan for fear of the reprisals which might fall on their friends in Jerusalem, and compromised upon a last demonstration of their hoarded resentment. As the galley sailed they hoisted her ensigns and "shot stones out of their bombards at the towers of Joppa [sic] and left the port with loud shouts of defiance . . ." [76]

While still in the Holy Land, unarmed, and hopelessly outnumbered, the pilgrims had to endure as best they could. Occasionally one or another would be goaded to retaliation which might well prove a costly satisfaction, but was sometimes allowed to pass unresented. Only rarely was there likelihood of a general brawl, but one of these occasions is described by Felix in his account of the journey to Jordan.

The pilgrims had settled down to an uneasy sleep upon a hillside, when, in the darkness, some young hangers-on of the Saracen escort began to steal in among them and snatch away their scrips. First one of these was filched; the thief was pursued and the scrip recovered. Then another was taken; it contained "bread, cheese, smoked meat, and hard-boiled eggs," and if it were not Felix's own the list is remarkably precise. Whoever the owner was he "began to cry aloud and call upon the other pilgrims to help him. Whereupon the pilgrims arose, and many of them ran furiously towards the Saracens, and so much noise and riot began that the Saracens were forced to keep off the pilgrims with staves and swords, and both sides picked up stones . . . there were endless numbers of stones there, exceeding smooth and fit for throwing. So each stood over against the other and shouted." The galley captains and the greater Calinus intervened, and had with difficulty restored quiet when a Saracen began once more throwing stones from the security of some hiding place. This roused the pilgrims to a higher pitch of fury; some yelled to the Calinus and the captains to defend them, others threw stones at the escort who drew their swords. The awkward and even dangerous situation was brought to an end by the Calinus and the galley captains ordering all to mount and ride on.[77]

Sometimes the pilgrims relieved their feelings in safer and more stealthy ways. Near the Franciscan house at Jerusalem there was a great heap of stones to which Saracen women came "to burn incense upon a stone, and bury loaves of bread." Felix watched their "superstitious observances" with disapproval, and "several times went to this pile of stones when I did not fear that any Saracen would come thither, and scattered the stones which had been put together to receive the fire, turned out the things which they had hidden beneath the stones, and so left the signs of my vengeance there." [78]

Yet in spite of tyranny on one side, resentment on the other, and some malice on both, Christian and Moslem could meet on occasion in casual good fellowship or real amity. In the old days of the Christian kingdom there had been a sharp distinction, in the minds of the Saracen, between the visiting crusader or pilgrim and those others, the Franks d'Outremer, whose home was in Syria. Even in the days when Saladin's victories had sharpened the enmity of East and West, the chivalric Usāmah, though he will salt his anecdotes of this or that Frankish knight with pious maledictions—"May Allah have no mercy on him!"—had nevertheless many good friends among them, and especially among the Knights Templars themselves. These, for their part, found nothing amiss in the Moslem praying in their church with his face turned toward Mecca, though a well-meaning but inexperienced stranger from Europe might be shocked to the soul at the sight.* [79]

In the fifteenth century it was the Christians who were excluded from any part of the Haram ashsharîf, but besides this, the Saracen had become too familiar a figure for even the most orthodox pilgrim to be stirred to any such frenzy of reprobation, and those passing tourists of a fortnight would follow the ancient custom of the Latin kingdom and share with Moslems the public baths. Margery Kempe and Brother Paul speak with more warmth of approval of the kindness of individual Saracens than they display toward the majority of their fellow Christians,[80] though this is perhaps due to that disposition toward the *"amor de lonh,"* which is a trait often to be observed in superior persons of all ages.

In the narrative of Felix Fabri there is frequent mention of pleasant intercourse between Moslem and Christian. After an expedition to the Valley of Jehosaphat, during which the pilgrims had let off some of their theological steam by much laughter, "at the madness of Mahomet," and by some jibes at their Jewish guide, Felix returned to take supper with "his lords," who were entertaining, as well as their chaplain and two Franciscans of Mount Sion, "two Jews, one Saracen and one Mameluke . . . and we supped merrily together—albeit we were of different faiths and customs." [81]

Chance encounters might be as pleasant. When picnicking at the fountain near Bethsura the pilgrims were joined by many Saracens who passed along the great road to Gaza and the south. "To those who stopped beside the fountain and

---

* Usâmah's story, told to illustrate the "harshness" of the Franks, is amusing and at the same time revealing. The stranger knight twice tried to drag the kneeling Moslem round so as to face the east. After the second attempt he was ejected by some Templars, friends of Usâmah, who apologized for the ignorance of their overzealous fellow Christian. Usâmah, courteously protesting that he had prayed enough, left the church, and noticed outside the stranger, trembling with horror and indignation.

drank we gave some of our bread, and very many Saracens sat down with us. At last there came one with a basket full of most excellent and sweet grapes, to whom we showed our scrips full of bread, which exchange pleased him much, and so we ate and drank in that place with them even unto the going down of the sun." [82]

To speak to women even was not always so fraught with danger as the pilgrims had been taught. We have seen how obliging the daughters of a surly Saracen father could be. When, on their way to Sinai, the pilgrims were at Gaza, "there came into our courtyard certain Saracen damsels with their attendants, with their faces veiled according to their custom, and wished to see us. So we came out of our tents and huts into their presence, and they laughed and talked in the Saracen tongue." As the pilgrims felt themselves at a disadvantage they asked, through an interpreter, that the veils might be raised. After a great deal of laughter the ladies ordered their women to unveil, and the pilgrims instead of black veils saw faces "black as coals," and understood why their request had caused so much merriment. Entering into the frolic spirit of the interview they made pretense of being frightened; then "asked their mistresses also to raise their veils. They did so, and they were fair and beauteous ladies," and also, we have Felix's word for it, "modest and respectable." [83]

Of our pilgrims, two, de La Brocquière and Felix, went beyond this pleasant but casual good fellowship, and came to close quarters and terms of real friendship with individual Moslems. For de La Brocquière, this was of the essence of his lonely adventure, in which, like Charles Doughty, he, a Christian, and known for a Christian, became a member of a Mecca caravan. It was not only that the rough Turkoman riders, after laughing to see him take out his written list of Turkish phrases, combined to teach him, by constant repetition, all the words which he would find necessary in supplying the needs of himself and his horse. A closer comradeship by far existed between him and the Mameluke Mohammed, who seeing the Frank alone and ignorant of the ways of oriental travel, took charge of him, taught him, fended for him, and saved his life (though de La Brocquière did not learn this till they parted) by refusing to consent to a plot to kill him. It would be unlawful, the Mameluke declared, to kill one with whom they had eaten bread and salt, and besides, "God made Christians as well as Saracens." [84]

Friar Felix, though coming into contact with Moslems only as one among a number of pilgrims, yet by the power of his candor and humanity, was able to cross the debatable ground which lay between the two religions and races. The donkey driver who kissed him and laughed for joy to see him return was the first friend whom he made among the Saracens. Ameth, the governor of Bethlehem, a man acceptable to both Christians and Arabs, was another; on the journey down to the Dead Sea Felix's mule bolted and gave him a bad fall. Ameth, letting the rest go on, himself attended to the Friar, using upon him some strange eastern skill of massage and showing "as much kindness . . . as the most tenderhearted Christian could have done." "I pray God," says Felix, "that He have mercy upon that Gentile Saracen, even as he had mercy upon me." [85]

"Sabathytanco, the upper Calinus," the Friar respected. He was "a tall man, wealthy and of austere morals, but he was hard upon the pilgrims . . ." and not always true to his bargain. Elphahallo, the lesser Calinus, on the other hand, it is safe to say that Felix loved. Already of a great age— Felix believed him to be over eighty—and suffering from a rupture, he yet journeyed between Palestine and Egypt, escorting batch after batch of pilgrims, not, as Felix declared, risking his life for the sake of reward but because of his love toward the Christians from beyond the seas.

Felix was not the first who had recognized the old man's nobility of character. A German noble, determined to snatch the Moslem from eternal damnation, had gone to the length of kidnapping him, conniving with the galley captain at Alexandria to slip out of harbor on a fair wind in the middle of the night, with the unsuspecting Saracen on board. So he was brought to Italy, presented to Pope Nicholas V and to the emperor, and much worked upon to change his religion. This he utterly refused to do, and was finally shipped back from Venice loaded with gifts and much impressed, says Felix, with "the great liberality and glory of the Christians."

Without resorting to such drastic measures the Friar did his utmost by argument and discussion to turn this "single-minded and upright Saracen, abounding in moral virtue," from the path of error, and the more eagerly because the old man admitted to a high opinion of the Christian faith. But he could never succeed, for it was Elphahallo's conviction that "all men may be saved in the faith wherein they are born, provided they keep it pure . . ." while he condemned with equal sternness the Mameluke or other renegades from Christianity, and those who forsook the Moslem faith; an opinion which Felix held to be a deplorable error, but entirely failed to shake.[86]

When, on the borders of Egypt, the Calinus turned back, leaving the pilgrims to go on alone, the parting was grievous. The Christians felt, says Felix, that they were losing the guidance of one who had been like a father to them. They must have known, humanly speaking, that they would never see the old man again, and that the absolute of the separation would be mitigated only by such chance letters and messages as might be carried by travelers across the leagues that lay between Germany and the Holy Land. And besides all this Felix, at least, must have been convinced that not even death would restore this friend whose faith condemned him to eternal torment. At the parting he confesses "with shame . . . that some of the pilgrims were in tears." Some of the pilgrims—the reader is sure that the Friar was one of them.[87]

## CHAPTER VIII

# LAST DAYS IN THE HOLY LAND

O N July 22 the pilgrims, having spent the night in the Church of the Holy Sepulcher, gathered at the Franciscan convent on Mount Sion. There, in the infirmary, "in a great chamber which the brethren call the Venetian Chamber," the conclusion of the pilgrimage was formally announced in the presence of the governor of Jerusalem, the greater and the lesser Calini, the two Venetian captains, the Father Guardian, Brother John of Prussia, and various high Moslem officials. When this was done, those who intended to make the pilgrimage to Sinai were invited to remain in order to discuss the terms of a fresh contract, this time with the Moslem authorities direct, but in the presence of and before the departure of the captains, so that if the infidel screwed his demands too high the pilgrims might refuse them and return by sea.[1] The rest went off to prepare for the road, for at once after dinner they would leave Jerusalem.

Felix, of course, was one of those eighteen who stayed in the Venetian Chamber to thrash out the terms of the new agreement. When the conference was ended he came out to find "everyone running to and fro, and packing up for the journey." He turned to, and helped the servants to carry out the baggage of "my four lords," and to load the donkeys which already stood waiting.

The parting was, he says, "not without tears." He grieved not only to see "his lords" go, and at the thought of the dangers before them, but also because of "my own lone-liness and the misery which I was about to undergo in crossing the boundless waste of the dessert . . ." He gave

them a letter which they were to deliver to his dear friend,
Prior Fuchs, and the lords bestowed on him a handsome sum
toward the expenses of his journey to Sinai.[2]

A certain amount of readjustment, both physical and mental, was necessary for those pilgrims who remained in Jerusalem. The Hospital, half-ruinous though it might be in these
days, was now far too large for their diminished numbers;
indeed it seems only to have been kept open for the regular
summer pilgrim season.[3] Sometimes pilgrims put up at the
house of that Christian of the Girdle known as the Gazelus,
who acted as dragoman to the convent, and also had the
right of supplying wine to the pilgrims.[4] He was not, however, popular as a host, and the pilgrim lords tried hard to
persuade the prior of Mount Sion to take them in at the
convent; he refused, though he made it clear that Felix was
welcome there still. The lay pilgrims therefore joined von
Breydenbach's party at the pleasant house of Elphahallo, the
lesser Calinus. "In this house there were three chambers,
besides a little solar chamber, and in the midst thereof was
a hall or court of fair size, wherein stood vines covered with
bunches of grapes, while beneath the house was a great
cistern for the ceremonial bathings of the Saracens." Here
all the lay pilgrims found a lodging; the Calinus gave up two
of the three rooms to them, keeping one only for himself
and his brother, and leaving the pilgrims free use of the house,
"so that they went in and out, slept and ate there, buying
what they wanted, and cooking . . . at their own pleasure." No wonder that von Breydenbach, whose standard
may well have been high, recommended it as a lodging possessing two great conveniences, plentiful water and quiet.
But besides the material improvement in the situation of
the lay pilgrims, all who remained in Jerusalem must have
experienced the enjoyable sensation of finding themselves
promoted for the status of mere tourists, almost, it might be

said, of trippers, to that of visitors who sojourn in foreign parts.

Brother Paul belonged to a company even more select. He, a Franciscan who had lived for over a year in the Franciscan house, could almost rate himself as a resident. He had in fact intended to stay longer, but the prior and convent, and we cannot wonder at them, had decided otherwise. Just before the arrival of the summer pilgrims, among whom were Felix Fabri, von Breydenbach, and the rest, the prior had visited Paul in his cell, and after politely belittling the comforts of the convent, and as politely acknowledging the pleasure and profit which the brethren had derived from Brother Paul's company, invited him, in the most honorable terms, to leave them. The request was so framed that not even Paul need take offense, but might rather preen himself upon the confidence which the convent reposed in him, wishing to entrust him with a mission to the court of the emperor.

Before the invitation was accepted, the arrival of the summer pilgrimage presented Paul with an alternative. He was invited by the chamberlain of Mainz to join them in the Sinai pilgrimage; more than that, von Breydenbach mentioned " 'a good benefice left by the landgrave of Hesse, and to that I will promote you, when by the grace of God we come homeward.' "

On hearing this, says Paul, "my spirit revived, and my heart leapt up, rejoicing in me, and I said, 'Would that this might be!' " But first he must have another interview with the prior. He reported the suggestion, leaving it to the other to make the decision. "If it pleases you, so be it, if not, tell me candidly, quite apart from my own convenience, and I will willingly give up the idea for the sake of the obedience I owe." [5]

The prior however agreed with alacrity. If the main object was to induce Brother Paul to leave Jerusalem, that had been obtained. The matter was settled with satisfaction to all—the only drawback being that Brother Paul was now reduced to a mere visitor. Yet he was one who could boast, and did, of a whole series of repeated devotions at every Holy Place in Jerusalem, and of more visits to the outlying ones than any ordinary pilgrim could number: "Twice visited I the Mount of Fasting, and the Fountain of Elias, thrice the city of Jericho, twice [but he should have said "thrice"] the river of Jordan, twice the monastery of St. Jerome in the great wilderness . . ." and so on.[6]

The Franciscans, for their part, seem to have felt a certain relief at the ending of another pilgrim season, and at being, as it were, once more en famille. They celebrated this by giving a party; but not, as might have been expected, to any representatives of the many Christian sects in Jerusalem. One evening three great Saracen lords rode up to the convent to enjoy the friars' hospitality and the fresher air of Mount Sion. They were the greater Calinus, the governor of Jerusalem, and that same Vaccardinus, or Fakhreddin, who was the friend of Emir Yeshbek and the special protector of the Franciscans. The friars, as was their custom upon such occasions, chose the coolest place in which to entertain their guests; this was the church itself, and there carpets were spread, and cushions strewn, so that the Saracens might sit at ease in their own fashion.

"When they were settled," says Felix, who helped to wait on them, "the brethren brought them a repast in a tin dish, biscuits made with spices, some loaves of their bread, honey-cakes, and fruits, grapes, almonds and melons, with cool water to drink . . ."

After conversation with the friars the visitors turned to questioning the pilgrims through interpreters; the answers to these questions the Moslems "heard . . . with wonder, and seriously discussed what they heard with one another; for they were grave and ancient men, with long beards and of much experience . . . and of a noble presence."

Besides conversing and answering questions both the

friars and pilgrims took advantage of the visit to petition
for redress of grievances. The Franciscans were promised
that a Saracen who had attacked two of their number should
"never trouble any Christian again"; the pilgrims were confirmed in their contention that the Saracen caretaker at
the Church of the Ascension had erred in demanding a fee
for admission; he also, the visitors said, would not do such
a thing again. But they added, giving friendly warning,
" 'when you are walking abroad always . . . have some
Saracen with you, that rude boys, whom we cannot hold in
check, may not annoy you.' " 7

The party would, it seems certain, have been an unquali-
fied success, but for the unfortunate effect of the supper
upon several of the company. The *Informacōn for Pylgrymes* warned Englishmen against "melons and such cold
fruits, for they be not according to our complexion." 8
Felix was to discover the same for himself. He had "both
at dinner and supper . . . committed excesses in eating too
greedily of melons . . ." which, he explained, "at Jerusalem
are very large and very sweet." Retribution followed; next
day Brother Baptista, the convent's Infirmarius, had to take
him in hand. He was up again the day after, and hearing that
two of the pilgrims at Elphahallo's house had also suffered,
with "a stick to lean upon, I went down from Mount Sion
with great trouble, because of my weakness . . ." Not feeling well enough to walk back to the convent, he spent the
day there, "but in the evening two knights brought me up,
well amused and almost whole again . . ." 9

The pilgrims did not intend that their time in Jerusalem
should be spent, apart from necessary preparations for the
desert journey, in social gatherings, however pleasant. They
had the opportunity now of seeing places for which the
crowded program of ordinary pilgrimage allowed no time,
and so, two days after the departure of the homing pilgrims, they met together in order to decide what they

should do. Unfortunately, according to Felix, "the devil sowed tares." Some pilgrims, and the Friar among them, were all for bold plans and long expeditions. These wished to visit the Sea of Galilee and Nazareth; they spoke even of going so far as Damascus. All these things had been possible earlier in the century, and were to be so later; de La Brocquière had visited Nazareth, the Sea of Galilee, and Mount Tabor on his way from Beirut to Damascus, finding Nazareth, which Felix specially longed to visit, only "a big village, built between two mountains," with its church in ruins, and the place of the Annunciation "pitiful to see." [10] Von Harff also was to pass through northern Syria in spite of the disorders which followed the abdication of Qâ'it Bey.

Felix was sure that if all had been as enterprising as himself and his fellows it could have been done, although both the Calini and the Father Guardian threatened worse dangers on the way to Nazareth than ever were to be met in the desert.* The more cautious or fainthearted among the pilgrims seized upon this advice, adding also that if some went to Galilee they might find, on their return, that the rest had already started for Sinai. "But herein," says Felix with some heat, "they were mistaken, for they might have gone three times over before we set out from Jerusalem . . ." [11] Without, however, a sufficient number to subscribe toward buying off Arab hostility, the expedition would have been too expensive, and so was finally given up, but the difference of opinion engendered so much bad feeling among the pilgrims that harmony was never completely restored. They had already, for convenience, divided themselves into three companies, two of eight and the third of six men. Now, though the first two remained on good enough terms, the third, that

---

* In this they may have been correct. Relations between the Mameluke sultans and the Turkoman power in Asia Minor were worsening, and disagreement between these reacted on the Bedouin tribes. Our pilgrims were to meet, as they went down to Sinai, an Egyptian army on its way to northern Syria to deal with trouble there. Fabri, X, 442. Cf. Walther, p. 192 and n.; S. Lane-Poole, *History of Egypt,* p. 347.

to which Felix belonged, and which contained presumably the more daring spirits, kept aloof, so that "they had two kitchen fires in the . . . house, two kitchens, two cooks, and separate buying of provisions . . ." In the third company one of the knights, Peter Velsch by name, revealing unexpected domestic gifts, took charge, "with two poor German Jews to help him," of the cooking and catering. Unfortunately the soreness which the disagreement had left behind, besides being responsible for these cumbrous domestic arrangements, caused many things to be "left undone which we might easily have done had we been all of one mind." [12]

The pilgrims might perhaps have done more, but certainly they managed to do much in their weeks of waiting. Some of their expeditions we have already anticipated—their visit to the Madrasah al'ashrafîyah, Qâ'it Bey, and to the House of Pilate—but besides these and more vigils in the Church of the Holy Sepulcher, for which they now had, as it were, an out-of-season ticket at the reduced fee of 5 ducats for all, there were walks in and around Jerusalem, visits to places of both sacred and profane interest, and the arduous journey down to the Dead Sea.

More than one of these expeditions, though not so risky as the entry into the temple, had to be undertaken with circumspection. Since the Saracens "in the early morning, and in the evening, when the sun is less hot . . . go out into their gardens and walk about outside the gates . . ." the pilgrims, when they wished to make a complete circuit of the city, so as to see the old walls from the outside, must, like

"Mad dogs and Englishmen
Go out in the noonday sun,"

and so they did, carrying a "packed lunch" and walking through "the exceeding great heat." When they had made their tour they returned, as they had started out, by the Fish Gate, the present Jaffa Gate, and Felix went with the rest to the house of Elphahallo, "and we refreshed ourselves there, for we were hot, tired and exceeding weary." [13]

Another hot afternoon they were led by a Jew, "in a half-secret fashion," to see the buildings close to the temple upon its southern side, going first to a ruined Christian church, and thence into the cryptlike buildings which lay below the madrasah and the Mosque al-Aqsa, and which are still known as the Stables of Solomon. These, besides their archaeological interest, provided a not unpleasant thrill of danger, as they ran beneath the Haram enclosure itself. There was even an opening in the vault used by the Saracens for getting rid of the sweepings of the court above. "Had we not," says Felix, "been afraid, we might have climbed up over the rubbish into the courtyard of the temple." [14]

Another day the greater Calinus, having exacted from each of the pilgrims an advance payment of 5 ducats for the Sinai journey, arranged, as a sort of "luck-penny," a visit to the crusader Church of St. Anne, a mosque now, and therefore not usually shown to pilgrims. The Calinus did not himself guide the party, but sent his son, "Abre," a youth of nineteen, and a servant. With these to lead them the pilgrims set off just before sunset "through secret lanes in Jerusalem" and were let into the empty mosque, where the whitewash, as it flaked from the walls, showed below it the old wall paintings of the story of Joachim and Anna. In the days of Ludolph von Suchem these had not been washed over, nor, apparently, were Christians forbidden to enter, for Ludolph had been amused to hear old Baguta, the Saracen woman who acted as guide, interpret the pictured episodes, with tears in her eyes, as representing the life of Mohammed, pointing out especially, says Ludolph, "the painting of the trees for paradise wherein Mahomet kissed girls . . ." [15]

Once, by a lucky chance, and the friendliness of a young Saracen, Felix and his companions were admitted into a place not usually seen by pilgrims. As they passed the Tower of David one day and stopped to stare up at it, the castellan's son signed to them with his hand that they might enter. In they went over bridge and drawbridge, through two iron doors into the court of the castle where women, sitting sewing, covered their faces at the sight of strangers and scurried away. The friendly young man showed them over the whole place, so that the knights could run a professional and respectful eye over the thick walls, the numerous towers pierced for war engines; there was a moat too, once deep but now silting up, and on the east given over to growing the castellan's vegetables.[16]

The greatest of the pilgrims' expeditions, during this period of waiting, was that to the Dead Sea. This, as in Felix's first pilgrimage, was often combined with the visit to Jordan, but in 1483 it had so far been omitted, why, Felix does not say. And now the two Calini deplored a rich variety of arguments against the expedition. They feared danger to the pilgrims from Arabs, from "many harmful and poisonous animals . . . such as lions, bears, wild boars, snakes, worms, and the like," which were reputed to abound on the shores of the sea. They suggested that the sultan, jealous of his own monopoly of the precious drug "tyriak," had forbidden visits to the place of its origin.[17] They spoke also of the pestiferous stench of the waters, pointed out that there was "nothing beauteous there . . . nothing pleasant," and as a final "somewhat theological" argument, urged that the Dead Sea had no shadow of claim to any sanctity, and that the pilgrims ought to be content with having visited the blessed river Jordan. Four of the pilgrims were wrought upon by all this reasoning, but the rest persisted; Sabathytanco yielded, and sent for that "brave and faithful Moor," Ameth, governor of Bethlehem, to provide donkeys, and himself, as one on good terms with the Arab tribes, to escort the pilgrims.

Next morning, so early that it was still dark, Ameth, accompanied by slaves with mules and donkeys, was at the door of the Franciscan house. Felix, never backward when there was prospect of an excursion, "ran down in the dark from Sion to Millo, to the house of Elphahallo, in which their lordships the pilgrims lay," and finding all asleep there, roused them by hammering on the door with a stone.

It was still starlight when the company started, and by the time the sun rose they were far down the Kidron Valley. But the heat grew and the pilgrims were glad to reach the monastery of St. Saba. Here was a convenient halting place, in which to pass the hottest hours of the day, and besides, St. Saba was, as it still is, one of the noted curiosities of the Holy Land.

The pilgrims were welcomed by the few Greek monks, but when they went into the monastery they had a bad fright, for they found there "many Arabs of the desert, both husbandmen and highway-robbers." At once they suspected their guide of a plot against them, but he, seeing this, brought to them the sheik of the Arabs and with him "promised that we should be safe both in our bodies and goods. If, however, we chose graciously to bestow a fee or small present upon them . . ." The pilgrims took the hint. A few "madini" changed hands, the Arabs promised to escort the Christians down to the Dead Sea, and the pilgrims could, with minds at ease, take out scrips and wine bottles, while the Greek monks brought cold water, so that they might wash their feet and drink. In an atmosphere of peace and friendliness they then sat down to eat, sharing their biscuits with their guide and the Arabs.

The heat of the afternoon was spent in pleasant sleep in the shade—or was so spent by all but Felix. He, insatiable of experience, went off, and "rambled about by myself through all parts of the monastery, both down in the valley and up above, and narrowly examined all the caves and huts of the holy monks of old with great admiration, and also with peril of falling as I climbed up and down over rocks and crags . . ." The place—"one of the most wondrous things which I have seen in all my travels"—fascinated Felix, and he explored eagerly the three tiers of caves, each cave separate "like the cells along one side of a dormitory"; the ruins of more cells and of greater buildings on the cliff top above; the church itself, "standing upon a rock which hangs in the air without any foundation," from under which rock "flows out a stream, but a very small one, of living water, whereby the monks there support life . . ." [18]

The reputation of the Dead Sea was such that the medieval traveler found it difficult to keep his head and exactly record his own observations at the sight of it. "It is always smoking, and dark like Hell's chimney." [19] The stench of it prevented any coming near.[20] A feather would sink in it, but iron would swim.[21] Here was to be found that poisonous snake, the Tyr, from which tyriak was made, blind but so venomous that if it bite a horse the rider dies,[22] so strong and fierce that "it is said to throw itself through a board three fingers thick when it is angry." [23]

Our pilgrims reached the shore at sunset, and had little time to stay, but that little was enough. Felix and some others scrambled out along some ruins till they were able to look down into the water and there "saw, touched, and tasted it." Here we come to real experience, if a little heightened by imagination. It was "clear, but exceeding salt and thick." A man "who puts his hands into it feels a pricking . . . as though they were full of fleas and gnats . . . and this he will suffer for many hours . . ." Felix went so far as to take some of the water into his mouth; the effect, he says, was that of boiling water.[24] All told, the Friar's description agrees not too ill with that of the modern traveler who said that the taste was like sea water mixed with Epsom salts and quinine, that it acted on the eyes as pungently as smoke, and that it produced upon the skin a sensation resembling that of prickly heat.

The pilgrims were allowed no longer stay, for the escort "with loud shouts" were urging them to come away, and they, looking about at the surrounding desolation of salt-white rocks and stones by the shore, and beyond ground "black . . . as though it had been burned up with a devouring fire," were not sorry to turn their backs on that place of wrath.

They had hoped to spend the night in those ruins which were commonly known, though Felix was critical of the identification, as the monastery of St. Jerome. They did manage to explore the buildings, and to see and admire the wall paintings in what had been the church; but according to the Friar, the place offered three disadvantages as a camping ground: the smell of the Dead Sea could still be detected here, there were scorpions among the stones, and the ruins harbored a great company of bats, which, the pilgrims had been warned, were in the habit of biting off the noses of visitors and flying away with their prey. "Men who have long noses are in greater danger than others." The pilgrims kept their hands over their noses while they explored the buildings, but to protect them while sleeping presented more difficulty. The party, therefore, mounted again and rode away, over wide, dull flats toward the hills, reaching, a little before midnight, a safe place at the head of a valley. Then, having supped, "where each man sat down to eat, there he lay down to sleep, and there we slept till morning in our clothes as we were, save only that we took off our gaiters and shoes." [25]

In addition to these excursions which Felix shared with all the pilgrims, he was able, like Brother Paul, to accompany the Franciscans in their rounds of the Holy Places outside Jerusalem. On the Feast of the Transfiguration he went up with them to the Church of the Ascension on the Mount of Olives. After Mass a variety of interesting sights offered themselves: the church itself; a view "as far as the Dead

Sea, and far and wide over the Holy Land"; and the curious and amusing spectacle of eastern Christians at one of their superstitious practices. For in the church a group of these men were, with laughter, trying to embrace one of the polished marble columns so that the fingers of one hand might touch those of the other, a feat which these "super-stitious Easterns" believed to promise great good luck, but "unless a man has rather long fingers, he cannot touch one hand with the other . . . After them we Westerns played the same in jest . . . and I was just able to join the tips of my two longest fingers with a strong hugging and pres-sure." [26] The eve of the Assumption was likewise celebrated by the convent. A tent, roofed and hung with tapestries, was carried to the place of the Dormition,* an altar set up with "costly stuffs . . . paintings, images, monstrances, and . . . candles," and boughs of palm and olive, grass and flowers strewn till the place was "a beauteous holy grove." The sound of complin sung in the open there attracted both Sara-cens, who looked on openmouthed, and eastern Christians who pressed in and followed up the Latin rite with a service of their own. These competitive observances were prolonged throughout the night at the Church of the Sepulcher of the Blessed Virgin outside the walls, with great satisfaction to Felix who was convinced that "no place was more beauti-fully adorned than ours, nor was any singing more solemn"; besides being solemn it was so loud "that the voices and howls of the other Christians were not heard." [27]

But in addition to his share in the liturgical excursions of the friars, Felix was able, in their select ecclesiastical com-pany—a reverence of parsons indeed—to enjoy an expe-dition in which the lay pilgrims did not participate. Gregari-ous though he was, and friendly toward all, an opportunity of escape from lay society was as great a relief to him as to a fourth form master at a boarding school are the intervals

---

* The Church of the Dormition is on Mount Sion and is the supposed site of the house of the Blessed Virgin in which she died.

when he can smoke a pipe in the company of his colleagues and contemporaries. So, the Friar, having a great desire to be alone at Bethlehem, permission was obtained from the Father Guardian, and he slipped away with two of the Franciscan brethren. The secrecy of the expedition, the congenial society, the freedom to explore, all made it a memorable occasion. This time he could turn aside to see a village not usually included in the Bethlehem pilgrimage but interesting to Felix because mentioned in the Old Testament—"to the best of my ability, I passed by no place known to me from the . . . Scripture without visiting it." Not only did the village possess biblical associations but it was remarkable for its wine. "I never," says Felix, "remember to have drunk better wine." 28

At Bethlehem that night, sleepless with excitement, Felix was able to make his way, by a door luckily left unlocked, into the Chapel of the Nativity itself, and to keep vigil there; it was an experience that moved him deeply. Morning Mass was followed by an expedition to the Church of the Shepherds, and a tour of the village during which he "scanned it narrowly." After dinner he and his two companions rode out on hired donkeys through "such lovely country that I have not seen its like throughout all the Holy Land," among fruit trees of every kind, and by the side of the little rill which watered the place, and so to the three great pools, known as the Pools of Solomon. Here they came unexpectedly upon the workmen, "architects, clerks of the works, overseers, and masters," employed upon the great irrigation undertaking of the Sultan Qâ'it Bey, an interesting but slightly unnerving encounter, for Felix had no safe-conduct; it was therefore thought best to make an unostentatious but prompt withdrawal.29

Another morning, after long hours of vigil in the Church of the Holy Sepulcher, Felix conceived the idea of an impromptu expedition. He approached three young friars, who also had watched all night in the church, with the suggestion of an outing in the Valley of Jehosaphat. They were willing, provided the visitor would make it all right with their Superior. So the three "went down into the street of the cooks, wherein I bought," says Felix, "for the brethren and for myself, pastry made with eggs, cakes, meat pies, roasted meat, bunches of grapes, and figs. With these provisions we went down into the valley, crossed the brook to the farm . . . and there sat down in the shade under the olive-trees, and breakfasted merrily together." [30] The place of this merry breakfast was the Garden of Gethsemane.

Yet even in such expeditions Felix did not reach the highest pitch of enjoyment of which he was capable, for he was one of those sociable individuals who yet find them-selves, on occasion, the best company of all. So that chapter of the *Evagatorium* which is headed "F.F.F.'s Lovely Pil-grimage" is the account of another excursion undertaken on a moment's impulse, but this time alone.

The impulse came to him as he stood, after matins, "in the upper walk of the cloister . . . as the day was breaking. While I gazed down into the Valley of Gehinnon, I was seized with a longing to go that very morning so far down the valley that I should no longer be able to see the Mount Sion . . ." If that were a mere whim it was easy to find a serious pretext—the positions of "the well of En Rogel" and of "the stone Zoheleth" needed investigation. "And thence I might go yet further down the valley, and see whether the brook Cedron [Kidron] hath running water in it in the lower ground . . . After this I might climb up the Mount of Offence . . ."

He thought to ask of the Father Guardian a companion from among the friars, but refrained, for "I did not dare to awaken that venerable man, who was still asleep." It was therefore alone, and a little fearful, that he set off, comfort-ing himself with the thought that the Saracens would not leave their beds till the sun rose, and by that time he would be far from the city.

Being the man he was he did not go far without breaking his fast upon some most excellent, ripe figs which he found in a garden below Mount Sion, while the fountain of Siloam in its rocky cleft provided him with a drink, as well as the refreshment of a wash. Then down he went again, following the course of the Kidron, the only man awake and abroad in the young day, for "the sun had now risen, and was shining on the tops of the mountains, but where I was it was still partly dark, and dripping with morning dew."

He reached the point which had been his first object to attain, for as the valley turned he at last lost sight of Mount Sion. Next there was the course of the Kidron to investigate; did it here, as some said, run underground? When he had satisfied himself that the bed of the brook was quite dry, he began to search for the well and the stone, but found neither, "only a cistern and many rocks." Leaving these problems unsolved he climbed the Mount of Offense where, among other historical associations, he recalled the tradition that in this place Solomon built a house for his concubines. Felix was ready to accept the supposition as probable; if the " 'threescore queens and fourscore concubines, and virgins without number' " of the Song of Solomon are to be taken literally, "without any spiritual meaning, he must needs," the Friar considered, "have had many houses for so many women." From the mountain Felix came down again "at a quick pace," to the "Pyramid of Jehosaphat" in the valley, which he examined "with great care . . . climbing in through the window," not from idle curiosity but in the interests of biblical archaeology, in order to decide for himself if he could accept the theory which identified it with Absolom's pillar.

That was the end of the Friar's happy and solitary excursion; "when I had seen these things, I crossed over the brook Cedron, went up to the Mount Sion, and came in to dinner full of sweat and in a burning heat." And he adds with some pride, "when the Father Guardian and the brethren heard that I had visited all those places unmolested, they were astonished." [31]

The last two days of the pilgrims' stay in Jerusalem came, and preparations for the journey took the place of sight-seeing. We shall not now inquire into these preparations, which belong to the account of the desert journey, except in so far as they were concerned with the collection and disposal of those sacred relics and secular mementos which, carried through the desert upon camels, overseas in the hold of a ship, and upon horseback across the Alps, would be at last unpacked and displayed to the wondering, awe-struck, or delighted eyes of the pilgrims' friends.

Many pilgrims, doubtless, had like Felix brought with them rings and other jewelry, whether their own or not, to lay upon the Holy Places, but rich men took pleasure also in buying such articles in Jerusalem, thus obtaining not only a ring or an ornament which had touched the sepulcher or the rock of Calvary, but one which was of fine and curious foreign workmanship. So, in de Caumont's luggage traveled home to France a large collection of pretty and costly objects, including a whole batch of thirty-three silver rings, and six rings of scarlet chalcedony, good for stanching blood, all of which had been laid upon the sepulcher.[32]

These were a layman's purchases. Priests like Felix and William Wey, remembering their brethren and the convent at home, looked for things of another sort, and Jerusalem, like any great tourist center used to catering for the taste of visitors, was able to provide these also. Felix bought "three costly cloths for our sacristy, wherewith to cover the chalice . . . one of these cloths is white, another blue, and the third yellow." [33] William Wey brought back with him, and at his death bequeathed to the monastery at Edington, a greater and more curious assortment of mementos, for there were curtains of blue buckram and cloth "stained" (i.e., painted) with the Temple of Jerusalem, the Mount of

Olives, and Bethlehem; there was "a crucifix in paper closed with boards"; leaves of parchment with pictures of the temple and Mount of Olives; a whole quire of paper "with the painting of Our Lord his Passion"; there were wooden models of the Chapel of Calvary, the Church of Bethlehem, and more curious, of the Mount of Olives and the Valley of Jehosaphat.[34]

Both lay and ecclesiastical pilgrims had a fancy for taking home with them articles which recorded the measurements of some or all of the Holy Places. For de Caumont these took the form of "girdles of silk and gold thread with the measurements of the Holy Sepulcher." [35] "Behind the choir" in the church at Edington was to be found a priest's version of this type of memento in "a board" containing "the length of our Lord his sepulcher, with the height of the door, the breadth of the door, the length of our Lord his foot, the deepness of the mortise of the cross, and the roundness of the same," brought home by William Wey.[36] Even a poor or miserly pilgrim could afford to follow the example of John Poloner, who paced the distances between the Holy Places "with the greatest care I could," [37] or of Margery Kempe, who gave as something worth giving to her host in Italy, "the measure of Christ's grave." [38]

Actual relics were, of course, most desirable acquisitions. In 1506 the pilgrims were entertained by the Franciscans to "a right honest dinner" in the cloister, just before their departure. After dinner in came "a basin full of folded papers with relics in each of them" which were distributed among the guests.[39] What these relics were we do not know, but since they were presented by the Franciscans themselves they can hardly have included those chippings from the Holy Places which the pilgrims were warned that they must on no account appropriate.

That warning was first given at Ramle, and repeated at Jerusalem. But in spite of exhortations, in spite of the unpleasant consequences in which a relic hunter might involve both himself and his companions,[40] and in spite of precautions taken to safeguard the holy objects, precious and venerated fragments of the Holy Places of Christian worship did go homeward in the luggage of the pilgrims. In the Franciscan convent that "part of the pillar at which Christ was scourged" was "made fast to the wall by iron bars," but William Wey took back with him a piece of it, as well as "a stone of the Mount Calvary, a stone of the Sepulcher." [41] The Armenian priests kept a lynx eye upon their share of the stone which was rolled to the door of the sepulcher, but one of their number smuggled into the church a German knight who shared Felix's first visit to Jerusalem, in order that he might help himself to a piece.

There was no embargo, from the Christian side, upon nails or pieces of the copper sheathing of the Golden Gate. If a pilgrim chose to run the risk, he might take what he could find of such things; von Harff, who as we have seen appropriated some of these relics when let into the Dome of the Rock, reported the gate as much cut about, doubtless by earlier collectors, or by the Moslems who were willing to trade bits of the desired commodities to the more cautious among the pilgrims.[42]

The eagerness with which the pilgrims sought many of the relics was due not only to the sanctity of these, but to their reputed curative and protective properties. Roses from Jericho were said to be of assistance to barren women; [43] reeds from St. Catherine's fountain at Sinai to women in labor; [44] a piece of stone from the Church of St. Anne in Jerusalem to pregnant women.[45] Water from Jordan had many remarkable properties which not only made it desirable for use at baptism, but which also created a demand for it among "warlocks and witches." [46]

German knights had a keen, and according to Felix, a special interest in relics of the Holy Innocents; ". . . in our company an exceeding rich nobleman," having failed to discover any such among the dust of the cave at Bethle-

hem, approached the greater Calinus with an offer of 100
ducats for an entire body. When he learnt that the sultan
reserved to himself the monopoly of these, so great was the
German's desire to acquire one that he even considered
making the Sinai pilgrimage in order that "he might buy a
child when he came to Cairo."

Felix himself did not "set much value upon new relics
. . . especially those which have been bought from Saracens or from eastern Christians . . ." and in this matter of
the Holy Innocents had such grave doubts that he made
inquiries—we may guess of his friend Elphahallo—and
learnt that the Saracens of Egypt did a brisk trade in fakes
of this particular class of relics. Dead bodies of young or
stillborn children were procured, then "Saracens and Mamelukes . . . slash them with knives . . . embalm the bodies
. . . and sell them to Christian kings, princes, and wealthy
people . . ." [47]

The Friar's own selection of relics was irreproachable,
with the possible exception of that piece of the stone of the
sepulcher mentioned above, which its owner, dying during
the voyage home, bequeathed to him.[48] The rest, which he
collected for himself, were of a different kind. Two days
before the pilgrims were to leave Jerusalem, he "rose early
before sunrise, and having said matins . . . stole out of the
convent alone." His purpose was twofold; he wished to take
a last look at the Holy Places round about Mount Sion, in
the Valley of Jehosaphat, and on the Mount of Olives. But
besides that "in each of these places I picked up pebbles,
marked them, and put them into a bag which I carried with
me . . . Moreover, I gathered some of the thorns which
grow in the hedges on the side of the Mount of Olives and
of the Mount Sion, and I bound twigs of them together, and
wove them into a crown of thorns . . ." All the hot day
he labored, "picking up little stones at the holy places," and
on the way back bought to contain them that "oblong basket," the safe passage of which with its contents through

the customs of Egypt was to cause him much anxiety.[49]

In addition to all these objects, whether secular in their character but sanctified by contact with the Holy Places or commemorating these pictorially or surreptitiously detached from or harmlessly gathered at them, the lay pilgrims took home with them, unless de Caumont is an exception, a variety of articles of the kind that any tourist may bring home with him from foreign travel. The Gascon knight, young, rich, and noble, brought back with him gifts "for my wife, and for the lords and dames of my country," the inventory of which fills a number of pages, and consists of thirty-five articles, many of them collective. In the hutch (i.e., the raised chest) of cypress wood, the three chests of cypress wood, and the two chests of painted wood were packed—as well as the rings which had touched the sepulcher, as well as bits of the Golden Gate and of the manger at Bethlehem, and a bottle of Jordan water—lengths of red damask, of cloth of gold, of black camlet, of white satin; rosaries of ivory and of black musk; purses of silk and gold thread; gloves of white deerskin; birds of Cyprus to perfume the house; * with so many other charming things that the reader is tempted to wonder whether the devout young sire de Caumont did not spend part of his time in the Church of the Holy Sepulcher bargaining with the merchants there.[50]

Livestock was occasionally picked up and taken home by the pilgrims. We have already noticed the parrot, which caused much embarrassment to its owner upon Casola's return journey. Henry of Lancaster, Earl of Derby, took back another parrot, whose cage with its hook and cord are duly

---

* Or perhaps "birds of Chypre." These were objects made in the shape of birds and covered with feathers and filled with sweet-scented gums or powders. "Poudre de Chypre" was composed of orrisroot, musk, and civet. The "birds" were sometimes provided with cages of gold or silver wire. V. Gay, *Glossaire Archéologique du Moyen Age* (Paris, 1928), p. 169, under "oiselets de Chypre," and H. Havard, *Dictionnaire de l'Ameublement* (Paris, 1887–90), III, 1032, under "oiseau."

noted among other items of the earl's household expenditure, but which miscarried, in some mysterious way, during the journey home and never reached England.[51] The earl also acquired a leopard, for whose transport considerable preparation was needed; a "caban" had to be made for it, a "matte" bought, and during the voyage generous rations of meat were drawn for it.

Nor was it only in the Holy Land that the pilgrims collected their strange assortment of souvenirs. Felix and his companions were to amass and to smuggle through the Egyptian customs many things acquired in Egypt. Henry of Lancaster, not content with his parrot and leopard, carried home from Rhodes a human trophy, a converted Saracen, whom the earl caused to be baptized with his own name, and provided with a pilgrim's gown and a pair of shoes.[52] From Rhodes too in 1494, the noble Captain Agostino Contarini carried away, as a relic of the siege, a stone bombard ball. On the same voyage Casola condescended, while at Crete, to follow the example of the other pilgrims and, half disdainfully, one imagines, to lay out a few ducats on "work done in cypress wood, and . . . articles of devotion painted in the ancient style." [53]

On August 23 the pilgrims met while it was still dark outside the Church of the Holy Sepulcher, having determined overnight "to make one last general round of all the holy places in Jerusalem and its neighbourhood." They accomplished their task, taking the Holy Places in the city, the Valley of Jehosaphat, and the Mount of Olives before dinner, and spending the afternoon in a tour of the Valley of Siloam, Mount Gihon "and . . . Mount Sion above and below." The reader will not be surprised to learn that all this was done only "by working very hard." [54] At night, fatigued but indomitable, they entered the Church of the Holy Sepulcher for the last of all their vigils there. When they came out next morning the dragoman, donkeys, and camels were waiting at the Franciscan house to begin the first stage of the desert journey.

But here, for the time at least, we must leave Brother Felix, concluding with the words which he used to conclude the first part of his book:

## "DEO SIT LAUS.

Finit peregrinatio Iherosolymitana."

# Notes

## Chapter 1

The spellings but not the words of all quotations from English sources of the fifteenth and sixteenth centuries have been modernized.

1. Haeberlin, *Dissertatio*, p. 2.
2. Fabri, *Wanderings*, VIII, 615. (Hereafter referred to as Fabri.)
3. Haeberlin, pp. 3–6.
4. Fabri, *Tractatus de civitate Uemensi*.
5. Haeberlin, pp. 5–30.
6. Fabri, *Evagatorium*, I, 4.
7. La Brocquière, p. 32.
8. Heyd, II, 464–465.
9. *Ibid.*, pp. 460–461.
10. Newett, *Casola*, p. 358, n. 17.
11. *Ibid.*
12. Kempe, pp. 9–10.
13. *Ibid.*, p. 25.
14. *Ibid.*, p. 9.
15. *Ibid.*, pp. 35–36.
16. *Ibid.*, p. 67.
17. *Ibid.*, pp. 105, 69.
18. *Ibid.*, p. 201.
19. *Ibid.*, p. 181.
20. Caumont, p. 19.
21. *Ibid.*, p. vi.
22. *Casola*, Introd., p. 53.
23. Lannoy, ed. Potvin, p. 51.
24. *Ibid.*, p. 67.
25. *Ibid.*, p. 99 n.
26. *Voyage de la Saincte Cyté*, pp. 63 n., 71; cf. p. 81.
27. "Advis directif pour faire le passage d'oultre-mer par le frère Brochart," *Monuments pour servir à l'histoire des provinces de Namur, de Hainaut et de Luxembourg* (Brussels, 1846), IV, 227.
28. La Brocquière, p. 63.
29. *Ibid.*, pp. 60–62.
30. Rochechouart, p. 177.
31. *Ibid.*, pp. 177–178.
32. *Ibid.*, p. 246.
33. *Ibid.*, p. 242.
34. *Ibid.*, p. 238.

35. *Ibid.*, p. 266.
36. *Ibid.*, p. 270.
37. Wey, Introd., I, i.
38. *Ibid.*, pp. 155–156.
39. *Voyage de la Saincte Cyté*, pp. 2, 6.
40. *Ibid.*, pp. 22, 47.
41. Brasca [f. 43b].
42. *Ibid.* [f. 48b].
43. Davies, *Bernhard von Breydenbach*, Introd., p. ii n.
44. Fabri, VII, 431. Cf. *ibid.*, VIII, 629.
45. Walther, pp. 1–2.
46. *Ibid.*, p. 32.
47. *Ibid.*, pp. 151–152.
48. *Ibid.*, p. 196.
49. *Ibid.*, pp. 157–160.
50. *Ibid.*, p. 248.
51. *Ibid.*, p. 23. "Appropinquantibus autem nos terminis Mantuanis."
52. This "terrible spirit" appears to have played the deuce with the Friar's Latin. The sentence runs: "Irruit in me spiritus terrens, stans motus, expectans socium."
53. *Ibid.*, pp. 24–26.
54. *Casola*, p. 230.
55. *Ibid.*, p. 261.
56. *Ibid.*, p. 154.
57. *Ibid.*, p. 285.
58. *Ibid.*, p. 137.
59. *Ibid.*, p. 135.
60. *Ibid.*, p. 166.
61. *Ibid.*, pp. 251–253.
62. *Ibid.*, p. 249.
63. Harff, pp. 173, 167.

## Chapter II

1. *Evag.*, I, 25–26.
2. *Ibid.*, p. 26.
3. *Ibid.*, p. 27.
4. Wey, I, 7. Cf. *Informacōn* [f. 12a].
5. *Evag.*, II, 66.
6. *Ibid.*, I, 29–30.
7. *Ibid.*, p. 5.
8. Raynaud, Docs., p. 249.
9. *Casola*, pp. 48–52, 61–62, 73.
10. *Ibid.*, p. 51.
11. *Ibid.*, pp. 23–27, 59. Cf. *Rev. de l'Orient Latin*, *loc. cit.*, pp. 246–247.
12. *Casola*, pp. 41, 26–27.

13. *Rev. de l'Orient Latin, loc. cit.*, pp. 238–239. 1302 here is obviously, I think, an error for 1392.

14. *Expedition of Henry Earl of Derby*, pp. 278–279.

15. *Casola*, pp. 35, 46–47.

16. *Ibid.*, p. 95. But Felix Fabri seems to have paid the full fare.

17. *Ibid.*, pp. 66, 48.

18. *Ibid.*, pp. 99–100. Cf. Wey, I, 98, and *Informacōn* [f. 9b].

19. *Casola*, p. 94.

20. *Informacōn* [f. 9b]. *Casola*, pp. 153–154.

21. Wey, I, 4. Fabri, VII, 88.

22. Fabri, VII, 88–89.

23. *Ibid.*, pp. 87–90. Breydenbach's contract [ff. 8a–9a] follows much the same form with the addition of a clause concerning the carrying of an interpreter.

24. *Casola*, pp. 58, 69.

25. *Voyage de la Saincte Cyté*, p. 24.

26. *Ibid.*, p. 66.

27. *Ibid.*, pp. 99–101.

28. *Ibid.*, p. 104.

29. *Casola*, pp. 295, 317.

30. Fabri, VII, 97.

31. *Excerpta Cypria*, p. 18.

32. *Voyage de la Saincte Cyté*, p. 25.

33. *Informacōn* [f. 12a].

34. *Ibid.* [f. 11b].

35. *Voyage de la Saincte Cyté, loc. cit.*

36. *Ibid.*

37. *Informacōn* [f. 11a].

38. Brasca [f. 49a].

39. *Informacōn* [ff. 9a–9b].

40. *Casola*, p. 12. The author thus translates Brasca's "qualchi boni lactuarii." The translation quoted above, "aromatics flavoured with rose and carnation," is also hers, from Brasca's "aromatici arosati e garifolati." But if garifolati means cloves and not carnations, the items mentioned would seem to be spices rather than perfumes, and certainly they occur in a list of eatables.

41. *Informacōn* [f. 11b].

42. Brasca, *loc. cit.*

43. Harff, p. 71.

44. *Voyage de la Saincte Cyté*, pp. 11–16, 22.

45. Fabri, VII, 11.

46. *Voyage de la Saincte Cyté*, p. 29.

47. Fabri, VII, 125–137. *Casola*, pp. 155–160.

48. Lane, pp. 9–10. Of the 120-pound oar only one third was inboard, and this was weighted with lead to give balance. The rowers mounted on "low sets of steps" in front of the thwarts in order to put their oars in the water.

49. *Casola*, p. 158. Fabri, VII, 153–154.

50. Fabri, VII, 152–153.
51. *Ibid.*, pp. 150–151. Cf. Brasca [f. 61a].
52. Fabri, VII, 158–162.
53. *Ibid.*, pp. 154–156, 160.
54. *Ibid.*, p. 180.
55. *Ibid.*, pp. 13–14.
56. *Voyage de la Saincte Cyté*, pp. 35–36.
57. *Ibid.*, p. 42. Cf. Fabri, VII, 21. The former says that twenty pilgrims turned back. Fabri has forty.
58. *Evag.*, I, 38, which reads "ita disposuimus nos ad recessum, introferentes in galeam ea, quae emeramus." The translator of Fabri, VII, 19, gives this as "we made ready to start, removing ourselves into another galley which we had bought." It is clear however from the *Voyage de la Saincte Cyté*, pp. 42–43, that the pilgrims continued their journey in the galley of Contarini.
59. Fabri, VII, 259.
60. *Evag.*, I, 41. Cf. *Voyage de la Saincte Cyté*, pp. 59, 101.
61. *Evag.*, III, 242–243.
62. *Voyage de la Saincte Cyté*, p. 104. Fabri, VII, 24.
63. *Evag.*, I, 45–46. Fabri, VII, 28–29.
64. *Evag.*, I, 48. Fabri, VII, 32–33.
65. *Evag.*, I, 49–50. Fabri, VII, 34–35.
66. Fabri, VII, 37.
67. *Voyage de la Saincte Cyté*, p. 116.
68. Fabri, VII, 44–46. Felix says "the feast of St. Othmar," i.e., November 16; not, I think, as in the translator's note, October 25, which date is that of the translation of the saint and would not allow for the fifteen days Felix spent in bed at Venice.

## Chapter III

1. Fabri, VII, 49–50.
2. *Evag.*, I, 2.
3. Fabri, *loc. cit.*
4. *Evag.*, *loc. cit.*
5. Ludolphus, p. 9. Fabri, VII, 115.
6. Fabri, VII, 125. Ludolphus, p. 15.
7. Ludolphus, p. 17.
8. *Ibid.*, p. 19.
9. Newton (ed.), *Travel and Travellers*, pp. 6–13.
10. *Ibid.*, pp. 17–18.
11. Kimble, p. 220.
12. Fabri, VIII, 376.
13. *Ibid.*, pp. 168, 204.
14. *Evag.*, I, 3.
15. Fabri, I, 110.
16. Kimble, p. 183.

17. *Ibid.*, p. 240.
18. *Ibid.*, pp. 200–203.
19. Poloner, p. 26.
20. Wey, Vol. II (map).
21. Kimble, pp. 140–141. Beazley, III, 9, 512.
22. Beazley, III, 513. Kimble, p. 193.
23. Fabri, VII, 135.
24. *Evag.*, I, 65. Fabri, VII, 53–54. Where "cappam" is translated "cap." Fabri, IX, 178.
25. Fabri, VII, 56.
26. *Ibid.*, pp. 70–71.
27. *Ibid.*, p. 75.
28. *Ibid.*, p. 77.
29. Walther, p. 30. Torkington, p. 6.
30. Fabri, VII, 79.
31. Harff, p. 51.
32. Fabri, VII, 79–81.
33. *Ibid.*, p. 84.
34. Torkington, pp. 7–8.
35. Fabri, VII, 91.
36. *Ibid.*, pp. 92–93.
37. *Ibid.*, p. 99.
38. Torkington, p. 13.
39. *Casola*, pp. 146–152. Fabri, I, 108–109. *Voyage de la Saincte Cyté*, p. 23.
40. Walther, pp. 58–59.
41. *Ibid.*, pp. 54–55. Fabri, I, 100.
42. Harff, pp. 60–61.
43. *Casola*, p. 142.
44. Fabri, VII, 95–96. Felix does not mention by name that "one of their captains" whom the Venetians wished to honor by this statue, but the date, and his remark that though the artist had been chosen, the casting was not yet begun, make it, I think, almost certain that he refers to the Colleone statue.
45. *Casola*, p. 131.
46. *Ibid.*, p. 129.
47. Harff, p. 51.
48. Walther, p. 51.
49. *Casola*, p. 145.
50. *Evag.*, III, 433.
51. Harff, p. 65.
52. *Casola*, pp. 339–340.
53. Fabri, VII, 107, 111.
54. *Ibid.*, pp. 164–166.
55. *Ibid.*, p. 168.

## Chapter IV

1. Röhricht, pp. 163–164, 82 n., 376.
2. *Evag.*, I, 85. Fabri, VII, 81–82. Where "Johannes dictus Schmidhans, armiger" is translated "John surnamed Schmidhans, a man-at-arms."
3. *Evag.*, III, 172–173.
4. *Ibid.*, I, 169. Fabri, VII, 190.
5. Fabri, VII, 166–167.
6. *Ibid.*, pp. 180–181.
7. *Evag.*, I, 139–140.
8. Fabri, VII, 176–177.
9. *Ibid.*, pp. 174–175.
10. *Ibid.*, p. 82.
11. *Ibid.*, p. 134.
12. *Ibid.*, p. 185.
13. *Ibid.*, pp. 186–187.
14. *Ibid.*, p. 188.
15. *Ibid.*, pp. 190, 201.
16. *Ibid.*, p. 191.
17. *Ibid.*, p. 194. But I quote from C. D. Cobham's translation, *Excerpta Cypria*, p. 38.
18. Fabri, VII, 194–195.
19. *Ibid.*, pp. 195–200.
20. *Ibid.*, pp. 203–204.
21. *Ibid.*, pp. 207–210, 212.
22. "Un Pèlerinage," p. 72.
23. *Ibid.*, p. 80.
24. Fabri, VII, 202.
25. Lannoy, ed. Potvin, p. 140. Cf. *Archaeologia*, XXI, 412–413, and La Brocquière, p. 10. Lannoy speaks of a good anchorage four (Potvin) or three (*Arch.*) miles out. But from what Felix and Walther say, it would seem that on this occasion the galleys lay nearer in.
26. Fabri, VII, 218.
27. *Casola*, p. 226.
28. *Voyage de la Saincte Cyté*, pp. 58–59.
29. Fabri, VII, 222. Brasca [f. 49a].
30. "Un Pèlerinage," *loc. cit.*
31. Guylforde, p. 16. Cf. *Casola*, pp. 234–235.
32. Fabri, VII, 226–227.
33. *Ibid.*, p. 234.
34. Breydenbach [f. 26a].
35. Fabri, VII, 232.
36. Walther, p. 98.
37. *Ibid.*, p. 99.
38. Fabri, VII, 240–243.
39. *Casola*, p. 236.
40. Fabri, VII, 246. Cf. La Brocquière, pp. 32–33, and *Casola*, p. 237, who

thought that they were dismounted in order to pass a Moslem burial ground.

41. *Casola*, p. 238. Cf. Walther, p. 104. Fabri, VII, 246.

42. Fabri, VII, 248–255. Felix recites no less than twenty-seven articles of this exhortation. Von Breydenbach [f. 27a], gives five, of which one is the same as the first in Felix's list, 2–4 are exhortations to devotion, and only the fifth touches on the interesting topic of behavior toward Moslems, in a warning against treading upon Moslem graves.

43. Fabri, VII, 255. Cf. *Casola*, p. 238.

44. Fabri, VII, 258–259.

45. *Ibid.*, p. 265.

46. *Ibid.*, p. 266.

47. *Ibid.*, p. 268.

48. Cf. Lannoy, ed. Potvin, p. 142.

49. Fabri, VII, 280.

50. *Ibid.*, p. 281.

## Chapter V

1. Fabri, VII, 283–284.

2. *Ibid.*, IX, 60.

3. *Casola*, pp. 244–245. Ludolphus, p. 106.

4. "Un Pèlerinage," p. 81.

5. *Casola, loc. cit.*

6. Fabri, VII, 285.

7. *Ibid.*, p. 397.

8. Brasca [f. 14a].

9. Fabri, IX, 102.

10. *Casola*, Introd., pp. 96–98, 244.

11. Harff, p. 192.

12. Walther, pp. 309–310.

13. *Ibid.*

14. Fabri, VII, 311.

15. *Ibid.*, p. 201.

16. Walther, p. 149.

17. Fabri, VII, 287, 299, 300, 305–306, 311.

18. *Voyage de la Saincte Cyté*, p. 59 n.

19. *Casola*, pp. 244–245, 384–385, n. 76.

20. *Voyage de la Saincte Cyté*, p. 81 n.

21. Walther, p. 137 n.

22. Fabri, VIII, 606–607. Walther, pp. 127–128 n.

23. Walther, pp. 123–124.

24. Fabri, VII, 299.

25. *Ibid.*, p. 366.

26. *Casola*, pp. 258, 249, 271.

27. Fabri, VIII, 439–440. *Ibid.*, IX, 117.

28. *Ibid.*, VII, 292.

29. *Ibid.*, p. 290. Cf. Brasca *passim.*
30. Fabri, VII, 297.
31. Harff, p. 193.
32. Fabri, VII, 304.
33. *Ibid.*, p. 308.
34. *Ibid.*, VIII, 333–335.
35. *Voyage de la Saincte Cyté*, p. 76.
36. Fabri, IX, 137–138. Cf. Harff, p. 205.
37. Fabri, VIII, 444–445. Cf. Harff, p. 206.
38. Rochechouart, p. 243.
39. Fabri, VIII, 466.
40. *Ibid.*, pp. 465–469.
41. *Ibid.*, pp. 492–493.
42. *Ibid.*, p. 524.
43. *Ibid.*, pp. 527–528.
44. *Ibid.*, pp. 532–533, 537–538.
45. Rochechouart, p. 241. *Casola*, p. 259.
46. Fabri, VIII, 340–341. *Casola*, p. 258.
47. Fabri, VIII, 424–426. *Casola*, p. 276.
48. Fabri, VIII, 342–346.
49. Rochechouart, p. 251.
50. Fabri, VIII, 365. Breydenbach [f. 30a].
51. Fabri, VIII, 404, 407–410. Cf. Brasca's plan [f. 58b]. *Casola*, p. 277. Rochechouart, pp. 252–253. Harff, p. 201.
52. Fabri, VIII, 414–415.
53. *Ibid.*, p. 386.
54. Caumont, pp. 50–52.
55. Fabri, VIII, 609.
56. Harff, p. 202.
57. Guylforde, p. 41.
58. Fabri, VIII, 346, 383.
59. *Ibid.*, p. 430.
60. *Casola*, pp. 278, 392, n. 87.
61. Fabri, VIII, 429. Walther, p. 143.
62. Fabri, IX, 84–85.
63. *Ibid.*, pp. 86–88.

## Chapter VI

1. *Voyage de la Saincte Cyté*, pp. 82–83. Fabri, VII, 48.
2. *Casola*, p. 262.
3. Fabri, VIII, 548.
4. *Ibid.*, pp. 549–551.
5. *Ibid.*, pp. 600–602. *Voyage de la Saincte Cyté*, p. 81.
6. Fabri, *loc. cit.*
7. Rochechouart, pp. 259–260.
8. *Casola*, p. 263.

9. Guylforde, p. 36.
10. Fabri, VIII, 560–561.
11. *Ibid.*, p. 565.
12. *Ibid.*, p. 552.
13. *Ibid.*, p. 575.
14. *Ibid.*
15. *Ibid.*, pp. 630–632.
16. *Ibid.*, pp. 637–638.
17. *Ibid.*, p. 641.
18. *Ibid.*, IX, 1–2.
19. *Ibid.*, p. 5. *Voyage de la Saincte Cyté*, pp. 86–88.
20. *Voyage de la Saincte Cyté*, p. 87 n.
21. Walther, pp. 146–148. Cf. Harff, p. 222.
22. Brasca [f. 38a].
23. Walther, p. 121.
24. *Casola*, pp. 266–267.
25. *Ibid.*, p. 266.
26. Fabri, IX, 6.
27. *Ibid.*, pp. 10–11.
28. Harff, p. 222.
29. Brasca [f. 40a].
30. Cf. Anglure, p. 36.
31. Walther, p. 120. Whose "balliantes" I take to be a misspelling of "baliantes." *Casola*, p. 268.
32. Walther, *loc. cit.*
33. Fabri, IX, 14–18.
34. *Ibid.*, p. 19.
35. *Ibid.*, p. 20. *Voyage de la Saincte Cyté*, p. 102.
36. *Casola*, p. 268.
37. Fabri, IX, 32–33.
38. *Casola*, p. 268.
39. Fabri, IX, 41–43.
40. *Ibid.*, pp. 44–45. Cf. *Voyage de la Saincte Cyté*, p. 91.
41. *Evag.*, II, 61. Fabri, IX, 45.
42. Fabri, IX, 48-49. Cf. *Voyage de la Saincte Cyté*, p. 91. Anglure, p. 38. *Casola*, p. 269. Walther, p. 121. Harff, p. 225.
43. Fabri, IX, 53–65.
44. *Ibid.*, p. 69.
45. *Ibid.*, p. 81.
46. *Ibid.*, pp. 30–32.
47. *Ibid.*, VIII, 400, 532. Rochechouart, p. 253.
48. Fabri, IX, 10.
49. *Ibid.*, VIII, 356.
50. *Ibid.*, p. 372. Ludolphus, pp. 103–104.
51. *Casola*, p. 276.
52. Fabri, VIII, 394.
53. *Ibid.*, IX, 248–249.

54. *Evag.*, II, 152. Fabri, IX, 161.
55. Walther, pp. 137–138.

## Chapter VII

1. Lannoy, ed. Potvin, p. 143. *Archaeologia*, p. 337. Brasca [f. 14b].
2. *Casola*, p. 251.
3. Fabri, IX, 225.
4. *Ibid.*, p. 226.
5. Lannoy, ed. Potvin, p. 142.
6. Fabri, IX, 226.
7. Brasca [f. 14b].
8. *Casola*, p. 251.
9. Brasca, *loc. cit.*
10. Fabri, VIII, 334.
11. Guylforde, pp. 43–44.
12. Fabri, IX, 245. Cf. Guylforde, *loc. cit.*
13. Anglure, p. 20.
14. Fabri, VIII, 496; cf. p. 486.
15. *Ibid.*, IX, 257.
16. *Ibid.*
17. Harff, pp. 208–211.
18. Fabri, IX, 124–125.
19. 'Abd al-Rahmán, pp. 144, 286, n. 3.
20. *Casola*, p. 253.
21. 'Abd al-Rahmán, p. 288.
22. Fabri, IX, 126, 245.
23. *Ibid.*, pp. 243–244.
24. *Ibid.*, p. 126.
25. Brasca [f. 14b]. *Casola*, p. 251.
26. Fabri, IX, 111. Brasca [f. 15b].
27. *Casola*, *loc. cit. Voyage de la Saincte Cyté*, p. 104.
28. Fabri, VII, 261.
29. Brasca [f. 14b].
30. Rochechouart, p. 273. Cf. Brasca [f. 15a].
31. *Casola*, p. 258.
32. La Brocquière, p. 70.
33. Brasca [ff. 14b–15a].
34. Rochechouart, p. 273.
35. Brasca [f. 15a]. Harff, p. 125.
36. Fabri, VII, 243.
37. *Ibid.*, p. 396.
38. *Ibid.*, IX, 206–207.
39. *Ibid.*, pp. 2–3.
40. Harff, pp. 129–132, 129 n.
41. *Evag.*, III, 449.

42. *Burchard of Mount Sion*, pp. 104, 106–107, 102.
43. Rochechouart, pp. 255–257.
44. *Casola*, p. 391, n. 87.
45. Fabri, IX, 156.
46. *Ibid.*, pp. 621–623.
47. Rochechouart, p. 255.
48. Fabri, X, 384.
49. La Brocquière, p. 58.
50. Davies, Introd., p. ix.
51. Fabri, IX, 116.
52. *Ibid.*, p. 245; cf. p. 385.
53. *Voyage de la Saincte Cyté*, p. 67.
54. Fabri, VII, 261–262.
55. *Ibid.*, IX, 249.
56. Rochechouart, p. 273.
57. Fabri, IX, 257.
58. *Ibid.*, VIII, 341.
59. *Ibid.*, IX, 3; cf. *ibid.*, VIII, 550.
60. *Evag.*, III, 97–98.
61. Kempe, p. 75.
62. La Brocquière, pp. 12, 66–67.
63. Rochechouart, p. 247. Cf. Fabri, VII, 300, 303.
64. *Casola*, p. 393, n. 89.
65. *Ibid.*, *loc. cit.*
66. Fabri, VIII, 606–607.
67. *Voyage de la Saincte Cyté*, Introd., pp. xxi–xxiii.
68. Walther, 163–165, 149.
69. Fabri, VIII, 602–603. *Ibid.*, IX, 201.
70. *Casola*, pp. 282–291.
71. Fabri, VII, 249–255.
72. *Ibid.*, p. 264.
73. *Voyage de la Saincte Cyté*, p. 63.
74. Walther, p. 104.
75. *Ibid.*
76. Fabri, IX, 98–99.
77. *Ibid.*, pp. 8–10.
78. *Ibid.*, VIII, 332.
79. Usāmah, pp. 176–177.
80. Kempe, pp. 74–75. Walther, pp. 154–155.
81. Fabri, IX, 132.
82. *Ibid.*, p. 205.
83. *Ibid.*, X, 444.
84. La Brocquière, pp. 63–64, 72.
85. *Evag.*, II, 178. Cf. Fabri, IX, 190–191. But "ipse misertus est mei" must refer to "the Gentile Saracen."
86. Fabri, IX, 105–107.
87. *Evag.*, III, 32.

## Chapter VIII

1. Fabri, IX, 92–93.
2. *Ibid.*, pp. 96–97.
3. Walther, p. 115 n.
4. *Ibid.*
5. *Ibid.*, pp. 171–178.
6. *Ibid.*, p. 186.
7. Fabri, IX, 112–113.
8. *Informacōn* [f. 11b].
9. Fabri, IX, 112–114.
10. La Brocquière, p. 45.
11. Fabri, IX, 109.
12. *Ibid.*, pp. 108–109.
13. *Ibid.*, pp. 117–119.
14. *Ibid.*, p. 130. Cf. Harff, p. 210.
15. Ludolphus, pp. 100–101. Cf. Fabri, IX, 132–135.
16. *Evag.*, II, 194. Fabri, IX, 212.
17. Cf. Harff, pp. 223–224.
18. Fabri, IX, 155–160.
19. *Burchard*, p. 59.
20. Guylforde, p. 53.
21. Fabri, IX, 172.
22. Ludolphus, pp. 116–117.
23. Harff, p. 224.
24. Fabri, IX, 164.
25. *Ibid.*, p. 177.
26. *Ibid.*, p. 137.
27. *Ibid.*, pp. 194–195.
28. *Ibid.*, pp. 195–196.
29. *Ibid.*, pp. 197–199, 202.
30. *Ibid.*, p. 149.
31. *Ibid.*, pp. 138–146.
32. Caumont, pp. 136–139.
33. Fabri, IX, 217.
34. Wey, Introd., I, xxviii–xxx.
35. Caumont, p. 137.
36. Wey, Introd., I, xxx.
37. Poloner, p. 4.
38. Kempe, p. 78.
39. Guylforde, p. 39.
40. Fabri, IX, 90; cf. *Ibid.*, 601.
41. *Ibid.*, VII, 297. Wey, *loc. cit.*
42. Harff, p. 211. Fabri, VIII, 459.
43. Röhricht, p. 22.
44. Fabri, X, 581.
45. Breydenbach [f. 37b].

46. Fabri, IX, 21–22.
47. *Ibid.*, VIII, 566.
48. *Ibid.*, VII, 319.
49. *Ibid.*, IX, 214, 217. *Evag.*, III, 204–205.
50. Caumont, pp. 136–139.
51. *Expedition of Henry Earl of Derby*, pp. 285–287, 292; cf. Introd. p. lxvi n.
52. *Ibid.*, Introd., p. lxvi.
53. *Casola*, p. 317.
54. Fabri, IX, 217.

# Bibliography

### Texts

'Abd al-Rahmán Al 'Alímí (Moudjīr Ed-Dyn). *Histoire de Jérusalem et d'Hébron*. Trans. H. Sauvaire. Paris, 1876.

Anglure, Seigneur d'. *Le Saint Voyage de Jherusalem du . . .* Éds. Bonnardot et Longnon. Société des Anciens Textes Français. Paris, 1878.

Baumgarten, Martin. "The Travels of Martin Baumgarten," *Collection of Voyages and Travels*. Ed. Churchill. London, 1744–46. I, 313–384.

Brasca, Santo. [Viaggio alla sanctissima cità di Ierusalem.] Begin. "Ad Magnificum Dom. Antonium Landrianum . . ." Milan, 1481.

Breydenbach, Bernhard von. *Peregrinatio in Terram Sanctam*. Mainz, 1486.

Burchardus de Monte Sion. *Burchard of Mount Sion*. Trans. Aubrey Stewart. Palestine Pilgrims' Text Society. Vol XII. London, 1896.

Caumont, Seigneur de. *Voyaige d'oultremer en Jhérusalem*. Ed. le marquis de La Grange. Paris, 1858.

*Excerpta Cypria*. Trans. C. D. Cobham. Cambridge University Press, 1908.

*Expeditions to Prussia and the Holy Land by Henry Earl of Derby 1392*. Ed. L. Toulmin Smith. Camden Society, N. S. No. 52. London, 1894.

Fabri, Felix. *Fratris Felicis Fabri Evagatorium in Terrae Sanctae . . .* Ed. C. D. Hassler. Stuttgart, 1843–49. 3 vols.

―――― *The Wanderings of Felix Fabri*. Trans. A. Stewart. Palestine Pilgrims' Text Society. Vols. VII–X. London, 1892–97.

Guylforde, Richard. *The Pylgrymage of Sir Richard Guylforde to the Holy Land*. Ed. H. Ellis. Camden Society, N.S. No. 51. London, 1851.

Harff, Arnold von. *The Pilgrimage of Arnold von Harff,*

*Knight.* Trans. M. Letts. Hakluyt Society, 2d Ser., No. XCIV. London, 1946.

*Informacōn for Pylgrymes unto the Holy Londe.* Ed. G. H. Freeling. Roxburghe Club. London, 1824.

*Information for Pilgrims unto the Holy Land.* Ed. E. Gordon Duff. London, 1893.

Kempe, Margery. *The Book of Margery Kempe.* Ed. S. B. Meech. Early English Text Society, O. S. No. 212. London, 1940.

La Brocquière, Bertrandon de. *Le Voyage d'outremer de La Broquière.* Ed. M. Ch. Schefer. Recueil de Voyages et de Documents pour Servir à l'Histoire de la Géographie. Vol XII. Paris, 1892.

Lannoy, G. de. *Oeuvres.* Ed. Potvin. Louvain, 1878.

——— "A Survey of Egypt and Syria," trans. J. Webb. *Archaeologia.* London, 1827. XXI, 281–444.

Ludolphus de Suchen. *Ludolph von Suchem's Description of the Holy Land.* Trans. A. Stewart. Palestine Pilgrims' Text Society. Vol. XII. London, 1895.

Newett, M. M. *Canon Pietro Casola's Pilgrimage to Jerusalem* . . . Manchester University Press, 1907.

Ousâma Ibn Mounḳidh. *See* Usāmah Ibn Murshid.

Poloner, Joannes. *John Poloner's Description of the Holy Land.* Trans. A. Stewart. Palestine Pilgrims' Text Society. Vol. VI. London, 1894.

Rochechouart, Louis de. "Journal de Voyage à Jérusalem de Louis de Rochechouart," *Revue de l'Orient Latin.* Paris, 1893. I, 168–274.

*Sarum Missal.* Trans. A. H. Pearson. London, 1884.

Torkington, Richard. *Ye Oldest Diarie of Englysshe Travell.* Ed. W. J. Loftie. London, 1884.

"Un Pèlerinage en Terre Sainte et au Sinai au XVe siècle," *Bibliothèque de l'Ecole des Chartes.* Vol. LXVI. Paris, 1905.

Usāmah Ibn Murshid. *The Autobiography of Ousâma.* Trans. G. R. Potter. London, 1929.

*Voyage de la Saincte Cyté de Hierusalem* . . . Ed. M. Ch. Schefer. Recueil de Voyages et de Documents pour Servir à l'Histoire de la Géographie. Vol II. Paris, 1882.

Walther, Paul. *Fratris Pauli Waltheri Guglingenis Itinerarium in Terram Sanctam . . .* Ed. M. Sollweck. Stuttgart, 1892.
Wey, William. *Itineraries of William Wey.* Roxburghe Club. London, 1857. 2 vols.


## LATER WORKS

Beazley, C. R. *The Dawn of Modern Geography* . . . London, 1897–1906. 3 vols.
*Cambridge Mediaeval History.* Vol. VIII. Cambridge University Press, 1911–36.
Davies, H. W. *Bernhard von Breydenbach and His Journey to the Holy Land. 1483–84. A Bibliography.* London, 1911.
Haeberlin, F. D. *Dissertatio historica sistens vitam et scripta Fr. Felicis Fabri* . . . Göttingen [1742]. (*Riedlin, E. respondent*)
Heyd, W. *Histoire du commerce du Levant au moyen-âge.* Edition française refondue et . . . augmentée par l'auteur, publiée . . . par F. Raynaud. Leipzig, 1923. 2 vols,
Iorga, N. "Les Aventures 'sarrazines' des français de Bourgogne au XVe siècle," *Mélanges d'histoire générale.* Vol. I. Cluj, 1927.
Jusserand, J. J. *English Wayfaring Life in the Middle Ages.* Trans. L. Toulmin Smith. London, 1889.
Kimble, G. H. T. *Geography in the Middle Ages* . . . London, 1938.
Lane, F. C. *Venetian Ships and Shipbuilders of the Renaissance.* Baltimore, 1934.
Lane-Poole, S. *A History of Egypt in the Middle Ages.* London, 1901.
Le Strange, G. *Palestine under the Moslems* . . . Palestine Exploration Fund. London, 1890.
Newton, A. P. ed., *et al. Travel and Travellers of the Middle Ages.* London, 1930.
Raynaud, F. "Les Consulats établis en Terre Sainte au moyen âge . . . ," Société de l'Orient Latin, Archives. Vol. II. Paris, 1884.

Röhricht, R. *Deutsche Pilgerreisen nach dem Heiligen Lande.* Innsbruck, 1900.

Stevenson, E. L. *Portolan Charts.* New York, 1911.

Warren, C. and Conder, C. R. *Survey of Western Palestine and Jerusalem.* Palestine Exploration Fund. London, 1884.

# INDEX